The Financial Executive's Handbook
for Managing Multinational Corporations

The Financial Executive's Handbook for Managing Multinational Corporations

LAMBERT H. SPRONCK CPA

A Ronald Press Publication

JOHN WILEY & SONS, New York   •   Chichester   •   Brisbane   •   Toronto

Library of Congress Cataloging in Publication Data:

Spronck, Lambert H   1916–
    The financial executive's handbook for managing
multinational corporations.

    "A Ronald Press publication."
    Includes index.
    1.   International business enterprises—Finance.
I.   Title.

HG4028.I53S67   658.1′599   79-27914
ISBN 0-471-05277-9

Printed in the United States of America

10 9 8 7 6 5 4 3 2 1

To

ANGELIKA

Preface

FINANCIAL MANAGEMENT AND CONTROL

This book has one major premise: A multinational company needs comprehensive, unified, and effective financial management to achieve continuing economic success. The basic elements of financial planning, control, budgeting, cost control, and reporting to executive management are fundamental to this proposition. Successful financial management of a multinational depends on establishing a strong controllership to conduct not only accounting and reporting, but also financial planning, analysis, and control.

A multinational company, an MNL, has to have a firm commitment, an organizational structure, and appropriate policies in order to initiate a program that will lead to comprehensive and successful financial management. It is essential to define the position of finance in the company's operations, its organization, functions, and the part it plays in planning major activities and profitable operations. Reporting results of operating performance to executive and middle management entails adherence to a rigorous time schedule throughout the organization. The cost and budgetary control system and the types of financial analysis and statistics significant to management have to be developed.

In writing this book I acknowledge the history and financial success of many MNLs who do not follow this type or degree of financial management control. But the need for more thorough financial studies has been recognized by a number of the same companies. Further, I appreciate that much of the basic information needed for my approach to financial management can be found in the existing accounting, cost, and other records of many of these MNLs.

In recommending a financial management program I assume that most MNLs' accounting and cost practices are fundamentally sound. But the best use may not have been made of the system, especially in the three areas—financial planning, reporting to management, and cost and budgetary control. My objective is to show how the information already available in the system can be developed or reorganized to achieve maximum benefits from financial management. A graphic presentation of this system of financial planning and control is shown in Figure 1.

Financial management control involves a five-point program:

1. Organize all the financial, accounting, and cost activities into one department and place the chief executive of this department, the chief financial officer, in a strong position in the company's management.
2. Initiate thorough in-depth financial planning to assess future plans of the company and use these plans to enhance current profits and continued growth.
3. Provide executive and middle management with the kind of financial reports and other information needed to guide their activities.
4. Revise and improve accounting and cost practices.
5. Establish a comprehensive system of cost and budget control.

This program is intended to achieve the following basic objectives towards which executives of an MNL have to direct their attention:

• Strengthen the finance organization.

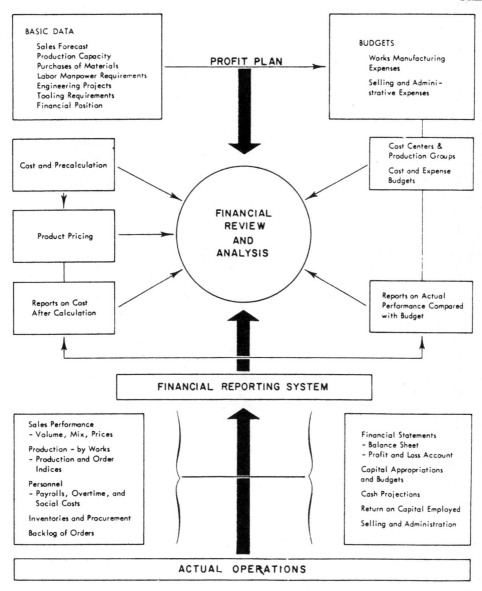

Figure 1. Financial planning and control system.

- Centralize and unify all financial, accounting, cost, and related information-producing activities.
- Strengthen the financial organization in the company's manufacturing plants and marketing branches in all foreign operations.
- Place greater emphasis on financial planning throughout the company.
- Provide executives with financial planning reports so that they can readily see the probable effects of future plans on the profitability of operations and on the technological requirements of the company.
- Improve the reporting of financial results to executive and middle management.
- Determine the cost and price of the product more accurately to improve the competitive position of the company and the marketability of its products.
- Make all levels of management more alert to cost and control, thereby employing men, materials, and machines most effectively.
- Improve and modernize the company's accounting and cost practices.
- Integrate all related activities into a single, effective system of financial management and information that will fully utilize the benefits and savings inherent in the company's manner of processing data.

The type of organization described in this book is intended to accomplish the first three objectives. The chief financial officer should spearhead the emphasis on financial planning. This task will be simpler when the basic tools, the profit plan and planning reports recommended later in the book, are used to explain to management future programs and anticipated results.

The objectives relating to reporting and cost control can be accomplished with a system of timely reports. One of the tangible results of the financial management program is the way the levels of management put these reports to use in directing and controlling their activities.

A financial officer's staff prepares and analyzes material concerning financial planning and the control of revenues, costs, profits, and assets. The staff prepares the monthly financial review and management reports, and investigates thoroughly available information in order to advise and assist the director of finance. It also prepares certain material that the chief financial officer presents to the president and the board of directors.

One further goal of this financial management program is to assure that operating plans or budgets for expenses are established on the basis of objective criteria, such as measured work standards. Changes in the methods of handling controllable manufacturing overhead expenses and classifying certain fixed and variable expenses are initial steps in studies of budget bases; these changes also improve the accuracy of product costing.

LAMBERT H. SPRONCK

New York, New York
January 1980

CONTENTS

The Financial Executive's Handbook
for Managing Multinational Corporations

INTRODUCTION

The World Of The Multinationals: Opportunities—Challenges— Adversities

Since World War II the world of the multinationals has been the land of opportunities and will continue to be into the twenty-first century. There are challenges and adversary situations, but above all, splendid economic opportunities for growth, individual gain, and most important, developing economies throughout the world. The impact of multinationals is fourfold:

- American multinationals on the international economy.
- American multinationals on the domestic economy.
- Foreign multinationals on the international economy.
- Foreign multinationals on their respective economies.

American and foreign investors abroad face obvious challenges:

- A country's nationalistic response to a foreign multinational company.

• The political risks of investing overseas in countries with unstable political allegiances, especially regarding their attitudes toward the multinational companies of certain nations.

• The possibility of nationalization of selected industries engaged in by the multinationals.

• The risk of expropriation by a host country.

In the face of these challenges and adversities American and foreign companies have continued to expand their overseas investments. This has been accomplished in some instances by the acquisition of foreign companies abroad, by mergers, and often by joint ventures. The form of corporate structure and the mode of operations often depend on the chemistry of various worlds involved — the political worlds, the economic worlds, the money worlds, even the saber rattling worlds influencing the governments of host countries.

The opportunities, challenges, and adversities vary greatly depending on the politics of the countries where the multinational operates or plans to do business. At a minimum there are four principal political worlds:

• The United States and those countries aligned with her either politically or philosophically.

• The European Economic Community, expanding strongly within its political sphere.

• Russia and the Eastern Block countries of Poland, East Germany, Czechoslovakia, Romania, Hungary, and Yugoslavia, obviously a political world of their own.

• China, a new and ominous political world with potentially far greater impact in its newly emerging position in world affairs.

ECONOMIC WORLDS The *New York Times* has divided the world into four economic divisions (Figure 2 lists these divisions in detail):

• *First World:* Industrialized democracies. This world in-

First World: Industrialized Democracies

Australia	Ireland	South Africa
Austria	Italy	Sweden
Belgium	Japan	Switzerland
Canada	Luxembourg	United Kingdom
Denmark	Netherlands	United States
Finland	New Zealand	West Germany
France	Norway	
Iceland	Portugal	

Second World: Communist Countries

Albania	Czechoslovakia	North Vietnam
Bulgaria	East Germany	Poland
Cambodia	Hungary	Romania
China	Mongolia	South Vietnam
Cuba	North Korea	U.S.S.R.

Third World: Developing Nations

Algeria	Guyana	Paraguay
Argentina	Honduras	Peru
Bahrain	Indonesia	Philippines
Barbados	Iran	Qatar
Bolivia	Iraq	Rhodesia
Botswana	Israel	Saudi Arabia
Brazil	Ivory Coast	Senegal
Cameroon	Jamaica	Singapore
Chile	Jordan	South Korea
Colombia	Kuwait	Spain
Congo	Lebanon	Swaziland
Costa Rica	Liberia	Syria
Cyprus	Libya	Taiwan
Dominican Rep.	Malaysia	Thailand
Ecuador	Malta	Trinidad and
Egypt	Mauritius	Tobago
El Salvador	Mexico	Tunisia
Equatorial Guinea	Morocco	Turkey
Fiji	Mozambique	United Arab
Gabon	Nicaragua	Emirates
Ghana	Nigeria	Uruguay
Greece	Oman	Venezuela
Guatemala	Panama	Yugoslavia
Guinea-Bissau	Papua New Guinea	Zambia

Figure 2 The world's economic divisions.

INTRODUCTION

Fourth World: Economically Troubled States

Afghanistan	India	Sierra Leone
Bangladesh	Kenya	Somalia
Benin	Laos	Sri Lanka
Bhutan	Lesotho	Sudan
Burma	Malagasy Rep.	Tanzania
Burundi	Malawi	Togo
Central African Rep.	Mali	Uganda
Chad	Mauritania	Upper Volta
Ethiopia	Nepal	Western Samoa
Gambia	Niger	Yemen Arab Rep.
Guinea	Pakistan	Yemen, People's
Haiti	Rwanda	Rep. of Zaire

Figure 2   Continued.

cludes most of the countries of Western Europe plus Canada, Australia, and of course, the United States.

• *Second World:* Communist countries. In addition to China, Russia, and the Eastern Block countries previously mentioned, these are Cuba, Mongolia, North Korea, and Vietnam.

• *Third World:* Developing countries. This vast category includes Brazil, Mexico, and practically every other country in Latin America. In Africa it includes Ghana, the Ivory Coast, Liberia, and Senegal. In Asia it includes Singapore and the Philippines. In the Near East — Israel, Iran, Iraq, and the United Arab Emirates.

• *Fourth World:* Economically troubled states. These include Afghanistan, Bangladesh, India, and Sri-Lanka.

The type of government of the host country obviously influences the economic world depending on whether it is a democracy, a communist power or a dictatorship. Needless to say, the degree of nationalistic tendencies has tremendous impact on the multinational company.

Saber rattling, still another factor in the worlds of the multinationals, is a way of life in those countries continually beset by war, military threats, or internal strife. Even with a peace pact, Israel, Egypt, and the Arab world would fall into this category. Iran, South Africa, Rhodesia, and other African nations have continuing internal strife.

The money worlds are groupings of countries with floating currencies. The European Economic Community, for example, has implemented the European Monetary System. The United States dollar is pitted against both these currencies and the Japanese yen. The French franc and English pound influence not only the countries with whom France and England trade, but also all their former colonies. The multinational is challenged to operate both in environments where currencies are anticipated to revalue strongly against the dollar and in countries where currencies are expected to devalue against the dollar. The multinational must consider the rate of inflation and the stability of prices and wages in the countries where it operates. The money worlds are of greatest significance depending on the banking and credit facilities available in various host countries as well as restrictions on trade, the movement of money, and remittability of dividends. The fundamental question is: can dividends and royalties be expected to be transferred or are funds blocked even to the extent that loans cannot be repaid?

OPPORTUNITIES The multinational has to formulate different policies and guidelines in order to operate successfully in the various worlds outlined above. Above all, it has to be able to brace itself against the adversities confronting it in certain of these worlds. Nonetheless the opportunities are there whether through import-export operations, doing business only with local distributors, or through investing in branches, subsidiaries, or joint ventures. The European Economic Community has a population of 260 million people. In Latin America, Brazil and Mexico provide outstanding opportunities for multinationals. In Russia and Eastern Europe the growth of trade shows tremendous potential for further development. China is now opening its doors. The Far East is vast and even in the Middle East and Africa opportunities exist if the multinational can show the proper amount of foresight, patience, and diligence required to do business under the prevailing conditions.

PLANNING FOR FINANCIAL MANAGEMENT OF THE MULTINATIONAL COMPANY

In succeeding chapters, the financial environment, money markets, and the methods of financing opportunities are discussed. In the planning phase many administrative functions in financial management of multinationals are identical to those of domestic operations. The use and sources of funds invested in foreign enterprises have to be explored and analyzed just as they are for a local investment. The reporting and control mechanisms required to assess and track the funds position of a company are managed as if all of its operations were conducted in United States dollars. Convertibility of foreign exchange, the handling of foreign exchange gains and losses on individual transactions, and the translation of financial statements are additional considerations in reporting and controlling the financial position of a multinational; but following the translation into United States dollars, the reporting and control documents remain essentially the same.

PLANNING FOR CONTROL

Establishing a controllership function in a multinational is identical to establishing control in a company with only domestic operations. The selection of managers in marketing and manufacturing facilities, the delegation of responsibility to division and local controllers, the decisions of products and pricing, the control over labor costs, wages, and productivity are basically the same. A significant difference is that the managers in a multinational are or should be drawn from the local population. The controllers may also be from the local nationals but they must speak the language of the MNL executive office in order to explain why results may differ from planned operations. Finally, the lines of communication are longer, but the essential problems remain; decisions have to be made about transfer pricing, determining costs, and selling and administrative expenses. Although annual budgets have to be prepared in foreign as well as local currencies, the annual budgeting process is essentially the same.

As the operating year proceeds, management reports have to be prepared comparing actual results with budgets, and the explanation of variances has to be communicated to the multinational executive office. The accounting and reporting requirements of the multinational's home country may differ from the statutory accounting and tax codes of the overseas countries. Provisions have to be made for auditing results pursuant to the accounting standards of the multinational's country as well as to the statutory standards of the host country. Finally, performance has to be evaluated according to the multinational's criteria, such as rate of growth, ratio of income to sales, and the return on capital invested. The understanding and communication of these performance criteria are among the most difficult tasks of the controller of a multinational company; communication is often impeded by the differing financial backgrounds of the parties involved, the language differences, as well as the great distance from the MNL headquarters.

IMPACT OF THE OECD

The Organization for Economic Cooperation and Development (OECD) was established in 1961 and replaced the Organization for European Economic Cooperation established under the Marshall Plan in 1948. The OECD is comprised of 24 industrialized countries: the United States, Canada, Japan, Australia, New Zealand, Austria, Belgium, Denmark, the United Kingdom, Finland, France, West Germany, Greece, Iceland, Italy, Luxemburg, the Netherlands, Norway, Portugal, Spain, Sweden, Turkey, Switzerland, and Yugoslavia. The OECD countries have only 20% of the world's population, but they account for two-thirds of the world's industrial production and foreign trade.

OECD meetings are concerned principally with world trade and economic cooperation. In 1976, the OECD turned to the language of trade and business and released guidelines for reporting the financial positions and results of operations of multinationals. Although the guidelines have no enforceable position in their respective countries now, any of the 24 countries could pass legislation that would change the guidelines into rules parallel to those applying to American companies registered pursuant to the Securities and Exchange Commission (SEC) Acts of 1933 and 1934.

The aftermath of Watergate and the investigations into questionable and improper payments of corporations in the United States has undoubtedly impressed the OECD. Professional standards of ethical behavior of multinational companies are now more seriously considered, and the OECD has approved a Code of Business Conduct. These guidelines contain four key provisions:

• No soliciting or rendering of bribes or improper payments to holders of public office.
• No illegal political contributions.
• No improper involvement in local politics.
• No discrimination because of national origin when filling responsible positions.

The code also recommends that corporations publish annually financial statements and other operating information. The statutes of many countries already require publishing such information. The following are the key recommended disclosures:

• Operating results and sales by geographical area; sales in the major lines of business for the enterprise as a whole.
• Significant new capital investment by geographical area and, as far as practical, by major lines of business for the enterprise as a whole.
• Policies followed on intragroup pricing. Corporations cannot use transfer pricing for modifying in a way contrary to national laws the tax base on which members of the group are assessed.

CHAPTER 1

Foreign Trade And Investment Abroad

Since World War II, multilateralism has significantly reduced visible and invisible trade barriers between nations. The organizational key to multilateralism is the General Agreement of Tariffs and Trade (GATT), an agreement to which nearly the entire noncommunist world is a party. Under the GATT, international trade matters are negotiated and settled in an open convention in Geneva, and any privileges granted by one country to another apply to the entire membership through the "most favored nation" principle. The objective is to prevent discrimination in the schedules, rates, or other matters involved in negotiating trade. By meeting together, member countries have standardized practices, procedures, and even customs procedures.

The GATT eliminated an invisible superstructure of trade barriers and simplified international transactions. Manufacturing companies can circumvent middlemen in foreign trade and simplify the mechanics of international commerce. Multilateralism enables many business and industry ventures in foreign lands to become profitable. National affiliates of a multinational can trade among themselves and thus form a truly integrated international system.

A multinational with resident affiliates in a number of trading countries can adjust marketing strategies within wide ranges when conditions demand it. These options provide the MNL with a degree of immunity from environmental adversities, internal business conditions, restrictive governmental policies, or disturbances in international affairs.

Potentially, the superiority of the multinational over its domestic rival lies in its ability to better plan marketing and production arrangements throughout the world. For example, the General Motors Corporation adjusts its production overseas to meet widely different markets with different marketing strategies. In Germany, General Motors markets a wide range of vehicles including high-priced models. In Brazil, the smaller, lower-priced Chevette is designed to attract a growing lower or middle class. In Malaysia, farmers use the Harimau, a utility vehicle costing under $1500, to carry their products to the local market. The multinational achieves economies by mass-producing the global and continental models and, at the same time, by taking advantage of local specialization in the production of any given model.

Many countries with financial incentive programs support or subsidize certain types of investment programs. These programs may be limited to particular industries or localities and may take the form of (1) government-guaranteed low-interest loans, (2) direct capital contributions (usually on a participation basis), (3) reduction of taxes or tax holidays for a number of years, (4) accelerated depreciation and write-off privileges, (5) special allowances for research and development, (6) foreign exchange and profit remittance guarantees, and even (7) governmental contracts to assure a minimum return on the contemplated investment.

The multinational endeavors to develop a degree of immunity to restrictive currency controls and at the same time to preserve operational flexibility. Separate legal entities in different countries provide options for carrying out a particular venture. If exchange restrictions of one country prevent a particular undertaking, the Swiss or Swedish affiliate of the company might not be similarly constrained; and several affiliates might combine into a consortium to meet the need. The legal means are reinforced by multinational distribution of capital reserves, as well as by the ability to borrow. With a balanced distribution of capital reserves and borrowing power, a multinational can pursue a wide variety of international investments, disinvestments, and transfers without violating currency and exchange controls of any particular country; this may be impossible for a company operating in a single country.

FORMS OF FOREIGN INVESTMENT

In certain countries and in varying degrees, visas for personal entry are difficult to obtain, imports of goods require lengthy customs clearance, and transfers of capital are restrictive. These problems are minor compared to the process of obtaining the right to do business in such a country. It is advantageous to have been located there for some years and to be legally established with local nationals who are well-known in the country. Lacking this advantage there are four options:

1 Qualify for a branch license.
2 Form a subsidiary company under the laws of the host country.
3 Create a joint venture with one or more local companies.
4 Enter into a license agreement with an existing firm.

Foreign Branches

From a legal standpoint, a branch is not a separate entity; it is a local office of a foreign parent company. The parent company is responsible for any legal action taken either by or against the branch. Licenses for branch operations of nonresident companies are sometimes restricted to branches with a responsible citizen of the host country serving as the legal custodian, who, with the power of attorney, assumes complete jurisdiction over the branch.

Foreign branches have other problems—business licenses may be of short duration, requiring frequent and expensive renewals; regulations and governmental surveillance may be restrictive; the taxable base may be so defined that the branch becomes taxable not on the basis of its own earnings or assets, but on the basis of the total profits or capitalization of the multinational as a whole.

Foreign Subsidiaries

Multinationals usually prefer to organize their affiliates as local enterprises under the laws of the host country. In certain countries there are organizations other than the corporation, legalgally separate from their owners, in which the owners' liability is limited to their investments in the enterprise. For example, German law provides for a limited liability company (GmbH) that resembles the American corporation in all features essential to management, yet it usually enjoys much greater freedom of action than does the German equivalent of the corporation (AG).

In order to qualify for incorporation in many countries, the law requires that local nationals hold a certain number of directorships or other key positions. Local citizens may have to control a specified portion, perhaps even half, of the capital invested in the affiliate. The necessary legal capital may, however, consist of existing assets such as land, buildings, equipment, production processes, and even goodwill. Monetary values can be assigned to these assets and the amount of the cash contribution is thereby minimized.

Joint Ventures

American multinationals have preferred wholly owned foreign subsidiaries. Complete control and ownership is consistent with their policies, even for American subsidiaries. The full success of worldwide strategy depends on complete control over all foreign units. Many foreign counries, especially the developing ones, have concluded that wholly foreign-owned enterprises do not contribute as much to the country's economic interests as do joint ventures. A shift from the whollyowned subsidiary to the joint venture is a trend in international business organizations.

Economically and administratively a joint venture is a partnership. An MNL joint venture is a business in which two or more economic entities from different countries participate either permanently or for a limited time. Participation involves equity capital and even control of manufacturing processes, marketing, patents, trademarks, and managerial expertise. A joint venture enables local capital to participate in profitable and productive undertakings in their own countries. A joint venture transmits techniques and managerial expertise more effectively and rapidly than wholly foreign-owned enterprises. It also eliminates the danger that the foreign investor will unduly dominate industry or improperly influence politicians. Finally, some countries prefer joint ventures as a means of strengthening their balance of payments position through minimizing dividend transfers and repatriating foreign capital.

From the standpoint of MNL public relations, joint ventures mean that the nation's people identify a joint venture with their own society. This is especially important in consumer goods industries because it directly affects the acceptance of products.

In labor relations, joint ventures enjoy certain advantages: the management of a joint venture can bargain with unions without being too vulnerable to anti-foreign attacks or other temporary foreign relations problems between countries. Employee morale is higher if it is known that local interests have a substantial share in the profits of the operation.

On the negative side, when individuals from different nations, and from different economic, ethnic, and cultural backgrounds join in a common effort, they often have conflicting views and value judgments, and different ways of looking at problems. The disposition of profits, and the need for reinvestment and the expansion of local operations are especially subject to controversy. Some local partners oppose liberal reinvestment policies and thereby undermine potential growth. In negotiating with a foreign partner, it is indispensable that policies on declaration of dividends and reinvestment decisions be understood fully.

Licensing Licensing enables a foreign firm to use an intangible asset such as a patent, a manufacturing process, or a trademark for the purpose of entering the foreign licensee's market. The licensor

13

enters the foreign market without export trading or capital investment. In return for the rights transferred, the foreign firm pays royalties normally based on its output or sales of the licensed product.

A licensing arrangement is a written agreement stating which rights are being transferred, the royalties or other considerations paid, where and how the rights are to be utilized, under which circumstances the rights are to revert to the licensor, and the degree of participation the licensor is to have in the specified operations of the licensee or in the marketing of the licensed products. The contract specifies the period of time; the size of the territory, the methods of control and payment; the applicable law in case of conflict; and if appropriate the method of arbitration.

In addition to providing an alternative to export-import trade and direct investment, licensing agreements also provide an inexpensive means for exploring and testing a company's growth potential in a particular foreign area before any investment is made. Licensing agreements entail greater risk than normal export operations but considerably less risk than direct investments. Licensing is often used in a transition phase from export to foreign manufacture in a company's international expansion, and is often succeeded by a more extensive commitment. Royalty agreements are specifically designed for gradual conversion from licensing to equity operations. They provide for a low or a declining royalty plus a stock purchase commitment in a new or existing establishment to succeed the licensing arrangement. The licensee acquires a partial ownership interest where local equity capital is not available in blocks sufficiently large to establish a joint venture facility. The facility may initially be financed by the American licensor and gradually converted into a joint enterprise under a royalty and stock purchase agreement.

Licensing has sometimes been defined as exporting of know-how, but it can also be described as a nonequity joint venture; it is a continous cooperative relationship between both parties for their mutual benefit.

There are several advantages associated with licensing. First, revenues increase with little or no commitment on the part of the licensor. Second, licensing helps manufacturers build goodwill and enhance the image of their products and reputations abroad before entering the manufacturing stage nationally. Third, in many countries the only way to protect a patent or trademark is to establish a licensing agreement with local capital and register the patents locally.

However, there are also problems with licensing agreements: inability of the licensor to insure quality control; limited profit potential of a licensing operation, especially in expanding markets; difficulty in charging a royalty commensurate with the value of the licensed development; and finally, the danger of training a potential competitor who may sever the license agreement in favor of developing a new competitive product, using the knowledge acquired through the license agreement.

BRAZIL—AN EXAMPLE OF INCENTIVES FOR FOREIGN COMPANIES

Multinational companies have had reservations about doing business in Brazil because of the country's 40% inflation rate per year and the rights of minority interests in a Brazilian firm. The new corporation law guarantees these rights but also establishes modern guidelines for joint ventures that encourage foreign multinationals to consider the minority partner option because of its advantages for financing.

Moreover the Brazilian government has successfully handled the endemic inflation; its monetary and fiscal policies have been described as monetary correction. Many companies, both Brazilian and multinational, have coped with inflation successfully in Brazil and have continued to grow and make profits at substantial rates.

Monetary correction is directly related to inflation. Inflation swallows profits in every company in Brazil. The Brazilian

Monetary Correction Law (No. 4357) allows companies to re-value the book value of their assets by the monetary correction index. When companies must sell, replace, or insure an asset, they are not taxed on the apparent gain but on the true gain. This means that inflation is deducted before the gain on the sales is established.

The concept of adjusting book values first applied only to the fixed assets of a company. It was then extended to the company's earnings. Today, after certain adjustments, a company pays taxes on the true earnings of the business, not on the inflated earnings. This system, which tries to create a realistic constant currency for business, is the way to live with inflation. Economists say that the system has a "refueling effect," that is, it tends to perpetuate inflation. When a country like Brazil has a 40% rate of inflation annually, the only choice is such monetary correction, known as indexing.

Indexing was introduced with the specific purpose of attracting investment from a public that was absolutely mistrustful of the system because of inflation. Brazil is one of the first large developing countries to employ indexing on such a vast scale. For example, returns from investments in term bank deposits are given in two segments; the larger is in monetary correction, the smaller is in interest. Investors pay tax only on the interest portion of the return.

The government determines the annual monetary correction index on the basis of an enormous matrix of calculations, considering the increases of at least 20 or 30 different indices of the economy, such as cost of living, wholesale prices, and cost of construction; it also takes account of internal matters such as exchange rates.

FOREIGN MINORITY CONTROL   When a company establishes a limited liability company—or Limitada—the charter of the company states that certain acts or decisions depend on the approval of a certain percentage of voting stockholders. For example, the charter may stipulate that to sell real estate belonging to the Limitada requires the approval of at least 95% of the quota stockholders; this protects minority participants. The stockholders may establish any type of restrictions in a Limitada charter.

When a company is established as Socieda Anonima (SA), which is a corporation in the broad sense, majority decisions rule. Protection of minorities in an SA is more difficult than in a Limitada; the minority position, accordingly, is not significant in making decisions. The new SA law establishes more protection for minority shareholders in that it recognizes and accepts the existence of shareholders' agreements. If minority and majority shareholders agree on certain points, these agreements may be registered in the company's books and must be observed by the company.

THE NEW CORPORATION LAW

The SA Law No. 6404 of December 15, 1976, regulates corporations in Brazil. The new law incorporates the idea of indexing, giving a standard format in accounting procedures for monetary correction in all SA companies in Brazil. One of the important new features of the law is a stronger protection of the interest of minority stockholders. For example, a central entity oversees the trading of shares within the country

If the majority partner departs from some of the clauses of the agreements, the minority partner can go to court and demand that the agreement be followed. The minority stockholder can expect specific performance under the minority shareholders agreements. This concept, which is modeled on United States legislation and, in turn, on Anglo-Saxon legislation, is new to Brazil and other Latin American countries.

The new law formalizes the concept of groups of companies, although it does not create a conglomerate. If a company operates under a group of companies it is obliged to present a consolidation, to pay consolidated taxes, and so on.

Brazil's Securities Commission has recently established that open companies should publish their corporate acts and annual balance sheets in the city where their head offices are located and also in the city whose foreign exchange negotiates the greatest number of their transactions. Open companies that have relevant investments in associated or controlled compa-

17

nies are bound to rules for preparing and publishing their balance sheets. The Securities Commission defines associated companies as those in which one corporation participates in at least 10% of the capital of another without controlling it; controlled companies are those in which one company has the power to elect the majority of the officers and rights that guarantee its influence in corporate resolutions.

BRAZIL—FISCAL INCENTIVES FOR FOREIGN COMPANIES

Fiscal incentives are available to multinationals if they locate in certain industrial sectors or geographical areas. The Brazilian government thinks that development is needed in basic industries and, provided that national security is not involved, it invites foreign firms to invest in these areas. Moreover, the Brazilian government, concerned with keeping its foreign trade in balance, has great interest in developing industries that will increase Brazil's exports.

The Industrial Development Council (CDI) of the Ministry of Industry and Commerce provides the following incentives to approved projects:

• Tax exemption on the imports of equipment, instruments, tools, and accessories that have no parts similar or complementary to those products produced nationally.

• (IPI) Excise tax exemptions for these goods; credit to the buyer of national equipment equal to the value of the IPI on this equipment; accelerated depreciation of nationally manufactured goods for income tax purposes.

• Preferential financial assistance from official banks and priority for review by the Council on Custom Policy for modifying import taxes to protect national industry.

Fiscal incentives are also granted for special export programs. Approval of these programs is granted from the Ministry of Industry and Commerce through the Commission for Concession of Fiscal Benefits and Special Export Programs (BEFIEX). These incentives cover many areas, from the reduction of import duty and exemption from IPI on the importation of machinery, equipment, instruments, tools, and accessories essential to a project, to rebate in profits taxable on the fraction corresponding to the export of manufactured goods, and the exemption of compulsory deposits on the import of these products included under the special export program.

Many government agencies in Brazil have been created to encourage companies to locate in certain areas. Under the Ministry of the Interior is SUDENE, which locates industry and projects in the northeastern states from Maranhao down to Bahia. The programs grant economic benefits, such as tax reductions and attractive financing, to companies that locate in these areas. For example, companies whose projects SUDENE approves may obtain a reduction of their income tax or an exemption from tax payment for as long as 10 years. They may also obtain a reduction of import duties on equipment needed to begin the project and a reduction of IPI and ICM value-added taxes. Multinational companies may participate in these programs, but they will receive less financing than majority-owned Brazilian companies. The tax incentives are the same for both.

Some of the agencies that provide fiscal incentives deal not with a particular region of the country but with a specific activity. SUDENE deals with projects in the fishing industry and comes under the jurisdiction of the Ministry of the Interior. Geimi deals with mining sections, Sunaman with the merchant marine, Carpe with the computer industry, and Embratur with hotels and tourism. Foreign investors with plans in these areas are assisted by the appropriate ministry in investigating available options and incentives.

CHAPTER 2

Foreign Acquisitions

The foreign acquisition is undoubtedly the most challenging and thrilling experience for the multinational manager. It requires thorough, time-consuming investigation of a different kind of company in a foreign land. It involves endless discussions with the management of the company to be acquired, with brokers and finders, the attorneys from both sides, the independent public accountants of both firms, and the internal auditors. Needless to say, no foreign acquisition is ever accomplished within an ideal timetable. Travel often involves long distances, time is limited, and, in addition, a foreign company is usually anxious to maintain secrecy and confidentiality until the deal is consummated. There is little time to plan, prepare, fully investigate or to report the findings according to a comprehensive checklist that includes financing, marketing, manufacturing, and legal matters. Meetings continue endlessly into the night. Overseas flights are numerous, but they seldom provide enough time for the complete audit and report that often accompany an acquisition in one's own country.

PLANNING FOR AN ACQUISITION

- Make a desk study of the country, its economy, politics, and attitude toward foreign business.

- Determine the industry in which the outlook for your entry seems feasible; determine whether you should start a new enterprise or buy an existing one.

• If you decide to buy a company, focus on the one you would prefer to acquire.

• Arrange to meet the real owner.

• Determine, after a preliminary discussion with top management of the company, the outline of a possible transaction. Explore the proposed transaction at the policy level.

• Assign a team to begin inquiry with a small group from the company's management, possibly along the lines of a basic checklist.

• Accept at face value the considerable data that have been supplied by company management.

• Draft a contractual acquisition in preliminary form. The draft will contain detailed representations by management and stockholders confirming the responses to the various questions raised on the subjects contained in the checklist; appended to the agreement will be financial statements reported by stockholders and management to be a true and fair view of the state of affairs. Agreements will also provide for an escrow or a withholding of a substantial portion of the purchase price following the time of closing, until a thorough investigation can be made to determine the completeness of representations and warranties.

• Commence an investigation, culminating in the release of the escrow or withheld purchase price after ascertaining the representations and warranties are true and correct. After the investigation and the closing, there will be a complete audit of the books.

The Financial Checklist   The following is the type of financial information to ask the seller and the key points to look for in a possible acquisition:

A Earnings

The company's earning history during the past five years.

Reasons for significant changes in sales revenues, returns, or profits in any of these years.

The principal product lines or segments of the business, and the profitability of each segment.

Annual sales, cost, and gross margin of each product line.

Projected sales and profits this year, and during the next three to five years.

Business outlook for these product lines, considering obsolescence of both the products and the technology to produce them.

B Product Volume Analysis

What factors affect volume changes on profits.

The indicated break-even point of this company. Comparison of this point with other companies in the same business and with comparable companies in the MNL home country.

C Cash Flow Earnings

Indicate cash flow earnings based on this formula: net earnings, plus depreciation and net of changes in working capital.

Extraneous factors affecting cash flow in recent years.

Effect of taxes, dividends, sale of assets, and acquisitions on the company's cash flow.

Significant changes in inventories affecting cash flow.

D Costs

Method of determining cost of sales; manufacturing cost charged directly to cost of sales as distinguished from overhead in cost of sales.

Types of cost systems—either job costs or process.

Are standard costs used?

Basis for setting standards.

Total number of employees and total payrolls, including direct, indirect, and administrative.

Approximate percentage of supplemental employee benefit payroll expenses to total payroll costs.

Amount of depreciation and amortization included in cost of sales.

Depreciation accounting policies.

Research and development costs whether reported as current operating expenses or deferred.

E Financial

The present cash position of the company—borrowings, overdrafts, lines of credit.

Local bankers and sources of capital.

Accounts receivable and average length of credit; aging of receivables.

Credit and collection operations.

What are the company's banking connections, both local and foreign?

Why does the company want to sell? Does it plan to use the capital in other enterprises?

What is the value of the company and what must you pay for it?

THE PREACQUISITION INVESTIGATION

Within time constraints, the preacquisition investigation demands optimum planning prior to the final negotiation of the deal. The investigating team is of prime importance; its role and responsibilities should be defined clearly and to the satisfaction of the management of both the seller and the buyer. The investigating team should consist of any brokers or finders involved in originating the deal, the attorney of both the buyer and the seller, the independent certified public accountants of both sides, and the internal auditors, especially of the acquiring company.

In addition to the requirements noted in the checklist, a number of special concerns should be considered when reviewing the operations of the foreign company.

- The timing of recognizing revenue.
- The policy on discounts and sales returns.
- The method of determining cost of sales.

- The separation of overhead expenses into fixed, semivariable, and variable.
- The compensation of key personnel, particularly officers.
- The amount of interest expense.
- The amount and rate of income taxes.

Areas of concern in evaluating working capital are: cash, trade receivables, advances or receivables from company personnel, inventories of raw material and finished goods, accounts payable, and short-term financing arrangements (including the availability of spot-cash loans).

In addition to land and buildings, areas of concern regarding fixed assets are leasehold improvements, both gross and net; operating equipment; and autos, trucks and other transportation equipment. Finally, the amount of future capital investment must be assessed. With respect to capital structure consider:

- Long-term financing.
- Commitments and contingent liabilities.
- Income tax liabilities, current and deferred.
- Stockholders' equity.

Major problem areas include:

- Owner compensation, direct and bonus.
- Perquisites of owners and officers.
- Land and buildings owned by major stockholders or relatives of officers.
- Special compensation arrangements with key officers.
- Pension and profit-sharing plans.
- Accelerated depreciation.
- Under-valued assets.

CORPORATE AND LEGAL MATTERS RELATING TO ACQUISITION OF FOREIGN COMPANIES

The legal and corporate matters concerning possible acquisition of a foreign company in many ways overshadow checklists described in the previous section. The following are essential in evaluating a foreign acquisition.

CORPORATE MATTERS

1 Examine all corporate documents of the company, including its charter, certificate of incorporation (or local equivalent), bylaws, and other state or provincial qualification papers; study the history of any amendments to these documents.

2 Determine the characteristics and provisions of all outstanding securities of the company, including any outstanding rights or options to purchase securities. Obtain copies of any prospectus issued in recent years. Inquire about the existence of any listing of the company's securities on any securities exchange and any instruments filed in connection with the listings. Note: Investigate matters in 1 and 2 for every subsidiary of the company.

3 Obtain a list of stockholders (or, if the company is publicly held, the principal stockholders), directors, and officers; inquire about all directors, principal officers, and stockholders.

Inquire about companies that might be described as "affiliates."

Inquire about any agreements among stockholders, such as voting trusts or other arrangements affecting control, agreements restricting alienability of shares, and the like.

4 Review minutes of the company for recent years (eventually a complete review should be made).

5 Inquire about all significant claims and litigation in which the company has been involved, whether as claimant or defendant, whether pending or concluded, and including

proceedings brought by any governmental agency; review all judgments to which the company may be subject.

6 Obtain a list of contracts of every kind (except agreements of purchase or sale of a product, or services made in the ordinary course of business and not involving more than a specified amount of money). "Contracts" is used here in the broadest sense and is intended to include every kind of written or oral agreement, including "gentlemen's understandings," regardless of subject matter.

7 Request that management furnish a comprehensive but concise description of the business in the management's own words. This statement should include a description of the company's principal product lines and the principal competition in each line. The management should also state its usual terms and conditions of sale, including warranties for each product line, its policy on product liability problems, extension of credit, and the like. (Note: This statement of management should be obtained even though it may overlap, in part, a more searching investigation under the heading of "marketing.")

8 Obtain a statement from management about the principal properties of the company, its understanding of the state of title of each, including information about ownership of rights and requirements for them, easements, and zoning restrictions bearing on the usability of each property. Obtain copies of any existing appraisals.

9 Inquire whether the company is materially dependent on patents or secret processes and, if so, obtain full information about its patent situation, including the need for processes or patents that belong to others. Obtain copies of all license agreements to which the company is a party, whether as licensor or licensee. If important, get copies of all patents.

10 Get a list of registered trademarks and a briefing on their significance. Obtain copies of all trademark license agreements to which the company is a party, whether as licensor or licensee. Inquire about any trademark problem areas,

such as a loss of trademark, dual uses, or inability to register them.

11 Obtain a list of all the company's governmental grants, licenses, franchises, and so forth.

12 Investigate investments in other companies, whether subsidiaries or not.

13 Review the scope of insurance protection.

14 Make a detailed investigation of the company's tax position, including any deficiencies alleged or threatened to be alleged, past compromises on disputed issues, status of audits of its returns, and so on. Extend the tax inquiry to taxes other than the usual income and franchise taxes.

15 Inquire about fixed and contingent liabilities (including obligations not required by accounting principles to be reflected on a balance sheet). Inquire about liabilities (including obligations recognized as only morally binding) not disclosed in the books. Question whether the scope of warranty of financial statements (audited or unaudited, for one or more years), inventory, receivables, undisclosed liabilities, and fixed assets are appropriate. Ask whether the company has continuing relations with other units or continuing warranty service requirements for past sales of units that require service, purchase, sale, or other contracts with the buyer.

16 Ask about any sales of the same business within the past five years and about any negotiations for a sale that did not transpire.

17 Obtain a list of locations where the company does business other than the jurisdiction in which it is incorporated.

18 Obtain copies of all employee benefit plans such as pensions, insurance, profit sharing, bonuses, and stock options or purchase arrangements; obtain details of any informal benefit plan.

19 Request that management describe the management structure and functions; obtain copies of policy manuals and organization charts and manuals.

20 Investigate banking connections.

LEGAL MATTERS

1 Study corporation laws applicable in the jurisdictions in which the company is organized and does a significant amount of business. Take special note of the laws bearing on corporate control, enforceability of relationships between stockholders, various capitalization possibilities, and the right of directors and management to indemnity in the event of acquisition.

2 Review applicable laws affecting foreign investments, including inducements as well as restrictions; foreign exchange matters; licensing new enterprises; exports and imports; extraction of raw materials; residence of foreign nationals; and preference for home enterprises. Also examine so-called antitrust laws and regulations, and laws regulating prices of products and services of any kind.

3 Investigate generally the procedural laws of the country and consider the feasibility of arbitration agreements.

4 Review exhaustively taxes, industrial relations, statutes, and jurisprudence.

5 Review past, existing, and proposed legislation that in any way discriminates against foreign-owned enterprises.

6 Consider enforceability under applicable laws of any contractual arrangements contemplated between "partner" stockholders, if any.

7 Consider legal and tax feasibility of the different forms in which the proposed acquisition transaction can be cast, for example, stock for stock, assets for stock, stock for cash, or assets for cash.

8 Ask about continuing relationships with outside consultants including, but not limited to, legal counsel. Request copies of all studies or opinions submitted during the last five years by outside consultants, including any opinions of counsel on material matters.

CHAPTER 3

Managing The Multinational

American companies tend to acquire foreign companies on the. most desirable terms, namely, 100% ownership. In recent years a number of companies have changed their position and realized that they can exert significant management influence on overseas operations even if they do not enjoy complete ownership. In many developing countries, laws require that foreign companies not own more than 50% of the voting stock and in some countries foreign companies cannot own more than 40%.

MANAGING AN ASSOCIATED COMPANY

An associated company is one in which the multinational owns 50% of the stock or less. The reason for this percentage of ownership is often financial; the MNL realizes that it does not necessarily need 50% of the stock to exercise a significant influence on the management of the company. In these situations, and in countries where laws prohibit foreign companies from owning more than 40 or 50% of the stock of corporations, the MNL and local management are often unclear about their relationship to each other. Managers need to know whether the multinational can require that the basic procedures of accounting, personnel, and so forth, apply to the associate.

An associated company in another country is first and foremost an independent entity with local stockholders who provide the balance of the capital; the multinational owns only 40 to 50% of this capital. The stockholders empower the directors to act and, further, to delegate to the officers and managers their appropriate responsibilities. When a managing director of an associated company needs to know who can approve the sale or acquisition of land, he or she must look within the company to the regulations governing the powers to effect such a transaction, and cannot look outside the company to the MNL which is an entirely alien corporation. In establishing an associated company the MNL makes an agreement with co-investors defining the limits of the authority of directors and officers that the stockholders feel are necessary to safeguard their rights. These rights incorporated in the bylaws and other corporate documents are the rules governing the conduct of the associated company and are binding on all the stockholders of that company, including the MNL.

The stockholders empower the managing director to act on their behalf and to refer back to them only certain decisions as specified in the corporate documents. In the normal operations of the associated company, innumerable ordinary decisions have to be made, and the directors empower the managing director to perform such acts on their behalf. The bylaws may specify that the sale of any substantial asset of the associated company must be approved by the majority of the stockholders; then no one is empowered to sell any substantial asset without referring the matter to the stockholders, even if the managing director is a prior employee of the MNL. On the other hand, stockholders are not concerned with hiring key personnel, such as a manufacturing plant superintendent; the managing director has this responsibility because it is part of the ordinary course of business.

The essence of the problem is to determine which responsibilities are delegated by the board of directors to the managing director and, in turn, which can be assigned to managers who report to him. The multinational safeguards its interests in the associated company by its position as a stockholder with a significant voice in the management of the company; the MNL makes certain that the basic agreements and bylaws protect its rights. The stockholders elect members of the board of directors and through them safeguard their rights in the company. The directors have a duty to advise the MNL and other stockholders of developments and to follow all stockholders' instructions about voting on matters coming before the board.

Two types of documents define these powers and responsibilities, and limit the authority of all officers and employees of associated companies:

1 The charter and the bylaws giving the general authority from the stockholders.
2 The delegation of authority, a document that specifies the powers, authorities, and limits that the directors grant to the managing director and also those which he can delegate to the officers and managers reporting to him.

The first document usually exists in the associated company, whereas the second is often lacking or unclear. It is important that the MNL develop a document that covers most normal business transactions and that distills from its own policy and procedures the types of powers, authorities, limitations, and reservations that apply to the board of directors, to the managing director or president, and in turn to those who report to him.

The instructions from the president of one MNL to one of its employees recently appointed as managing director of the associated company might define the relationship thus: "You must remember you are a manager of that company and in that position you represent all of the stockholders, not merely the company from which you were transferred."

The managing director of an associated company wears two hats, one being the director who represents its stockholder, the multinational company. In that capacity he has a duty to keep the MNL informed, to safeguard its interest, and to receive from the MNL instructions on how to vote on matters coming before the board of directors. He has the power to vote by proxy in the stockholders' meeting in accordance with the

MNL's wishes. In all other respects, he is the general manager of the whole company and represents not only the MNL but also the 40, 50, or 60% of the stockholders who are nationals of the host country. (See Figure 3.)

DELEGATION OF AUTHORITY

A multinational company should provide in its bylaws and related administrative procedures for delegating authority and power, and for limiting them according to the following guidelines.

PRINCIPAL ACTIONS

1   *Reserved to Stockholders*
Establish or change corporate structure.
Elect board of directors.
Determine and delegate powers and authorities to the board.

2   *Reserved to the Board of Directors*
Provide for managing and directing company affairs, pursuant to powers granted by stockholders.
Elect the officers of the company.
Delegate specified authority to the president or managing director.

3   *Reserved to the Managing Director or President*
Act personally, without further delegation, on ordinary matters.
Delegate to other officers and executives the authority to act in matters in the ordinary course of business.

REQUESTS FOR BOARD ACTION

Action of a board committee, the board of directors, or stockholders is required by law or corporate policy for certain types of authorizations, commitments, transactions and other undertakings, as follows:

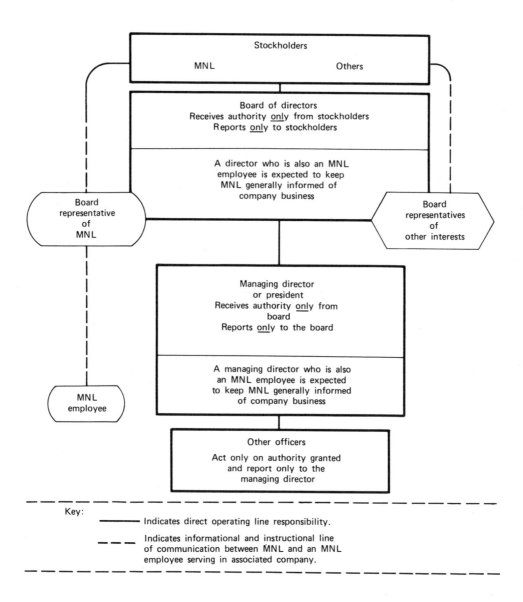

Figure 3. Organizational lines of authority in associated companies.

• Any change in the general scope of authority or of signers designated under resolutions currently in effect.

• Approval of specified undertakings, review of projects or programs the board has approved, or report of events or developments that may significantly affect corporate business.

GENERAL CORPORATE POLICIES

• Delegations of signature authority are subject to the provisions of any applicable statute, bylaw, or specific resolution of the board of directors or its finance committee.

• The managing director must be consulted promptly on certain important matters before verbal agreements are made or contracts signed that commit the corporation to a course of action.

• Ethical conduct of relationships and transactions is vital; conflicts of interest should be avoided.

• It is the MNL's policy always to comply with restrictions imposed by antitrust laws, as well as all other laws of the countries where the MNL conducts business.

• Contract forms must be approved by the legal counsel of the MNL, and be submitted to the secretary for review before they are signed.

• It is against corporate policy to execute contracts providing for automatic renewal in the absence of a termination notice. Exceptions to this policy are to be approved by the managing director.

ACTIONS RESERVED TO THE STOCKHOLDERS

• Elect annually the board of directors.

• Amend the certificate of incorporation (charter).

• Adopt or amend bylaws.

• Issue stock within authorized amounts.

• Effect any recapitalization plan or reduction in capital.

• Effect any increase, decrease, reclassification, or other adjustment in capital stock.

• Authorize the merger, consolidation, or dissolution of the corporation.

• Authorize the sale, lease, or exchange of any part of the company's assets in excess of 1% of its net worth.

• Employ annually the independent auditors.

• Authorize employee benefit or pension plans, basic changes, or substantial cost increases in existing plans.

GENERAL RESPONSIBILITIES AND FUNCTIONS OF DIRECTORS

As trustees of the company, the directors manage its business in compliance with the applicable laws, the bylaws, and the certificate of incorporation.

• Exercise prudent judgment, due care, undivided loyalty, and good faith in any act that affects corporate interests.

• Establish broad corporate objectives, determine basic policies, and appraise overall results.

• Protect corporate assets, promote their effective use, and approve changes (declare dividends, authorize issuance of securities, pledge assets on loans and convey property).

• Approve important financial matters (budgets, major appropriations, investments in new ventures, audits, and key executives' compensation).

• Refer to the stockholders those proposals that specifically require their approval; see that proper annual and interim reports inform stockholders of significant corporate developments.

• Perpetuate a sound board by holding regular elections and filling interim vacancies.

• Elect corporate officers, advise them, approve their actions, and audit their performance.

• Grant special authority to officers and executives to make commitments and sign contracts and other documents.

ACTION RESERVED TO THE BOARD OF DIRECTORS

• Qualify to do business under national and state laws.

• Authorize the purchase, guarantee, mortgage, transfer, sale, or disposition of securities of other companies.

• Authorize the purchase, mortgage, or conveyance of real estate or personal property.

- Fix the time and place of stockholder meetings.
- Fix the record dates for meetings, dividends allotments or exercise of rights, close transfer books, or obtain consents for any purpose.
- Authorize the inspection of corporate records.
- Fix the time and place for board meetings (does not begin any meeting until a quorum is present).
- Act without meeting, provided that prior written consent is given by all board members and filed with the board minutes.
- Designate and change membership of board committees; grant them powers and dissolve them.
- Elect officers.
- Fix compensation of officers.
- Grant officers or executives specific authority to make specific types of commitments or to sign specific types of contracts or other documents (or to delegate such authority).
- Authorize any change in the general scope of authority or in the signers designated under resolutions in effect.
- In the absence of a managing director, board action or delegation of alternate authority is required in matters not in the usual course of business.
- Authorize use of the corporate seal; prescribe and alter it.
- Authorize the listing on stock exchanges; approve or amend listing applications or agreements, subject to a policy review by all stockholders.
- Review financial reports.
- Accept corporate budgets.
- Review financial reports (sales, earnings, cash position, treasury stock, investments, borrowings, loans, contributions, etc.)
- Accept corporate budgets, subject to specific approval of particular undertakings as required by corporate policy.
- Approve and release the annual report to stockholders (after the audit committee has reviewed and recommended it). Authorize publication of earnings and dividends.

• Declare dividends.

• Review or act on such other matters as the managing director and board advise, according to the board's responsibilities to determine capital and reserves, vary working capital, and determine the use of working capital, surplus, or net profits.

• Authorize sales of real estate or grant of irrevocable easement and authorize signers of deeds or easements.

• Authorize the contribution budget.

• Inform stockholders of significant corporate developments through proper annual and interim reports.

• Report to the stockholders on such matters as:

Credit agreement notes.

Short-term borrowings.

Short-term investments.

Guarantees of affiliates' borrowing.

Loans to foreign affiliates.

Credit to foreign customers.

Leases of a specified number of dollars or more; exceeding a specified number of years).

• Authorize appropriations (and disposal requests) amounting to a specified number of dollars or more.

• Delegate to the finance committee authority to review, evaluate, and recommend to the board appropriations amounting to a specified number of dollars more.

AUTHORITY RESERVED TO THE FINANCE COMMITTEE

The board of directors at its first meeting held after the annual meeting of stockholders each year shall designate a finance committee that shall (a) consist of one or more directors, none of whom shall be an officer or an employee of the company or any of its subsidiaries and (b) have the sole authority to exercise the following functions of the board of directors:

1 To review and submit to the board with its recommendations (i) any proposed property appropriation or condemna-

tion "on budget" in excess of a specified number of dollars, (ii) any proposed property appropriation "not on budget" in excess of a specified number of dollars, and (iii) any appropriation or condemnation affecting real estate regardless of the amount involved, it being understood that all expenditures for any single project shall be covered by no more than one appropriation and that any series of expenditures relating to the same purpose shall be considered a single project.

2 To review and submit to the board with its recommendations any proposal to change the compensation of any employee or director of the company or any of its subsidiaries, including other allowances and emoluments not paid as salary, where the total compensation of such person is or will be in excess of a specified amount.

Note: Regarding The Finance Committee In Associated Companies

Finance committees should also operate in partially owned foreign subsidiaries and include one MNL director. This provides the MNL with the means of reviewing major capital expenditures without circumventing the authority of the local board.

In associated companies, the finance committee can effectively provide the MNL with the opportunity to review and control them. In deference to the local stockholders it may not be possible or practical, because of long distances, to have the finance committee review financial proposals, particularly capital expenditures, down to such a low dollar level as the MNL may insist on in wholly owned subsidiaries.

It should be clear to local partners that the finance committee, including an MNL director, should review *major* financial matters. The definition of *major* depends on the size of the company concerned.

MANAGING DIRECTOR'S OR PRESIDENT'S AUTHORITY—GENERAL

1 The managing director can delegate general authority in ordinary business matters. For example, he can delegate authority to officers or other executives to sign routine contracts or other documents, or to act to the extent necessary for efficient conduct of the company.

2 Grants or delegations of signature authority are subject to provisions of any applicable statute, bylaws or specific resolution of the board of directors.

3 The managing director must consult promptly with the board before contracts are signed (or verbal agreements made) that commit the company to a course of action on certain important matters.

4 Contracts providing for automatic renewal in the absence of notice of termination are contrary to corporate policy.

5 The managing director cannot delegate authority in matters outside the usual course of business.

ACTION RESERVED TO THE MANAGING DIRECTOR OR PRESIDENT, WHICH CANNOT BE DELEGATED

The following are matters outside the ordinary course of operations that require the managing director's signature or, in the event of his temporary absence, the signature of another officer authorized by the board to sign:

• Conveyances or contracts for the purchase or sale of real estate.

• Easements, restrictions, or long-term licenses for the use of land, except those revocable without penalty at the will of the corporation.

• Leases for over a specified number of years or involving a specified number of dollars or more.

• Contracts or commitments of any kind regarding the purchase or sale of any business or segment thereof.

• Contracts or commitments for the purchase, sale, or license of patents; as well as out-of-court settlement of infringement claims.

• Guarantees, indemnities, and warranties, other than standard product warranties.

• Employment of outside consultants.

• Research and development projects in excess of a specified number of dollars.

• Commitments for advertising or sales promotion in excess of a specified number of dollars.

• Authorization of any substantial variation for established credit terms.

• Personnel change in any key job and any salary change.

• Authorization of appropriations in excess of a specified number of dollars (but less than a specified amount over which amount action is reserved to the board or the finance committee.

ACTION WITHIN AUTHORITY OF THE MANAGING DIRECTOR OR PRESIDENT THAT CAN BE DELEGATED TO OTHER OFFICERS AND EXECUTIVES

• Delegate to a senior officer the authority to approve appropriations (and disposal requests) of a specified number of dollars or fewer.

• Grant powers of attorney to designated persons with specific authority for particular purposes regarding property and interests of the corporation as in his judgment is proper:

(a)   In the regular conduct of corporate business.

(b)   To protect corporate interests in any emergency.

• Acting under general authority of the board, the managing director may personally sign, or delegate others to sign, bids, contracts, guarantees, and bonds for the sale of any goods or services of the corporation to any foreign government or agency of subcontractor thereof.

• Make contractual arrangements for the sale of goods or services.

• Make disbursements in the ordinary course of business, such as:

(a)   Open and close bank accounts.

(b)   Authorize bank signatures.

(c)   Establish petty cash funds.

• Carry on official communication with any branch of the government.

• Register documents by the corporation pursuant to statutory requirements.

• Make personnel changes—hire, transfer, promote, demote, or terminate employees.

• Establish salaries and wage rates.

• Enter into contracts with unions or other employee bargaining agencies.

• Take actions necessary to safeguard assets of the company.

• Delegate authority to other officers or executives pursuant to an appropriate summary of delegation of authority approved by the board of directors.

See Figure 4, a sample letter to the managing director of an associated company, immediately after the MNL acquired equity interest in the company.

Señor Mario Lopez Gonzalez
Managing Director
MNL Associated Company
Madrid, Spain

Dear Mario:

In accordance with our policy of treating foreign subsidiaries as independent corporate entities, we agree in principle with the general contents of the resolutions approved by your board of directors in their meeting of June 22, 1979. In a similar sense, you will agree, the powers conferred upon specific members of the board and upon management should be subject to certain checks and balances in order to ensure safeguarding our stockholders' interests.

Our company policy, in line with good business practice, provides that the managing director be given every authority by the board to carry out his duties in the ordinary course of business.

We also feel it is advisable that the scope of power conferred upon any one individual be specific in time as well as in amount. For example, it is clear that no one should have the power to dispose of any substantial corporate asset without the approval of a committee of the board of directors. We recommend that such a committee known as the Finance Committee be formed, and further, that it be composed of three members, one of whom will *not* be an officer of the Company.

It appears prudent that certain changes be introduced into certain of the articles of point four, "Extension of Powers to Señor ———, Finance Manager," of the board's resolution of June 22, 1979, as follows:

Figure 4. Sample letter to the managing director of an associated company.

Figure 4. Continued.

Number 2 of the fourth point should clarify whether the term "Company's personnel" (personal de la empresa) includes corporate officers. If so, it must be clear that the appointment of officers and the determination of their compensation is subject to the approval of the finance committee. In reference to numerals, in order to provide for the necessary checks and balances mentioned above, it appears prudent to limit the finance manager's powers to bind the company to an amount not exceeding U.S. $———— (approximately Pesetas ————.) Contracts for amounts over $———— should be entered into only after the approval of the finance committee.

In relation to the powers conferred to Señor ———— related to opening new bank accounts and closing existing ones, it is good business practice to submit such transactions to the approval of a board of directors' finance committee. Therefore, opening new bank accounts or closing existing accounts should be subject to the finance committee's approval.

It must also be made clear that the director of finance (or managing director) may not delegate authority in matters not in the usual course of business. Contracts such as those mentioned in the fifth point (punto quinto) relating to technical assistance should also be subject to approval by the finance committee. We, therefore, suggest that it be proposed to the board and approved that the discretionary powers extended to the Financial Manager, Señor ————, be controlled by the amounts and principles explained in this memorandum. Such controls, you will agree, will enable other responsible directors to have an equitable share in the responsibilities of managing your company.

Very truly yours,
T. P. LANE
Vice President
Chief Financial Officer

CHAPTER 4

The Financial Environment

The foreign exchange market in the United States from its beginning in 1789 until World War I was somewhat disorganized. In the last decade of the eighteenth century a market began to develop in foreign banknotes; New York City was the principal market for foreign exchange and became more important during the 1800s. Mail transfers were the means of foreign exchange between the United States and Europe in contrast to the personal courier system that was prevalent throughout Europe.

During the nineteenth century a closer relationship developed between foreign banks and certain banks in New York. Forward contract exchanges began to be transacted, and the volume of foreign transfers and commercial transactions between the United States and Europe increased. Following the colonial period, no business in London was transacted in dollars, and trade with Britain was financed exclusively by contracts in sterling on the other side of the Atlantic. Many foreign exchange transactions were negotiated directly between American importers and exporters through advertising in newspapers for the bills they wanted to buy or sell. A more advanced foreign exchange system developed at the turn of the century, but it was interrupted at the outbreak of World War I, when foreign exchange markets became chaotic. It was impossible to carry out foreign exchange contracts entered into immediately before the war, and it was difficult to carry out contracts with enemy countries during the war. The pound sterling was endangered by the increase of the London bank rate to 10% in August 1914. The need was evident for an active forward exchange market. A system of "Put and Call" contracts in forward exchange was started in New York. The forward exchange market, which transacted most forward business on the telephone, became an integral part of the foreign exchange market.

Foreign exchange markets did not change significantly between World War I and World War II, and the conduct of business between Europe and a rather parochial United States was neither dramatic nor newsworthy. The principal exchanges became stabilized only after the end of World War II when Bretton Woods brought forth the International Monetary Fund. The Bretton Woods Agreement fixed the price of gold in dollars and related parities of international currencies to the dollar, tolerating a valuation of only 2%. The Bretton Woods Agreement produced stability and confidence in the monetary system by replacing economic warfare with rules and machinery for international cooperation. Some say that the breakdown of international monetary arrangements was really one of the major causes of the Depression of the 1930s. The Bretton Woods Agreement provided for fixed exchange parities that member countries of the newly established International Monetary Fund were obligated to defend. The system also called for abolishing exchange controls over current transactions and for reducing trade barriers. The objective was the gradual restoration of full convertibility among foreign currencies.

The Bretton Woods Agreement worked well until the 1950s. Payment imbalances among major countries became very large and the Bretton Woods system did not provide strong enough incentives for sizable fluctuations in foreign exchange. The dollar was the principal reserve currency. Accordingly, international liquidity could only be expanded through more United States dollar deficits. As the deficits accumulated, confidence in the dollar began to erode. In December 1971, representatives from major countries met at the Smithsonian Institute and reached an agreement by that name, but by 1973 the Smithsonian agreement had practically disappeared; all currencies floated freely against each other and the dollar began to lose ground.

What, then, is the current system of floating rates? Imbalances in payments among countries are corrected by changes in the relative prices of their currencies rather than through movements of reserves. Governments do not concern themselves with imbalances of payments that cause large inflows or outflows of reserves and, in turn, undesired effects on the domestic monetary system. Countries with floating rates are in one sense protected against recession started in another country; domestic inflation and unemployment even become remedies for a trade deficit.

Massive shifts of short-term capital funds occur solely for profit. Some movements are induced by differentials in interest paid by various countries, or by promoting certain imports, or most likely by the unknown forces of speculative transactions.

FOREIGN EXCHANGE MARKETS

In the United States foreign exchange markets operate on three levels (a fourth, the Euro-currency market relates more to international markets). At the first, the retail level, contract agreements between commercial banks and their customers, whether corporations or individuals, cover commercial transactions that result in a purchase or sale of foreign currencies for immediate or future delivery; the transactions may be commercial or even speculative and represent a hedge on the part of an American or foreign transporter or importer, assuring him that the final costs or profits agree with those figured at the date of sale. The cost and profit margins are kept intact in terms of his currency on the date the goods are delivered.

The second level covers transactions entered into by investors who wish to speculate on the future movement of foreign exchange rates, one against the other, for the purpose of making a profit. This level of the foreign exchange market in the

United States consists of interbank transactions commonly referred to as the wholesale market for foreign exchange. An agreement exists in the United States exchange market whereby commercial banks do not deal directly with each other but rather through agents or brokers. Commercial banks obtain coverage of the risks entered into by their acceptance to buy or sell foreign currencies from their customers.

The third level is the dealing of commercial banks with the American central bank, the Federal Reserve Bank. Central banks intervene when necessary to maintain parity in a specific currency; under these conditions commercial banks buy and sell foreign currencies with the Federal Reserve Bank.

An American commercial bank contracts for the purchase or sale of a foreign currency from a corporation, thereby shifting the exchange risk from the corporation to the commercial bank. In an active market such transactions compensate for each other and the risk entered with one corporation covers the risk from another. Depending on the volatility of the market at the end of the day, the trader determines what he calls his position. The purchases of a given currency with delivery on a specific date are compared with sales of the same currency for the same date. The trader thereby determines if his position is long or short; that is, if he is holding that currency or if he owes it. Having determined his position he covers his risk, usually with commercial banks, or he speculates by maintaining his position in these currencies on his own.

A central bank of a country can intervene in a commercial transaction and thereby assume the inherent foreign exchange risk. When exchange rates were calculated on a fixed basis with currencies having a parity fixed to the United States dollar, the risk to an exporter in an international transaction was minimal; the exchange risk was limited to the predetermined range. Since 1971, with the creation of a freely floating exchange, this risk has been intensified for the exporter and has led in many instances to a reduction in the number of foreign trade transactions. The importer or exporter can avoid the risk by passing it on to a foreign entity, such as a commercial bank.

The central bank of a country can better absorb risks than a commercial bank. It can evaluate the requests of all the importers and exporters and accordingly is in a position to compensate one transaction against another and cover part of the risk by itself. The central bank can also decide not to cover the risk if it would create an imbalance between the currency in circulation and the country's international reserve. A central bank wishing to diversify its reserves must accept the risk inherent in holding foreign currencies.

A national central bank can adopt certain strategies to cope with these situations and thereby influence the nation's foreign exchange rates and balance of payments.

Strategy 1   Maintain the spot rate at very near parity with little range for movement, thereby minimizing motivation to move funds into or from a currency in expectation that profit could be made from sudden changes in the exchange rate. This strategy maximizes stable markets. However, it may be difficult for the bank to protect its reserves from the impact of funds transferred abroad by those seeking higher interest rates. When domestic interest rates are higher than foreign interest rates, the cost is minimal.

Strategy 2   Seek to moderate or cushion any sudden movement in spot rates, trying limit changes in rates from .05 to .10% per week. There are several advantages to this method over Strategy 1. First, the small variance permitted in reserve encourages participants to enter the market in search of windfall profits; second, shifting funds abroad for higher interest rates is discouraged.

Strategy 3   The spot rate is allowed to move to the limit with minimum official intervention. This strategy reduces the use of rates in supporting the rate against potential speculation. However, movements in the exchange rate can be disorderly, for the rate might move quickly from one support limit to another.

Strategy 4 With only sporadic official intervention, expected fluctuations in exchange rates are an uncertain barrier to shifting funds. This strategy would tend to discourage shifts of funds on the expectations of changes in exchange rates and flows fo funds towards centers of higher interest rates abroad. This strategy encourages the least orderly market.

EUROCURRENCIES The final and probably most important part of this discussion is the market for Eurocurrencies. During the last few years this market has expanded rapidly; it is now the truly international credit market in the world. Foreign exchange markets operate through the United States dollar for the exchange, and arbitrage of currencies of major international countries has expanded this ability. The Eurocurrency market was formed because certain iron curtain countries wanted to hold dollar deposits outside the United States. During the last decade American banks have established numerous offices in Europe and have competed for dollar denominated deposits. American business enterprises in Europe have expanded tremendously, and European branch managers of American banks have earned greater profits on their dollar deposits.

The relationship between the Eurodollar market and foreign banks is difficult to fathom. It involves the foreign exchange cost of reconverting dollars into a foreign currency, or the risk assumed in not providing a reconversion. Banks and corporations do not operate in the same way; banks usually cover their exchange risks, whereas businesses may or may not. Large corporations operate in many currencies in several countries. The Eurodollar market, even more complex, involves official changes in policies, interest rates, forward rates, and so forth. These changes affect the level of domestic liquidity and the amount of international reserves held by a bank as well as the operations negotiated by the central bank itself or banks operating for it.

The Bank for International Settlements has been most significant in bank operations in the Eurodollar market during the last decade, especially in gold operations. The Bank for International Settlements has encouraged all its stockholders to deposit dollars, gold, or other funds in its bank in order to invest these funds to secure the maximum rate of return. The Bank for International Settlements also plays an important role in stabilizing interest rates on different kinds of assets in the European market. It has switched its holdings from one country to another and from one kind of asset to another in order to maximize its profits.

One other relationship between international capital markets and foreign exchange markets is arbitrage for the sake of arbitrage: switching funds from one currency to another although the profitable use of the converted currency needs to be developed. Foreign exchange dealers of large commercial banks having control of considerable amounts of money are better able to switch funds from one currency to another. The major part of the European market is denominated and conducted in dollars even though these dollars are not the same as those from the United States with regard to law, exchange control, and debt reimbursement. These differences may explain why rates of interest on loans made in Eurodollars vary from those charged on ordinary dollar loans in the United States. Loans are made in Eurodollars from a larger pool of deposits than are available to any one American commercial bank, hence the more attractive interest rates.

THE WORLD BANK   The idea of the World Bank started with plans for rebuilding the countries devastated during World War II, with the purpose of developing resources and productive capacities of the world, especially of less-developed countries. After four years the charter of the World Bank was signed by forty-four countries. Concurrently, the International Monetary Fund was also signed at Bretton Woods, New Hampshire in July, 1944. The International Monetary Fund is a regulatory agency composed of members from over a hundred countries for the purpose of stabilizing world exchange rates and financing balance of payment deficits. A member of the World Bank had to be a member of the International Monetary Fund. The "Bretton Woods

Twins" could thereby regulate exchange rates, encourage world currency stability through the Fund, and provide capital lending facilities through the Bank.

The Export-Import Bank was established to foster United States foreign trade, which had faltered during the Depression years of 1929 to 1933. The Eximbank was founded by Executive Order 6581 under terms of the National Recovery Act of 1934. It was a "risk-sharing" institution that might, for example, extend as much as $100 million in credit for financing trade with the Soviet Union. Its preferred stock was held by the Reconstruction Finance Corporation; the common stock was held by the State and Commerce Departments, the Reconstruction Finance Corporation, and the Agricultural Adjustment Administration.

Between 1945 and 1950, the Export-Import Bank and the World Bank became rivals because foreign applicants pit one bank against the other. During this period the United States was the only major and significant banker in the world. The Eximbank's primary purpose was to support and encourage foreign trade of the United States, and not to promote the economic development of foreign countries. The banks differed in these areas:

• The World Bank scrutinized more carefully the credit worth of its applicants.

• The interest rate in 1950 at the World Bank was 4.5% on long-term investments; at the Eximbank it was 3.5%.

• Eximbank favored granting loans to countries that were politically aligned with the United States.

• Open bidding on projects was required by the World Bank whereas American products or services were tied to the loans granted by Eximbank.

• The World Bank could make loans only to its members.

The Banks both complement and compete with each other. But if the Eximbank was considering a long-term loan that the

World Bank wanted, the World Bank, through its governmental membership, could and would exert pressure on that member to let the World Bank finance the transaction.

The World Bank group consists of the International Bank for Reconstruction and Development (IBRD), the International Development Association (IDA), and the International Finance Corporation (IFC). The International Bank for Reconstruction and Development is the core or "mother" to this World Bank group. It comprises over a hundred nations and its capital subscription is determined by consulting each new member. Prior to membership, the prospective member must be a participant of the International Monetary Fund. The purposes of the IBRD are:

1 To assist in reconstructing and developing territories of members by facilitating the investment of capital for productive purposes, such as restoring economies destroyed or disrupted by war, reconverting productive facilities to peacetime needs, and encouraging the development of productive facilities and resources in less-developed countries.

2 To promote private foreign investment by means of guarantees or participation in loans and other investments made by private investors and when private capital is not available on reasonable terms, to supplement private investments by providing, on suitable conditions, finance for productive purposes out of its own capital, funds raised by it, and its other resources.

3 To promote the long-range balanced growth of international trade and to maintain equilibrium in balance of payments by encouraging international investment for the development of the productive resources of members, thereby assisting in raising productivity, the standards of living, and conditions of labor in their territories.

4 To arrange the loans made or guaranteed by it in relation to international loans through other channels so that the more useful and urgent projects, large and small alike, will be dealt with first.

5 To conduct its operations considering the effect of international investment on business conditions in the territories of members and, in the immediate postwar years, to help achieve a smooth transition from a wartime to a peacetime economy.

The International Bank for Reconstruction and Development is the heart of the World Bank and the competitor of the Eximbank. As the IBRD began to grow and more subscriptions were paid into the treasury, the Bank tried to make loans rather than guaranteeing them. Throughout its history, the IBRD has never paid a dividend because the member nations thought that it should be a nonprofit organization.

In the place of dividends, "Profits" were retained as earnings and used to enhance lending capabilities. As time went on, the Bank, through its own activities in the developing world, became increasingly aware of the urgent need for an institution that could provide development finance on more lenient terms that would bear less heavily on balance of payments of developing countries. To achieve this goal, initiated largely by the United States, the International Development Association was formed in 1960. Most other industrialized members of the World Bank or IBRD, as well as many of the developing member countries, soon joined the Association. At the end of December, 1973, it had 112 members, divided into two categories. The 19 "Part I" countries represent the developed or high-income members (that is, the United States, The United Kingdom, Germany, France, Norway, Sweden, Japan, Canada, etc.). "Part II" countries comprise IDA's poorer or relatively less-developed nations. These 93 countries include Afghanistan, Brazil, Burma, China, Chile, Ghana, Haiti, Honduras, Kenya, Nepal, Panama, Togo, Uganda, and Zaire.

Capital funding for the International Development Association is based again on subscription. The amount is determined by consulting its members, and depends on the economic strength of the member and its classification as either a Part I or Part II country. Each Part I country pays its entire subscription in convertible funds; the balance is paid in the member's own currency and may not be used by IDA without that country's consent. To date, $906 million has been subscribed in convertible currencies that the IDA can use for lending.

The Association makes concessionary loans to its poorest member-countries based on sound, productive, high-priority economic projects. The concessionary loans thus far have been for terms of 50 years and bear no interest. After a ten-year grace period, 1% of the credit is repaid annually for 10 years; during the remaining thirty years, 3% is to be repaid annually. Under the Articles of Agreement that provide the terms for IDA it says that terms should be more flexible and weigh less heavily on the balance of payments than those of conventional loans.

In summary, the purposes of the International Development Association are to promote economic development and increase productivity, thus raising the standard of living in the less-developed areas of the world included within the Association's membership, especially financing their important development requirements on more flexible terms that bear less heavily on the balance of payments than those of conventional loans; thereby the IDA furthers the developmental objectives of the International Bank for Reconstruction and Development and supplements its activities.

The third member of the World Bank group is the *International Finance Corporation.* The IFC was formed in 1956 to finance private enterprises of members of the IBRD and to protect private investors from government intervention. Loans by the IBRD and IDA are made to governments whereas the IFC makes loans to the private sector. The IFC will neither solicit nor accept a government guarantee of its investments. It can make a direct investment in the stock (equity sharing) of an enterprise as well as a loan to it; the IFC can purchase stock outright, and it can also help underwrite a stock issue. The corporation thus developed another area of capital markets by giving support to private finance corporations.

Since mid-1969, under the direction of Robert McNamara, president of the World Bank, the IFC has shifted its emphasis to a financial development institution for private use as compared to one for special situations; the IFC, generally, shows greater interest in the development of capital markets and development loan companies.

IFC members are also members of the IBRD and in 1979 there were 96 members. Again, subscription to capital stock was necessary and originally $100 million was subscribed to, with a par value of $1000 per share and with the issuance of 100,000 shares. Although the IBRD and the IDA use the same staff, the International Finance Corporation has its own staff and its own funds.

The president of the World Bank serves ex-officio as chairman of the board of directors of the IFC and he has been appointed to act as president of the IFC. The directors of IFC are the executive directors of the World Bank, and they are appointed or elected by at least one government that is a member of IFC.

Private investors should look upon the IFC as a catalyst for meeting financial needs. With private investments and capital it tries to finance industrial development in less-developed countries in association with the corporation.

THE EXPORT-IMPORT BANK OF THE UNITED STATES

The Export-Import Bank of the United States was established during the Depression to improve the balance of payments of the United States, assist export sales, and help domestic business create employment. It is a bank, and not an institution for economic aid like the International Bank for Reconstruction and Development. The Eximbank finances overseas applicants so that they might purchase American goods or services. The dollars loaned never actually leave the United States, and the repayments of principal and interest come from overseas.

American commercial banks traditionally have not been interested in overseas business because of the risks involved. The Eximbank does not compete with domestic commercial banks; it usually provides a direct loan for the first 45% of the purchase price and guarantees the next 45% provided by a cooperating commercial bank. Today, American banks are interested in overseas business but still turn to Eximbank because this cooperation offers more attractive terms.

The Export-Import Bank was first established by executive order as a District of Columbia banking corporation in February, 1934, and named the Export-Import Bank of Washington. The United States was beginning the Reciprocal Trade Agreements program that required financing for its success. The government also wanted to "prime the pump" with exports as a means of alleviating the Depression.

On March 9, 1934, a second Export-Import Bank of Washington was established by executive order to finance trade between the United States and Cuba. On May 7, 1936, the second Bank was abolished and its commitments were transferred to the first Eximbank. Although the Eximbank has consistently financed foreign trade of the United States, it has changed its methods as domestic and world situations changed. As Europe prepared for war in the late 1930's, international trade closely followed the course of international politics; many countries could no longer import from their traditional sources. At this time overseas buyers began to request assistance from the Eximbank, whereas until then the Bank had dealt almost exclusively with American exporters.

During World War II Eximbank financed several key activities, such as the steel industry of Brazil; it also lent $25 million to the Universal Trading Corporation, as agent for the Chinese government, to finance construction of the Burma Road.

When World War II ended, the United States began to furnish large-scale credit assistance to many foreign countries to rehabilitate their economies. The administration sent a bill to Congress that would establish Eximbank as an independent agency of the United States government with authority to lend up to $3½ billion. The Export-Import Bank Act of 1945 was signed on the same day as the Bretton Woods Agreement Act to show America's determination to participate in international trade and to finance and support other countries. This act, except for a few amendments, is basically the law under which

Eximbank operates today. Eximbank then embarked on a program of large-scale lending in the form of reconstruction loans to almost every allied country in Europe.

In the immediate postwar period, Eximbank loaned some $5 billion to Europe and China, covering purchases in the United States of equipment needed to reestablish economic activity. The USSR was not included because of political differences between the two countries, growing problems in the United States, and America's failure to gain Soviet friendship and cooperation at the peace table, which had been expected as a result of the major Lend-Lease program to the Soviet Union during the war.

Under the Lend-Lease program, the United States had supplied aid to the Allies on a scale that was too large for them to purchase, and had removed the dollar sign from this aid so as not to complicate postwar settlements. After the Allies' victory in Europe, the Soviet Union sealed its occupation zones, ringing down Churchill's famous "iron curtain," and proceeded to strip Eastern Europe of industrial and agricultural materials for reparations. With the establishment of the Marshall Plan in 1948, Eximbanks's responsibility for reconstruction was reduced. The Bank's resources were then called upon to finance projects in the developing world. In the late 1950s, the United States confronted a persistent decline in its balance of payments; increased exports were one way of coping with this problem.

Eximbank Operation Today

Eximbank today recognizes that credit is as important a competitive tool as price, quality, or service. For American exporters to compete in foreign markets they must be provided with credit facilities as good as those available to exporters in other countries. New extension and improvement programs were inaugurated in the four basic activities of the Bank: direct credit to foreign borrowers, export credit guarantees, export credit insurance, and discount loans. The Eximbank also makes special foreign trade loans to governments with dollar shortages.

The inflow of principal, interest, and fees on long-term and other credits that the Eximbank extends directly to foreign borrowers, plus sales of loans abroad less payments to participating foreign holders of loans, contributes annually to the favorable side of United States' balance of payments. In addition, a million in dollar payments is received by suppliers or their banks on sales financed under the Eximbank's guarantees and insurance programs, also to the credit side of the United States payments balance.

Funds for the Eximbank's operations derive from a number of sources, among them the sale abroad of certificates of beneficial interest in individual loans. Capital stock and accumulated reserves used in the business of the Bank provide over $2 billion in funds. The Eximbank has also sold certificates of participation in its portfolio, debentures, and short-term discount promissory notes, which are all in the public money market.

The Eximbank requires that the proceeds of its loans be used to pay for goods and services procured from the United States. By contrast the World Bank is primarily interested in furthering the economic and social development of particular countries, and namely, the less-developed countries of the world.

Before granting any loans, the Eximbank considers how the applicant meets the following policy requirements:

• The Bank's primary purpose is to promote the United States' export and import trade.

• The Bank supplements private capital but does not compete with it.

• Loans of the Bank are generally for specific exports, projects, or services.

• The Bank evaluates possible adverse effects on the country's economy once the project will have been completed, and reckons the possibility of promoting foreign competition and its ensuing effects on American manufacturers.

• The Bank must have reasonable assurance that the borrower can secure income to service the debt owed the Bank and be able to get the necessary foreign exchange. All loans plus interest must be paid in dollars.

Direct Loans and Financial Guarantees (Participation Financing) of the Eximbank

To qualify for a direct loan or financial guarantee the borrower must:

• Give "reasonable assurance" of repayment.

• Give proof that the project supported by the loan will be economically, financially, and technically sound.

• Give assurance that the project will not adversely affect the economy of the United States or the country in which the project is located.

The purposes of the direct lending programs are:

1 To supplement private sources of financing when the private financial source is unwilling or unable to assume the political and commercial risks under current conditions.
2 To extend credit on terms longer than those private lenders can provide.
3 To enable American suppliers to provide terms on major projects that equal or better those offered by government-sponsored export financing institutions in other exporting countries.

The Eximbank's policy concerning direct loans is heading more and more toward "participation financing." Under this plan the borrower gets 50% of the loan in dollars and the remainder from a commercial bank. To encourage the commercial bank to participate, the Eximbank will supply it a financial guaranty, in the amount of the participation, that covers the possibility of the borrower's bankruptcy. This policy has a threefold purpose:

1 Assuring that the Eximbank's financial resources supplement rather than compete with private sources of export financing.

2 Extending the usefulness of the Eximbank's cash resources to the largest possible number of purchases and projects.

3 Assuring that private financial institutions will continue to provide export credits in the international arena.

Eximbank will gurantee medium-term (181 days to 5 years) loans made by American banking institutions to American exporters. The purpose of these commercial bank exporter guarantees is to encourage banks to assist American exporters who must provide deferred credit terms on their sales. Upon receipt of an overseas order, the exporter goes to his commercial bank and it determines the acceptability of the transaction for the amount or the credit terms proposed. If the bank desires guarantee coverage it can apply to Eximbank for coverage against the credit and political risks of nonpayment.

Because this program supports commercial banks, Eximbank relies to a considerable extent on the credit judgment of the commercial bank in approving the transaction. Banks experienced in export financing are granted discretionary and delegated authority, permitting them to commit the Eximbank to issue guarantees, within specific limits, without prior Eximbank approval.

Most major banks are involved with export financing, and therefore a master guarantee agreement is issued to them by the Eximbank. If discretionary or delegated authority is not being used, but prior approval by the Eximbank is desired or required, the bank submits the necessary financial and credit data with a formal application to the Eximbank.

When a particular shipment is made, the Eximbank's guarantee is issued to the commercial bank upon notice from the bank that it has purchased the buyer's promissory notes without recourse to the exporter. The commercial bank makes the loan to the exporter without recourse, being protected by the Eximbank's guarantee against defined credit or political loss.

Under the terms and conditions of this coverage, the Eximbank requires that the buyer pay the exporter 10% of the total price on or before delivery. At the same time, the exporter must retain not less than 10% of the financing for his own account and risk.

The Cooperative Financing Facility, another program by which the Eximbank assists American exporters, enables the Eximbank to make credit available to small and medium-sized purchasers of American equipment and services through banks in their own countries. The Eximbank will lend half the funds at a low rate of interest. Bank "X" then provides the other half of the financing from its own resources and extends the loan at its own risk. At the same time, if Bank "X" wished to borrow its half of the financing, the Eximbank could assist it by guaranteeing repayment to another lender of these funds. This program has the following benefits:

1 It extends Eximbank financing to small and medium-sized enterprises that might not otherwise be able to purchase American goods. The familiarity of the local bank with the customer's credit standing and local market conditions enable it to evaluate the loan request quickly.
2 It allows the local bank to broaden its lending capacity, increase its resources, develop new relations with existing customers, and attract new customers.
3 It helps American suppliers expand their exports and services to enterprises that lack experience in financing overseas purchases. Many enterprises find working with their own bank the most convenient way to obtain their financing.

The Bank also offers the Medium-Term Discount Program and the Short-Term Discount Program to assist financing sales that require repayment terms of 12 months or longer, and 364 days or shorter, respectively. The Bank similarly urges the exporters and private banks to use this program only when other sources of funding are not available. The Eximbank will make advance commitments for discount loans of up to 100% of the principal amount or discounted value of eligible export debt obligations that arise from the financing of current American exports or services.

Under the lease guarantee program, one of the special support programs that the Eximbank is involved in, the Bank will cover full payout leases and nonpayout leases. The Bank will also arrange financing for engineering, planning, and feasibility studies. The Eximbank recognizes that historically the export sale generally follows as a consequence of the feasibility study. Further, the bank offers some excellent services such as helping the Export Finance Counsel, getting credit information for American commercial banks, and providing professional training in international finance for American commercial banks. The Eximbank also has extremely strong ties and influences with the Foreign Credit Insurance Association (FCIA), the Domestic International Sales Corporation (DISC), the Private Export Funding Corporation (PEFCO), and other domestic and international financial institutions.

We now have a clear idea of the Eximbank's programs of direct loans, participating finance, guarantees, medium-term guarantees, discounted loans, and services and facilities that the Bank can offer. All of these assist American exporters and indirectly assists in a positive balance of payments effort.

THE EURODOLLAR MARKETS

DEFINITION AND CHARACTERISTICS OF EURODOLLARS Eurodollars are deposits of United States dollars in interest bearing accounts of a foreign bank. Other currencies such as the deutsche mark and the yen are also part of the Eurodollar market, which is an international pool of liquid capital denominated in convertible currencies. The distinguishing characteristic of a Eurocurrency is that it is deposited in a bank in a country to which the currency is not "native."

This is the key: the dollar must be outside the borders of its country of origin, as when an American depositor maintains dollar balances in the foreign branch office of an American bank. Transferring a dollar balance from a bank located in the United States to its London branch creates Eurodollars. Other countries outside Europe maintain a flourishing trade in dollars and a major new market is developing in Asia. Singapore's role in the Asiadollar market is like London's in the Eurodollar market.

ORIGIN AND GROWTH OF THE EURODOLLAR MARKET

The unique quality of the modern money market and the reason for the Eurodollar market derive from the disparity of interest rates of different countries. Banks in the United States are subject to the regulations and guidelines of the Federal Reserve System. Interest rates in the United States were until 1979 lower than those available in the Eurodollar market. The bulk of dollars traded outside the United States occurs in Europe, mainly in London, and is the primary means of transmitting short-term funds across the national boundaries and, more recently, medium and long-term funds.

A form of the international money market has existed for a long time, and a highly developed market existed before and after World War I, with London as the center. After the Second World War, a number of European banks (particularly British banks) revived the practice of taking dollar deposits and, instead of placing these dollars in New York, lent them to other European banks to finance international trade. As a result, a market began to develop for dollars outside New York. Various state banks in Eastern Europe placed dollars with Moscow's Narodny Bank in London and with the Banque Commerciale pour L' Europe du Nord in Paris, preferring to keep their dollar balances safe in Europe rather than risking balances blocked in New York. As these dollar balances grew, banks made every effort to lend these funds at more attractive yields than could be obtained by the usual operations of investing dollars in the New York market.

The market has flourished primarily because the banks operating in it have been able to establish interest rates at levels that have been strongly competitive against their domestic banking counterparts on both sides of the Atlantic. At the same time, American and European monetary authorities have been invaluable in developing the market through their introduction of various artificial barriers to the free flow of funds across national boundaries.

The foreign banks have been free of self-imposed regulations common in nearly all domestic money markets. As a result, the Eurobanks have the opportunity of circumventing these restrictions and thus they attract business because of both cost and maturity. The absence of reserve requirements against deposits traded in the market also works to Eurobanks' advantage. Almost all domestic banking systems have obligatory reserve requirements for deposits.

Eurodollar deposits are free of reserve requirements and can offer more attractive rates. Some countries, particularly the United States, forbid payment on interest on deposits with a maturity of less than 30 days. This ruling was the result of the chaotic conditions of the 1930s that led to unsound banking practices in America, and has given Eurobanks an open door to attract depositors by paying interest on these short-term deposits. Also, throughout the 1960s the Federal Reserve Board of the United States put a ceiling on the rate of interest that American banks could pay on time deposits with maturities greater than 30 days. This "Regulation Q" undoubtedly gave, from time to time, a great impetus to the development of the Eurodollar market. Throughout most of the 1970s, interest rates in Europe were higher than interest rates in the United States, which enabled European banks to attract dollar deposits.

HOW A EURODOLLAR LOAN IS MADE

A holder of $1 million deposit (A) in an American bank is attracted by the interest yield on a deposit in the Eurodollar market. The holder's time deposit matures and it becomes a demand deposit in the United States, and the funds are then transferred to Europe. A's demand deposit in the United States becomes Eurobank I's demand deposit. Demand deposits in the American banking system remain unchanged but, through the intermediation of the Eurobank, a dollar denominated deposit has been created in the Eurodollar market. Since this deposit is a perfect substitute for the time deposit previously held in the American bank, then the world supply of "dollars" has been increased by this transfer of funds. However, it should be stressed that the Eurodollar deposit cannot be used for settling debts by writing checks—the deposit is only a liquid asset.

Eurobank will be anxious to convert its demand deposit (noninterest bearing) into an interest bearing asset by using the deposit for loans. Let us assume that the entire $1 million is lent to another Eurobank that temporarily needs funds and is consequently willing to offer a slightly higher rate than Eurobank, which paid for those funds. Eurobank instructs the American bank to debit the demand deposit and credit the account of Eurobank II. Again, the American banking system is left unaffected. Thus, Eurobank I, in the same manner as A, has converted a demand deposit into a time deposit, but by so doing has brought into existence another $1 million of dollar denominated deposits, bringing the total of Eurodollar deposits to $2 million. This process may be repeated a number of times.

EDGE ACT BANKS

The American banking legislation known as the International Banking Act received approval of Congress in mid-August of 1978; President Carter signed the bill without ceremony or publicity. This legislation ended a debate within the American banking community that pit the internationally active regional banks together with the Federal Reserve against the large New York banks and their allies among foreign banks already established in the United States.

The International Banking Act permits foreign banks to open branches or agencies under the administration of the Comptroller of the Currency, with the same rights and privileges, and subject to all the same duties, restrictions, penalties, liabilities, conditions, and limitations that would apply to a national bank under the National Banking Act.

The rules of deposit acceptance resemble those currently applying to Edge Act subsidiaries of American banks. In effect, foreign banks can operate in their "home state of operations" on a fully competitive basis with American banks, but like American banks headquartered in the same state, branch offices cannot be established in either state to take domestic deposits except under the rules of the Edge Act. This means they can only take deposits from foreign sources or when related to international trade.

CHAPTER 5

Financing Import-Export Trade

One problem in exporting is not knowing the buyer or his country. Banks provide this information through their export department or through correspondent relationships with large metropolitan banks. Two basic questions must be answered to export sucessfully: Does the buyer's country allow unrestricted payment for imports? Is the buyer financially able to pay for the merchandise?

Countries in a good position regarding balance of payments and foreign exchange normally do not restrict payments on imports. Yet, in every South and Central American country there is some form of payment restriction, ranging from simple exchange permits in Venezuela to absolute control of import payments in Argentina, Uruguay, and Chile. It is possible to ship goods to a reputable customer and still not receive payment due to a decree of the country of import to suspend payments on all or part of the debt. This type of decree, known as a moratorium, terminates or suspends payments, and the decree of a sovereign country is final.

When the country of import is economically stable and does not restrict payments, the credit decision relies on the buyer's financial capacity and integrity. The exporter protects his investment by requiring the importer to establish a letter of credit or to arrange for a documentary sight draft shipment.

Letters of credit are usually used when the exporter has some serious doubt as to either the financial status of the customer or the ability of the country to make available to the importer sufficient foreign exchange to make the payment on time. A letter of credit is a protective device that minimizes the impact of unknown factors and at the same time facilitates payment. A letter of credit is arranged by the importer, who has his bank inform a bank in the country of export that it will pay a certain amount of money against receipt of certain documents, that is, evidence of shipment. The exporter's bank then informs the exporter, the beneficiary of the credit. The domestic bank may, if requested, add its guarantee of payment to the exporter, a process known as confirmation. The principal value of the letter of credit sale is that payment can be made to the exporter while the goods are in transit. Because all governmental regulations must be complied with before the document is issued, the exporter receives payment without delay.

If the exporter is not concerned with the stability or regulations in the importing country, a letter of credit may not be necessary. The most commonly used alternative procedure is documentary collection, whereby the shipper presents documents covering the shipment to the importer, through the banking system, with a draft drawn on the buyer for the amount of the order. This device protects the shipment since the customer cannot obtain title to the merchandise until payment is made to the local bank.

Shipments on consignment are less protected but can sometimes be covered by insurance. Export Credit Insurance can be obtained through the Foreign Credit Insurance Association (FCIA) which is operated under the guarantee of the Eximbank. This insurance protects against non-payment due to commercial and political risks and facilitates financing credit sales through commercial banks.

With a commitment from FCIA to insure a shipment, an exporter can arrange to have a bank purchase the insured receivables, thereby freeing working capital by financing these medium and long-term sales. FCIA sales range from 180 days to three years, medium-term transaction, to sales on terms exceeding three years, which are considered long-term. FCIA rates are confidential but generally average about 1/4% of the insured portion of any sale.

FCIA, recognizing the problem of paper work, has instituted innovative steps such as prequalification of foreign buyers and a master policy for exporters. Prequalification utilizes FCIA's vast sources of credit data to establish limits for foreign buyers so that the turnaround time of coverage approval is reduced.

These plans greatly assist American exporters to obtain orders despite the competition from exporters in other countries, which sometimes have superior means to stimulate exports. The Eximbank also provides services that are designed to enable exporters to offer competitive payment terms.

The Eximbank services are usually offered in conjunction with the participation of an American commercial bank, thereby enabling the private sector to help increase exports and still have the assurance of the Eximbank guarantee.

• The Eximbank places primary emphasis on export assistance, with secondary concern for economic progress of developing nations.

• The Eximbank is the only government institution undertaking direct lending in industrialized as well as less-developed countries.

• The Eximbank enables American firms that deal in capital goods to participate in channeling direct loans to prospective customers.

• Proceeds of Eximbank's loans and credits can be spent only in the United States.

Eximbank's principal methods of assisting exporters are making and guaranteeing long-term direct loans to investment projects abroad while requiring the purchase of American equipment; providing medium-term financing in conjunction with commercial banks and discounting export debts of commercial banks; and guaranteeing exports of marginal risk not normally acceptable to FCIA and the commercial banks. The Eximbank and FCIA assistance, though controlled by the federal government, is available even to the smallest exporter.

LETTERS OF CREDIT

Major international commercial banks provide a variety of services designed to assist corporations in the conduct of international business. Among these services are making spot and future foreign exchange contracts, executing international transfers of funds through networks of correspondent banks, handling inward or outward collections, and arranging for participation loans or loan guarantees from various government agencies, such as the Eximbank, AID, and Overseas Private Investment Corporation. Two of the most frequently used services involve letter of credit transactions and banker's acceptances financing.

As previously noted, the most significant barrier to international trade is the lack of credit information on prospective customers located in different countries. The exporter is hesitant to ship merchandise to a foreign company with which he has had only minimal previous dealings. The importer is reluctant to pay an unknown foreign company for goods before their shipment or arrival. The solution to both problems is a letter of credit, which assures the shipper that he will be paid if he complies with his part of the contact and also assures the purchaser that the shipper will not be paid until he fulfills the contractual terms

The letter of credit is a document issued by the buyer's bank, authorizing the seller to draw in accordance with certain terms; it stipulates in legal form that all such bills will be honored. It sets forth under what terms and conditions the person in whose favor the letter has been opened may draw drafts against such credit, at the same time guaranteeing the payment or acceptance of such drafts as they comply with the letter's terms.

A letter of credit involves four parties: (1) the importer who applies for the credit to facilitate purchase of his goods; (2) the importer's bank, which has added its credit to the importer's; (3) the bank on which the drafts are drawn and consequently the bank that pays the shipper of the merchandise; and (4) the beneficiary, who has shipped the goods and will receive the money from the paying banks.

The process starts when the importer, or account party, applies to the opening bank for a letter of credit. The opening bank writes a letter of credit for the account party worthy of the credit and sends the credit directly to the beneficiary or to a correspondent bank, which either advises or confirms the letter of credit to the beneficiary. If the letter of credit is confirmed by the correspondent bank, the bank adds its guarantee of payment to that of the account party and the opening bank; if the letter of credit is advised the correspondent bank does not guarantee payment. After the beneficiary has received the letter of credit and complied with its requirements he presents the letter of credit, the draft, and the stipulated shipping documents to the correspondent; the confirming bank examines the documents to assure that all the requirements of the letter of credit have been met; once satisfied, it can pay the beneficiary the amount that he is owed under the credit. Only the documents, and not the goods themselves are examined. If the correspondent bank had only advised the credit, it would still pay the beneficiary outright if the opening bank had sufficient monies deposited to cover the draft or it could pass the documents on to the opening bank, which would credit the correspondent's account for the proceeds. At the same time the beneficiary's account would be credited for the amount, and the account party's account would be debited notice or payment for the proceeds and commission charges. Along with the debit notice or payment receipt, the account party would receive the shipping documents that enable him to claim the merchandise. The denomination currency of the letter of credit can be that of either country involved depending on who is to accept the foreign exchange risk.

The letter of credit permits exporters to confidently deal with importers with whom they would otherwise not do business because ignorant of the foreign company's credit standing. At the same time letters of credit give importers a measure of protection since documentation concerning the shipment of goods has to be in order before the exporter is paid.

A fundamental idea of letters of credit is that banks deal in documents only and are merely responsible for assuring that the documents appear to be in order. A letter of credit is a contract between the account party and the issuing bank whereas the contract of sale is between the buyer and seller; each contract is independent of the other. The obligation of the bank to the buyer is to issue the letter of credit in accordance with its agreement with the buyer, honor drafts drawn against the letter of credit when presented with the proper documents, and examine the documents to ascertain that they do actually conform to the letter of credit. Thus the buyer must known his customer to some extent because letters of credit will not protect him against damaged or defective merchandise, or even worse, against fraudulent shipments of material that does not conform to the documents. In these instances the account party has recourse against the beneficiary only under the contract of sale. (See Figure 5.)

BANKERS' ACCEPTANCES

The use of a banker's acceptance as an instrument to finance the increasing volume of international trade has grown substantially since the end of World War II. A banker's acceptance originates in a commercial transaction in which the buyer of goods is obligated to the seller. Being from different countries, neither the buyer nor the seller knows the credit standing of the other and therefore they need a means of guaranteeing delivery of the goods and payment for them. Acceptance financing allows the multinational to go to its American bank,

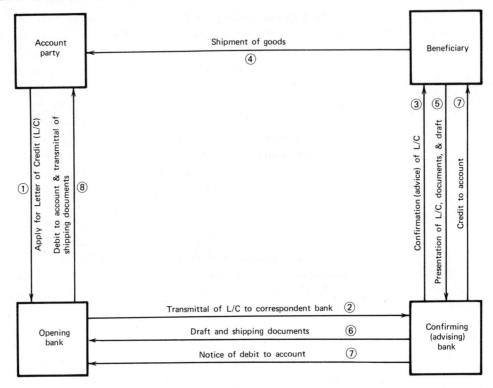

Figure 5. Letter of credit operations.

which assumes the obligation to pay the amount owed the seller at a specified date.

The contract binds the parties and defines obligations in a document known as a "time draft." The importer or exporter, as the case may be, makes a time draft payable at an American bank. The draft becomes the written order to pay a certain amount of money in dollars (although any currency can be used in an acceptance) to a certain party sometime in the future. When the instrument is presented at the bank and found to be in order, the draft as a contract will be stamped "accepted" and signed by an official of the acceptance bank. In this action the bank unconditionally assumes the liability for payment of the item when it comes due, even if the initiating party of the acceptance fails to repay the bank. Thus, a banker's acceptance is a time draft drawn against a bank and accepted by it.

In acceptance financing, an importer of goods approaches the exporter's bank with a request to grant acceptance credit. When the bank agrees to extend financing to the importer, it sends a commercial letter of credit advising him that the credit has been established and tells the exporter to draw a time draft on the importer's bank. Acceptance of the draft by the bank depends on a fee and a set of documents accompanying the draft, namely the invoices, bills of lading, and insurance policies. When the documents are certified by the bank of importer, the exporter can then exercise the draft he holds by cashing it, discounting it, or holding it until maturity.

The exporter or his bank then forwards the draft to the importer's bank, which determines that the accompanying documents are in order and accepts the draft, thereby creating a "banker's acceptance." The bank thereby irrevocably agrees to pay the obligation and the importer rather than the exporter becomes the credit risk.

The primary function of the acceptance is to enable the exporter of goods to obtain cash as soon as possible and at the same time to give the importer the option to defer payment until he receives and inspects the goods or even until they are sold.

In the United States, commercial banks, Edge Act corporations, foreign banks, and American agencies and branches engage in acceptance financing and other forms of international financing. Certain banks have more expertise in this area than others; an acceptance from one of these is known as a "prime banker's acceptance." Whether an acceptance is prime depends on the obligation of the acceptor and on trade at a prime rate. The participant who draws the acceptance and any unlimited endorsers are continually liable in the event that the acceptor, the bank, should default. The basis of the whole acceptance transaction is the expectation of cash that will enable the participant to liquidate his debt to the accepting bank. To the banks, each other's acceptances are attractive especially if the "paper acceptances" conform to certain Federal Reserve regulations. Commercial drafts and bills stemming from the following transactions are all eligible under the Federal Reserve regulations.

1 Import or export of goods.
2 Shipment of goods between foreign countries.
3 Storage of readily marketable staples in the United States or any foreign country.
4 Shipment of goods within the United States.

To be eligible, bankers' acceptances must mature within six months of the date of acceptance and bear evidence that the transaction is satisfactory to the local Federal Reserve Bank.

Acceptances are particularly adaptable to financing international trade. In the area of imports in the United States, coffee, sugar, iron and steel products, and wool and textile products are usually financed by acceptances. On the export side, acceptances finance the sale of American products such as grains, machinery, cotton, ore, oil, iron, and steel. In economic market trade between foreign countries acceptances are used for transactions involving oil, ores, metals, wool, cotton, grains, sugar, and rubber. As these materials become more and more scarce and vital to our economy, the acceptance is a means of guaranteeing delivery without prepayment.

MORE ON BANKERS' ACCEPTANCES A bankers' acceptance is a draft or bill of exchange, whether payable in the United States or abroad and whether payable in dollars or some other money, accepted by a bank or trust company, or a firm, company, or corporation engaged generally in the business of granting bankers' acceptance credits. This credit instrument finances both domestic and international self-liquidating transactions. Acceptances that can be discounted with (sold to) to Federal Reserve System are termed "prime" bankers' acceptances.

In addition to imports and exports, acceptances finance the following types of transactions:

1 Shipments of goods between countries.
2 Domestic shipments.
3 Domestic or foreign storage of readily marketable staples secured by an independent warehouse receipt.
4 Dollar exchange with banks of approved foreign countries.

In addition to assisting growth of world trade, bankers' acceptances are highly liquid assets held in commercial bank portfolios, thereby adding a great measure of liquidity to the banking system as a whole. Bankers' acceptances are negotiable loans that can be a liability to the balance sheet as well as an asset. Legal limits set by the Federal Reserve Board allow commercial banks to be makers of bankers' acceptances (a liability) or holders of acceptances (an asset).

The bank's obligation begins when an importer or exporter, or an agent of either, draws a time draft on an American bank to pay a certain amount of money in the commercial transaction in dollars, to a designated recipient (usually the party who draws the draft) on a specified date in the future after the date the draft is drawn or after the date it is presented to the paying or accepting bank.

This time factor is a direct function of Federal Reserve Board regulations and subsequent reserve requirements on its member banks. For purposes of banking system liquidity, the Federal Reserve Board has determined that it will only discount acceptances of its member banks that will mature in less than 180 days; the banking community usually restricts credit commitments in excess of 180 days. Although this discount is rarely used by member banks, it directly affects the ability of these banks to market their acceptances in the secondary market, for the Federal Reserve recognizes that dealers in bankers' acceptances often utilize this discounting device to increase their liquidity.

From an investment standpoint, it is said that not one investor in bankers' acceptances has ever lost the value of his investment if it was held to maturity.

Example. An American importer wants to buy coffee from a Brazilian exporter. The importer asks his bank to issue to the exporter a letter of credit stating the details of the shipment, the terms, and the amount of a time draft that the exporter may draw on the bank. The importer agrees to pay the bank when the draft matures, and he has received the shipment of coffee. Although the bank looks to the importer for payment under the terms of their agreement, the exporter, who draws the draft, remains contingently liable for the life of the transaction (nine months or less). The exporter discounts his draft at his bank in Brazil, which has been notified of the letter of credit agreement by the American bank. The shipping documents and the draft are sent by the Brazilian bank to the American bank, where the draft is stamped "Accepted"and signed by an officer. The draft, now an acceptance, becomes an irrevocable obligation of the American bank. In the usual case, the Brazilian bank will discount the acceptance with the American bank. The American bank may then sell the acceptance to a dealer at the posted bid price or to other persons or companies, or may retain it in its loan portfolio.

The same import could be financed by the American importer rather than the Brazilian exporter. In this case, the coffee would be shipped to the importer but released to him only upon payment of the contracted sum. To raise money for payment the importer would draw a time draft (based on the coffee or other commodities shipment) on his American bank. When the American bank had accepted the draft, payment would be made to the exporter, and the coffee would then be released for the importer to resell.

LEGAL LIMITATIONS   Federal Reserve Board interpretation of Regulation A states that the Federal Reserve Board cannot authorize a member bank to accept drafts drawn against it in domestic transactions in excess of 50% of the accepting bank's paid-up surplus and capital. It may authorize a member bank to accept drafts up to 100%, including both domestic and foreign drafts. The domestic drafts, however, are subject to the 50% limitation but this limit does not apply to drafts drawn on and accepted by an individual other than the bank and discounted by the bank.

This regulation allows the Federal Reserve Broad to restrict the initiation of banker's acceptances to banks that are multinational in their operations.

The Federal Reserve Board also states that, where a bank has been granted permission to accept an amount not exceeding in the aggregate 100% of its paid-up capital and surplus, that bank need not obtain additional authority from the Board each time it increases its surplus.

Most large multinational commercial banks are members of the Federal Reserve System and continually make bankers' acceptances in the area of 100% of paid-up capital and surplus liquidity.

On the bank's annual reports, bankers' acceptances are usually not prominently noted because they are recorded on the account books as loans and are grouped together with the other bank loans. The only figures reported are "outstanding acceptances" and "customer liability on acceptances." Bankers' acceptances appear in the outstanding acceptance figure only when they are sold in the secondary market. The acceptances outstanding, which at least equal and sometimes exceed the customer liabilty on acceptances, includes those acceptances initiated by the reporting bank and sold in the secondary market plus those initiated by another bank, discounted by the reporting bank with its endorsement. This endorsement means that the reporting bank assumes a "contingent liability" for payment at the maturity of the bankers' acceptances sold in the secondary market.

PRIME BANKERS' ACCEPTANCES AS AN INVESTMENT

There are many reasons for the popularity of prime bankers' acceptances as an investment for short-term funds.

Strong credit backing is derived from the guarantee of the draft by the accepting bank; the implicit backing of the firm drawing the check or draft, and the merchandise involved in the transaction. Moreover, banker's acceptance yields are usually 50 basis points or more higher than Treasury bill yields of comparable maturity. Acceptances are available in a broad spectrum of maturity dates, ranging from 1 to 270 days, with most bankers' acceptance activity concentrated in maturities of 180 days or fewer. Foreign investors holding a substantial percentage or the total amount of bankers' acceptances outstanding are attracted to acceptances because the income from an acceptance—which is subject to federal, state, and local income taxes for American investors—is free from federal income taxes imposed on foreigners. Numerous acceptances are endorsed by two banks rather than one, which provides additional safety.

Bankers' acceptances in face value from as little as $1000 up to $1 million or more. Finally, almost all banker's acceptance dealers trade acceptances at relatively stable posted interest rates, in contrast to the more rapidly fluctuating fields of most other short-term securities.

BANKERS' ACCEPTANCES AT THE ACCEPTANCE DESK OF THE FEDERAL RESERVE BANK

An article titled "Trading in Bankers' Acceptances: A View from the Acceptance Desk of the Federal Reserve Bank in New York," by Ralph T. Helfrich appeared in the *Federal Reserve of New York, Monthly Review,* of February, 1976. Later enquiries disclosed that this article has not been updated and that it is the latest and most reliable discussion of trading in bankers' acceptances from the viewpoint of the Federal Reserve Bank of New York.

The acceptance trading desk at the Federal Reserve Bank of New York is the focal point for providing general information on the acceptance market, assembling the standards and guidelines used in the daily operations of the acceptance desk.

Operations at the Federal Reserve's acceptance desk consists of two major activities. First, operations undertaken for the system under the direction of the Federal Open Market Committee (FOMC) and second, operations to invest funds for foreign accounts maintained at the Federal Reserve Bank of New York.

Acceptances are normally purchased each day for the Federal Reserve's own portfolio of outright holdings. Because acceptances are short-term, daily maturities of acceptances from the Federal Reserve's holdings are very large and the portfolio must be continually replenished to provide its share of a steady base for bank reserves.

Acceptance Desk operations for the Federal Reserve System are governed by directors from the FOMC. The new rules issued by the FOMC authorize the Federal Reserve Bank of New York to buy (outright or under repurchase agreement) and sell prime bankers' acceptances with maturities up to 9 months of acceptances that either arise out of the current shipment of goods between countries or within the United States, or arise out of storage within the United States of goods under contract of sales and expected to move into trade channels within a reasonable time and are secured throughout their life by a warehouse receipt or a similar document that conveys title to the underlying goods.

The authorizations announced on April 1, 1974, changed the type of acceptances the Federal Reserve can purchase as follows:

1 Maturities at the time of acceptance from six months to nine months, provided they meet other requirements, are eligible for purchase but not eligible for discount.
2 Domestic shipment acceptances without attached documents conveying title at the time of acceptance are eligible for purchase but not eligible for discount.
3 Foreign storage acceptances are not eligible for purchase but are eligible for discount provided the goods are readily marketable staples, are stored in an independent warehouse, and are secured at the time of acceptance by a receipt or other documents conveying title.
4 Acceptances financing the domestic storage of goods (any goods, not necessarily readily marketable staples) that are under contract of sale or expected to move into the channels of trade within a reasonable time, and are secured throughout their life by a warehouse receipt or similar document conveying title to the underlying goods, are eligible for purchase but are not eligible for discount.

5 Dollar exchange acceptances are not eligible for purchase but continue to be eligible for discount.

As can be seen, these new rules divide acceptances into those eligible for purchase and those eligible for discount.

Market Participants The market for bankers' acceptances with the counter market is composed of perhaps 10 to 15 firms, some with nationwide branches. Most of these firms deal in a variety of market obligations with acceptance trading constituting one relatively modest part of their overall activities.

A dealer firm trading in acceptances and desiring to establish a trading relationship with the Federal Reserve must meet certain financial, managerial, and operational criteria. Before the Federal Reserve trades with a dealing firm, the officers responsible for open market operations establish that the bank name is "prime."

To qualify its acceptances for purchase by the Federal Reserve, a bank must establish its name in the market and its acceptances must be considered "prime." A bank may market its acceptances however it chooses, but it is when sales are made daily to dealers reporting to the Acceptance Department that a bank's sales become known to the Federal Reserve. When a bank's acceptances move in the dealer market, the Federal Reserve can more easily reach the marketability of the paper and whether it is considered prime by the dealers. The volume and frequency of market transactions is also considered by the Federal Reserve before it decides to add a bank's name to the "acceptable" list of paper that can be purchased in the open market. The financial condition and the reputation of the bank are important ingredients in determining whether a bank's acceptances are considered prime.

A bank seeking to have its acceptance qualified for purchase by the Federal Reserve Bank also has to meet other standard criteria in the form of documentation. The requirements are somewhat different for agencies or branches of foreign banks and for nonmember commercial bankers than for Edge Act corporations and member banks of the Federal Reserve system.

It should be emphasized that the policy of the Federal Reserve Bank is to purchase in the open market only acceptances already established as prime acceptances; the lodging of the documents with the Acceptance Department would not in and of itself mean that the acceptance of the bank would be purchased immediately by the Federal Reserve. The documents merely put the Federal Reserve in a position to purchase the acceptances when such purchases are consistent wih the Federal Reserve's objectives, or when the Federal Reserve customer's accounts request that such purchases be made.

BACK-TO-BACK TAX CREDIT LENDING

In international banking regional banks compete with money center banks for prime customers. The business development officer of a regional bank must confront a typical customer's idea that "bigger is better." Back-to-back tax credit lending can be one answer to the challenge of the money center bank market.

The concept is simple; a domestic bank agrees to lend money to a multinational company's subsidiary or affiliate in a country that has a withholding tax on interest paid on an external debt. The multinational agrees to place an interest bearing deposit in the same amount as the principal on the loan with an offshore branch of the bank. The interest rate the bank receives on the loan is greater than the rate it pays on the deposit. With this spread the bank absorbs the withholding taxes which, in turn, can be credited against its tax liability in the United States.

The regional bank's marketing edge over the money center banks is the foreign tax credit limitation, which is unimpaired by taxes from a world wide branch network. The size of the limitation is a function of net foreign source income as a percentage of tax liability in the United States. Regional banks have a much smaller proportion of their physical assets overseas and are more likely to have a higher proportion of their tax credit available to commercial customers. The excess foreign tax credit limitation can be calculated and marketed as a potential resource.

When a multinational needs to put more funds into a subsidiary in a country with a withholding tax and also desires to reduce its worldwide tax liability, regional banks can provide the more advantageous credit terms

For example, to expand its South American operation, a multinational parent company had to put more capital into its Argentine subsidiary. With concern over the political situation in Argentina, some kind of loan seemed the only alternative to investing additional equity. The parent was willing to lend Eurodollars to its subsidiary at 6% interest. The business development officer of a regional bank proposed instead a back to back tax credit loan at 7^1/2% with the bank absorbing the 36% Argentine withholding taxes. The 7^1/2% was considerably less than the subsidiary would have to pay to secure funds on its own, even with the parent's guarantee. The parent company's investment decision was between two alternative returns on the loan, calculated as follows:

Alternative 1

Parent lends subsidiary $1,000,000 for one year at 6%	$60,000
Subsidiary pays interest income to parent less 36% withholding tax	(21,600)
Net return to parent on loan	$38,400 or 3.84%

Alternative 2

Parent arranges loan with regional bank for $1,000,000 for one year at 7^1/2% cost	$(75,000)
Parent deposits same amount with offshore branch of bank with interest income of 6%	60,000
Offshore bank credits subsidiary's amount with $1,000,000.	

Subsidiary pays interest income to parent less withholding tax of $21,600	60,000
Offshore bank absorbs withholding tax, which in turn is credited against regional bank's tax liability	— 0 —
Net return to parent on loan	$45,000 or 4.5%

The advantages of the back-to-back tax credit loan are: (1) that the parent gets cash savings in the entire amount of withholding taxes that the subsidiary would have paid to the Argentine government if the parent had made the loan; (2) these cash savings are traded off against the incremental interest expense to the subsidiary; and (3) the parent meets its objective of lending to its subsidiary at a considerable cash savings.

There are some additional reasons why the multinational company may find this type of loan attractive:

1 The bank places its name on the loan and thus provides anonymity for the customer. Foreign governments with controls on the repatriation of loan capital are more hesitant to prevent repayment of a loan to a bank than to a parent company. In the event of nationalization of the subsidiary's assets, it follows that obligations to banks are likely to be paid off before obligations to the parent of a nationalized subsidiary.

2 It is advantageous to fund the transaction with an offshore deposit. For reporting purposes, the company is required to make fewer disclosures if the bank formally assumes the loan than if the parent makes the loan directly.

3 Often the withholding tax rate on interest payments for bank obligations is less than the withholding tax rate on obligations to the parent. Because of the relationship of the subsidiary to the parent, a foreign country may deem the interest on an intercompany loan to be in fact a royalty or a dividend payment and therefore subject to a higher withholding tax.

ADVANTAGES TO THE BANK

This type of loan is attractive to the bank as well as to the customer. If the interest rates are properly spread, the loan can bring income to the bank without using funds. The risk is documentary rather than of credit. In the event of default, the bank retains the right of offset against the offshore deposit. The loan agreement usually has the parent guarantee payment of interest and tax receipts. Because the deposit is booked offshore, the bank is not required to keep reserves against it.

Further, back-to-back tax credit loans turn a useless excess commodity, the foreign tax credit limitation, into a generator of marketable income for the regional bank. Because money center banks have less capacity to absorb withholding taxes, they are unlikely to promote the sale of this type of loan. This gives the international officer of a regional bank the advantage of serving a customer's routine needs.

However, there are some areas of concern. Complete documentation is necessity. Moral obligation on the part of the parent is not likely to assure repayment of the loan to a subsidiary if the right of offset on a bank deposit is not properly executed. Since governments change their tax laws from time to time, the agreement should also provide adequate protection to the lender against these unforeseen changes. In the event of default, even with the right of offset against the deposit, the bank must still look to the parent for payment of interest. Excess income from foreign sources is a limited commodity even to regional banks. It is wise therefore, to allocate the tax credit to its most profitable uses.

The rate of return on capital employed (based on a ratio of loan to capital) is not very high on these loans and may in fact be lower than many other loans in the international portfolio. Because loans use capital, they should be considered in planning capital allocation and receive proper pricing of the ratio spread. In view of the savings to the customer and the limits of income from foreign sources against which the taxes can be credited, the bank must be sensitive to the rate of return.

Back-to-back credit loans are essentially marketing devices for regional banks with enough foreign source income to create an excess of foreign tax credit availability. By offering attractive savings and benefits to the customer as well as income to the bank, they improve the competitive stature of regional banks in the international marketplace.

FORFAITING—A NEW WAY TO FINANCE EXPORTS

Forfaiting is a special form of export finance that has evolved since the mid-1960s in trade with Eastern Block and developing countries. An exporter sells his claim on a customer arising from the supply of goods or services to a forfaiting agent "without recourse," meaning that the latter assumes the commercial, political, transfer, and currency risks connected with the debt. Although forfaiting (also known as no-recourse financing) can be rather expensive for the supplier, it does have definite advantages. He receives payment immediately, is relieved of all risks, and no longer has to worry about credit or collection arrangements. As a rule, forfaiting is restricted to trade receivables with maturities of up to 5 years. With the growing popularity of forfaiting a flourishing, international secondary market has developed with its center in Zurich, Switzerland.

In the past, banks conducted their forfaiting business through affiliated finance companies. Notes purchased were not resold and remained in portfolios; their volume was limited. Many European banks have since acquired controlling interest in finance corporations, which specialize in forfaiting business, operate as a unit, and are among the leaders in this specialized field. They are now in a position to offer expanded facilities in this area of export finance.

CHAPTER 6

The Multinational Finance Organization

THE ROLE OF THE FINANCE EXECUTIVE

Most important in the success of a financial management program is the stature of the chief financial excutive in the MNL's organization. This executive must hold a strong position in the executive and committee structure of the company, with a status equal to or greater than the executives in charge of the major operating activities.

The chief financial officer reports directly to the chief executive officer of the company. The position of the chief financial officer in the organization assures that matters of profit and loss receive first consideration in executive decisions. The chief financial officer is a member of the management and operating committees that report to the president or chief executive officer. Recommendations of the committee on operating or policy matters, whether they affect sales, engineering, or production, are made with appropriate consideration to their financial impact.

The position of the chief financial officer is also measured with regard to the effectiveness of financial control within the company. The part he plays in control is not through direct command but through setting realistic financial objectives and analyzing performance against these goals. His staff includes personnel who are competent in the fields of finance, cost, and accounting and who can analyze and interpret the financial data. This staff, together with centralized reporting, statistics, and record keeping facilities places him in a position to effect control simply by asking the pertinent questions, especially when the facts speak for themselves. The chief financial officer strengthens the efforts of top management and his fellow excutives in planning and decision-making; with timely reporting of results, he assists his colleagues in taking action to correct unprofitable performance.

ORGANIZATION OF THE FINANCE DEPARTMENT

The finance department consists of a strong central staff and a number of accounting, cost, budget and other operating responsibilities, as indicated in Figure 6. Analysis of financial, accounting, and cost data is directed toward better controls and cost savings. Financial action affects every phase of the compa-

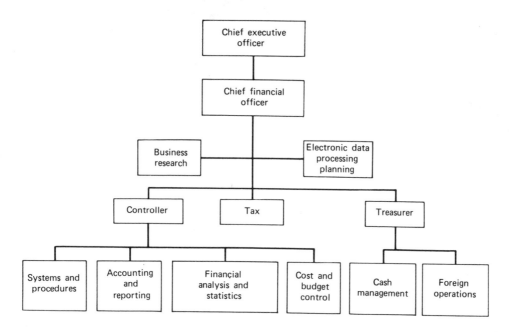

Figure 6. Organizations of the finance department.

ny's activities. With uniform policy and direction, results are reported accurately and the cost and budget control program is integrated into one uniform system.

Timely reports on planned versus actual results are best attained when a single staff is responsible not only for reporting financial matters and correlating planning data, but also for analytical studies and statistics.

This type of organization assures that accounting and record-keeping systems operate under the same policy direction as cost and budget control and financial reporting and analysis. More important than the centralization of record-keeping and statistical facilities is the knowledge and ability of the executives who head these analysis groups in various parts of the company. Drawing on the skills and training of these people the finance office can view the company as a whole and, at the same time, make objective analyses of any individual operation. Uniformity of approach to financial problems eliminates individual and sometimes conflicting interpretations of policy.

In a typical MNL the following items should be transferred to the finance office:

1 Sales statistics, from a sales department.
2 Cost estimating, from an engineeering department.
3 Cost accounting, from a production department.

Appendix B describes a representative multinational financial organization—with chart, functions, and position descriptions.

FUNCTIONS OF THE FINANCE DEPARTMENT   The finance office performs the following basic functions of financial management:

- Financial planning
- Reporting to management
- Costs and budget control
- Financial and statistical analysis

- Cost accounting
- Systems and procedures
- Treasurer's functions
- External reporting
- Taxes

FINANCIAL PLANNING Financial planning determines the direction of a company and the desired rate of return. It begins with a thorough analysis of the international, national, and industrial economic situation and of the strengths and types of competition. From this information a long-range forecast is developed and translated into the financial language of revenues, costs, earnings, and profitability. This long-range forecast includes related forecasts of facilities and machinery requirements, cash generated from profits compared with cash requirements; costs and pricing anticipated in future markets, as well as additional commitments that a company may contemplate. The chief financial officer concerns himself personally with this type of planning; but he has on his staff competent analysts who gather the information and assimilate it under his direction.

REPORTING TO MANAGEMENT Reporting to management is undoubtedly the most important continuing responsibility of a finance organization. The type, form, and composition of reports are usually the results of an evolutionary process in which basic requirements are adapted to the needs of operating management and special types of information. Reports to executives emphasize timeliness and highlight the key factors that affect operating profits, such as depreciation, underabsorbed overhead, taxes, rents, and interest. Complete understanding of these matters is an indispensable prerequisite to executive decision-making.

COST AND BUDGET CONTROL Controlling costs and budgets is interrelated with almost every other function of financial management. Inherent in such control is reporting the results to a broad base of middle manage-

89

ment. Many companies present interesting and informative reports in graphic form. The effectiveness of these reports can be enhanced by wider and more timely distribution of this information among shop superintendents and foremen and among supervisors in office and administrative activities. These persons are in a position to take corrective action when adverse performance is disclosed in current reports.

Equally important in cost and budget control is the use of measured standards or other objective criteria to establish budget allowances. Whenever possible, measured standards should replace those set only on the basis of past performance because the latter provide no target or basis for improved performance.

The functions of the finance office in cost and budget control are threefold. First, results must be reported frequently to key personnel who can make use of the information and take corrective action. Second, the finance staff should work out objective targets or standards of performance that they can expect from the company's employees. Third, the finance staff must carry on a long-term program to better inform key people in middle management and alert them to costs. When managers get a clearer picture of their part in the overall operations of the company, and when they see how shrinking profit margins hurt them as well as the corporation, they are often anxious to share in planning the financial aspects of their own activities. The objective here is to have a management team that makes detailed estimates of the cost of its own activities and then compares these estimates with the resulting cost.

THE MULTINATIONAL TREASURER

A treasurer's objective is to obtain the funds needed to conduct the business, to safeguard cash and other assets, and to find additional sources of financing through borrowing or equity capital. In a multinational company, the treasurer assigns these tasks to his counterparts in foreign locations, to managing directors and finance officers of the company's subsidiaries, associated companies, and branches. To control these often disparate activities, policies must be issued and guidelines set for every function of the treasurer. The key issues are how much to delegate and when, and which transactions require the approval of the multinational's treasurer.

INVESTMENT IN SUBSIDIARIES AND AFFILIATES

The chief financial officer an an MNL usually recommends the type of investment, the capital stock of a subsidiary, the disposition of earnings, whether dividends should be paid out or retained, and whether the dividends should be based on local legal books.

DEBT FINANCING

Debt financing is the responsibility of the treasurer, who must search for various sources of funds at the lowest possible cost so as not to impair overall financial strength. Short-term, local currency debt financing in foreign countries under specified borrowing limits is often delegated to foreign units.

PROTECTION OF COMPANY TANGIBLE ASSETS AGAINST LOSS

The treasurer is responsible for providing insurance coverage against all economically insurable risks of loss of assets, loss of earnings due to business interruption, and losses due to legal liabilities.

PROTECTION OF COMPANY ASSETS AGAINST LOSSES RESULTING FROM CURRENCY FLUCTUATIONS

The treasurer assures that assets denominated or measured in foreign currencies are adequately protected against the risk of loss resulting from changes in the dollar values of those currencies. To do this effectively the treasurer determines periodically the maximum amount of exposure the MNL should have in each currency under the circumstances then existing, and enjoins the management in each country not to exceed the established limit. The MNL treasurer assists the foreign management in maintaining the appropriate level of exposure when actions that can be taken within that country cannot bring the exposure within the desired limits.

CASH MANAGEMENT   The MNL treasurer is responsible for the effective use of cash resources throughout the entire company. The cash management function includes the coordination of the flow of funds worldwide with the objectives of minimizing the use and cost of borrowing and maximizing the use of surplus funds. The responsibility includes administering the flow of funds within the treasurer's office itself, between the treasurer's office and the operating entities, between the operating entities in different countries, between operating entities located in one country, and within the operating entities themselves. The treasurer determines the methods and timing of all transfers, both to and from the operating entities, in close cooperation with the divisions involved.

     The treasurer delegates to certain foreign banking centers the responsibility for the efficient flow of funds between operating entities located in countries other than the home country. By establishing standards the treasurer retains control of the methods by which various payments and transfers are to be made between operating entities.

BANKING CENTERS   When an MNL has more than one operation in a foreign country, the subsidiary or branch of the division most influential in the country is designated as the banking center. All banking transactions are channeled through this center and thereby sources of financing and opportunities for lower costs are maximized.

FUNCTIONS   Subsidiaries, associated companies, or branches within each country provide the banking center with financial information, including forecasts during the year, so that total financing requirements may be determined with reasonable accuracy. The banking center, acting on behalf of all profit centers through its designated representative (general manager, director of finance, treasurer or controller as appointed), is responsible for:

1 All bank and lease financing, obtaining local aid and foreign funds.

2 All legal book accounting and procedures.

**FOREIGN CURRENCY
TRANSACTIONS**

A typical MNL engaged in manufacturing and marketing moves substantial amounts of goods across country boundaries. These companies deal in many currencies other than the MNL currency in which its consolidated financial results are expressed.

The typical MNL is *not* in the business of trading or speculating in foreign currencies. Consequently, unless specifically approved no office may enter into a foreign exchange transaction not connected with its regular importing or exporting activities or with some foreign currency obligation, such as a foreign currency loan, without the express permission of the treasurer's office.

**FOREIGN CURRENCY
EXCHANGE RISK**

Any office that deals in more than one currency runs the risk of loss (or gain) when the exchange rates between currencies change. For offices within companies the most severe risk is that of a change in the exchange rate between the local currency and, for example, the United Staes dollar because the latter is the currency in which the company expresses its consolidated financial results. The terms "exposure to exchange risk" and "exposure" refer to the degree of vulnerability to the risk of loss (or gain) that would result from such a change in the exchange rate.

The MNL views exposure to exchange risk from an economic standpoint. This means that an asset is considered exposed if, when it is ultimately sold or disposed of, it will produce a higher dollar profit for the company as a result of a rise (or a lower dollar profit as a result of a decline) in a currency's exchange rate against the dollar. Similarly, liability is considered exposed if, when it is settled, it will produce a lower dollar profit for the company as a direct result of a rise (or a higher dollar profit as a result of a decline) in a currency's exchange rate against the dollar.

Economically, inventories are subject to exposure even if they may be shown in accounting records at their historical dollar cost because, if the local currency declines against the dollar, lower margins will be realized for a period of several months unless selling prices can be raised immediately to the full extent of the currency's decline. This is seldom possible.

Fixed assets are considered not exposed to exchange risks even from an economic standpoint because they tend to maintain their dollar value, net of depreciation, regardless of what happens to the exchange rate of the local currency.

Intracompany receivables and payables are partially exposed to exchange risk. Although these accounts are eliminated in the consolidated financial statements of the corporation, when they are settled they result in higher or lower taxes in the paying country; therefore, they lower or raise net income of the consolidated companies after taxes. Consequently intracompany accounts are included in exposure calculations.

The total company exposure in a particular currency may differ significantly from the exposure of the country whose currency it is. This is not only because of the effect of the intracompany accounts and their varying tax treatments but also because entities in other countries may have assets or liabilities denominated in that currency. Consequently, action taken by a country to reduce its local currency exposure can, under some circumstances, have a detrimental effect on the overall company position either in that currency or in some other currency. For this reason, overall exposure must be carefully monitored and controlled by the treasurer.

DEFINITIONS "Local currency" means the currency of the country in which the entity conducts its business.

"Foreign currency" means any currency other than the local currency.

"Foreign exchange transaction" means any purchase or sale of a foreign currency.

"Exposure" is the sum of the dollar values (local currency converted at the current book rate) of:

1 All assets that can be revalued for accounting purposes when the book rate for the local currency is changed (including intracompany receivables but excluding investments in subsidiaries and affiliates);

2 All inventories;

3 Forward contracts for the *sale* for foreign currencies; minus the dollar values of:

a All liabilities that can be revalued for accounting purposes when the book rate for the local currency is changed (including intracompany payables);

b Forward contracts for the *purchase* of foreign currencies.

"Transaction gains" (or losses) result when currencies are bought or sold at rates differing from the book rates listed in a company's financial manual.

"Translation gains" (or losses) result from revaluation of balance sheet accounts when the book rate is changed for either the local currency or a foreign currency in which certain assets or liabilities of the profit center are denominated.

CURRENCY RISK MANAGEMENT

To assist the treasurer in fulfilling his responsibility to protect against exchange risk those assets denominated or measured in currencies other than the United States dollar, the banking center's director of finance will accomplish the following tasks:

• Assure that the reports showing the exposure of all company offices in the country are prepared properly and submitted to headquarters on a timely basis.

• Prepare consolidated reports showing the combined exposure of all entities in the country in both local and foreign currencies and compile forecasts of future exchange exposure.

• Direct the purchase and sale of foreign currencies for all entities within the country.

• Take such actions as are authorized to keep total exposure in the local currency at desired levels.

• When necessary direct individual subsidiary branches to change their financial practices if this is required to keep local currency exposure within established limits.

PROTECTION AGAINST EXCHANGE RISK

The MNL treasurer notifies each country's local manage periodically of the maximum permissible level of exposure in local currency. This level will be determined both by the amount of investment necessary to sustain the volume and nature of the business in that country and, as a result, by an assessment of the risks of holding assets denominated in that currency.

If there is more than one profit center within the country, the designated representative of the banking center upon receipt of the country exposure limit will assign to each profit center its appropriate exposure level. This assignment generally will be made in proportion to the then existing economic exposure levels of the profit centers, that is, revaluable assets plus inventories minus revaluable liabilities. Once individual exposure limits have been assigned, observing them may require action to control more carefully revaluable assets or to increase revaluable liabilities and, most important, local currency borrowings.

Seasonal circumstances may cause limits to exceed by, say, 5 to 10% for one or two months. If such is the case efforts should be made to bring exposure sufficiently below the level in preceding or following months so that, on the average, exposure will be below the established limit. In keeping exposure at the proper level it will always be the responsibility of country management to try to maintain budgeted profit levels in dollar terms.

A REPRESENTATIVE MULTINATIONAL FINANCIAL ORGANIZATION

See Appendix B, Organization and Functions Charts and Position Descriptions, beginning on page 000.

CHAPTER 7

Money Management And Foreign Exchange

The multinational company's survival kit for exchange exposure is a risk management system designed to lessen the uncertainties and risks associated with periodic devaluation and revaluation of foreign currencies. A multinational's exposure lies primarily in its investments in foreign subsidiaries, branches, or affiliates; and secondarily in international trade transactions in which receivables or payables are denominated in foreign currencies. Exposure also arises from portfolio investments and long-term debt in foreign currency.

AN EXPOSURE-RISK SURVIVAL KIT

Following are some basic remedies found in a MNL survival kit:

Cash • In a currency prone to devaluation, keep cash at the minimum level required to support working capital needs. Forecast disbursements and receipts daily, weekly, and monthly; estimate when excess and shortfalls might occur.

• Transfer excess cash to a central location, whether local or in another country, by wire transfers, lockbox systems, or by instructing customers to remit funds to a specified country.

• Pool funds within a country and internationally so that locations with excess cash can provide liquidity to others requiring cash.

• Arrange swaps or parallel loans among sister locations.

• Remit excess cash to the parent company as rapidly as possible except when the potential gains from a revaluation exceed the opportunity cost of holding idle cash.

Accounts Receivable

If trade practices permit, invoices are denominated in a strong currency when a devaluation threatens. Invoices must be mailed immediately upon receiving orders and, if possible, before shipping merchandise. Discounts for early payments are offered if they are within a margin of the expected loss from devaluation. Payments of billing in a weak currency must be collected as soon as possible for conversion into a hard currency.

Inventories

From the start, do not tie up too much capital in inventory. Inventories can be a hedge in countries whose currencies are prone to devaluation and rapid inflation; when prices on goods to be produced can be priced upward after a devaluation. In countries where price control laws and regulations prevent price increases after a devaluation, inventories should be sold at all costs, even at a discount.

Accounts Payable

Payments are deferred when devaluation threatens weak currencies, barring damage to credit ratings. Orders are placed in advance and goods are even prepaid when revaluation appear likely.

Other Liabilities

Other current liabilities should be increased when devaluation threatens. Long-term debt with an interest rate quoted as a percentage of a prime or base requires estimates of the average prime or base rate over the life of the debt. The costs of compensating balances and other charges must be considered in assessing the debit situation.

Currency Risk Analysis It is useful to assign a risk factor to each currency, assessing the magnitude or likelihood of a devaluation or revaluation in the next month, quarter, or year. The following table lists devaluation potential for the Swiss franc and the Deutschmark during a certain period.

	Amount Of Likely Change	Within 1 Month	Within 3 Months	Within 6 Months	Risk Factor At Six Months
Swiss franc	15%	20%	50%	70%	10.5%
Deutschmark	10%	40%	60%	80%	8.0%

The risk factor for each currency is the "amount of likely change" multiplied by the "probability of change" within the time periods shown in each column.

The MNL assigns comparative rankings to foreign exchange exposures and schedules its priorities for action. This system also measures the cost of insuring against the risk of loss from a currency change. For example, if the cost of a six-month hedge of pound sterling is estimated to be 5% yearly, while the risk factor for the pound over the same period is only 4%, then hedging is too expensive an alternative. The risk factor also helps marketing executives in a particular country to estimate the magnitude of price changes needed to compensate in dollars for currency devaluation over a given period.

FOREIGN EXCHANGE TECHNIQUES Operating adjustments are often more advantageous than market hedges to cover exposure to loss in a weak currency. In adjusting foreign operations to reduce the exchange risk, subsidiary balance sheet items and cash flows between the parent and subsidiary are affected. Additional foreign currency debt is desirable for local subsidiaries, but in currencies prone to devaluation, balance sheet adjustment involves increasing the value of liabilities and decreasing the value of assets, both converted at the current rate. Increased liabilities generate cash or bank balances in the local currency, so exposure is not actually changed until these funds are invested in an asset account convertible at historical rate, later remitted in United States dollars to the parent corporation, or invested in assets denominated in other stronger currencies.

Adjustments to Reduce Assets

• Reduce holdings of devaluation-prone local currency, time deposits, and short-term investments. If local exchange controls permit, begin investing the funds in some less vulnerable currency or returning funds to the MNL.

• Reduce receivables, tightening credit terms and down payment requirements. Receivables could be sold to a factor, but this is more costly than tightening credit terms. Selling receivables to a captive finance company that is not consolidated in the parent's statement avoids having to report a book loss but does not reduce a devaluation's real economic impact. Receivables can also be used as collateral for additional debt.

• Reduce inventories. Reducing inventory does not minimize book exposure, and an economic exposure remains, depending on the price of the finished product and raw materials after devaluation. Some MNLs establish warehouses in strong currency areas, thereby reducing stock hold in devaluation-prone locations to a minimum.

Adjustments to Increase Liabilities

1 Increase payables in a devaluation-prone currency by increasing pruchases or delaying payment.
2 Local borrowing is less costly than hedging when the cost of hedging includes more than simple interest rate differentials. The cost of hedging is the effective interest cost of local funds plus the cost of investing these funds into a hard currency or low-risk asset, less the income received on this investment. This cost is compared with the estimated dollar cost of market hedges for the same period.

Use of Funds

• Invest in low-risk currencies with exchange regulations.

• Make intersubsidiary loans so that they are repayable. Funds may also be used for a hard currency investment.

• Invest in plant and equipment. The dollar value is preserved since local market valuation of new investments usually increases through inflation, thereby compensating for the devaluation.

• Remit funds to the parent, if possible, through payment of a dividend or as a return of capital, giving consideration to additional tax liability for the MNL.

• Purchase foreign source assets. Frequent devaluation, chronic inflation, and blocked funds lead to more and more purchases of real assets, machinery, automobiles, and raw materials. These assets, particularly imports, become more valuable over time owing to the combined effects of inflation and devaluation.

Revaluation-Prone Currencies

Currencies threatened with revaluation require the reverse action to reduce exposure: current assets are increased and liabilities are decreased. A positive net asset or long position in such a currency is the objective. Buy the revaluation-prone currency on the spot market and keep sizable investments and time deposits in that currency.

Market Hedges

The forward exchange contract is the basic means of covering foreign currency exposure. Hedges remedy the major risks implicit in devaluations, revaluations, or other types of parity changes, and also the less common risks of spot rate movements within the permitted fluctuation. Hedging enables one to meet future commitments or safeguard future income by buying or selling forward contracts, which offset or minimize the risk of exchange loss on assets or liabilities denominated in a foreign currency. Hedges are a form of insurance and they cost a premium.

Forward Exchange Contracts

A forward sale or purchase of foreign currency is a contract to deliver or receive a specified amount of that currency on a specified date at a specified rate of exchange. Its prinicipal variables are: the currency to be sold (or purchased), the amount of exchange to be delivered, the date of delivery, the rate of payment for exchange, and the dollar equivalent. An MNL may buy or sell foreign exchange forward to cover all or part of its book or economic exposure in a currency. This is not speculation; the MNL is simply guarding itself against a potential economic or book loss.

With a devaluation-prone currency, an MNL with a net asset or long position may sell that amount of the currency forward. Just before contract maturity, it enters the spot foreign exchange market and purchases currency sufficient to cover its forward sale. If a devaluation has occurred in the interim, the MNL pays less for the amount needed to cover its commitment. The amount of the contract multiplied by the difference between the forward rate in the contract and the current spot rate is a profit.

With a revaluation-prone currency, a company with a short position buys that currency forward. The MNL hopes that when the revaluation occurs the amount it pays to settle the purchase contract is less than the post-revaluation rate. The object is to repay its liability or short position in that currency at an exchange rate approximating the rate at which the liability was incurred. The cost of hedging has to be less than the amount of the parity adjustment; otherwise the hedge is useless or too costly.

Swaps A swap is made when a currency is purchased spot and simultaneously sold forward. In effect, two parties are lending foreign currencies to each other for a fixed period. For example, one party buys deutsche marks spot from another and simultaneously sells to the same party an equal amount of francs six months forward. In effect, the first party owns deutsche marks for that period while the other has the use of United States francs. The spot and future exchange rates are fixed in advance and no exchange risk is incurred. In a foreign exchange swap, both the money cost and the forward exchange rate differentials between the currencies over the agreed period are expressed in the exchange rate established for the return of currencies by each to the other on the six month forward date. Alternatively, these same factors may be expressed through an interest rate paid by one party to the other, or by a "spread" between the rates each pays to the others.

The foreign exchange swap is an essential part of the Eurocurrency loan and deposit market centered in London. In recent years MNLs have evolved a long-term swap technique that parallels the banking system. In a back to back loan an American MNL lends dollars to the American subsidiary of a foreign company. In turn the foreign company lends its currency to the foreign subsidiary of the American company for an equivalent term. The cost of money and forward exchange rate spreads are the difference between the interest rates applicable to each loan.

REPRESENTATIVE FOREIGN EXCHANGE POLICIES FOR MNL SUBSIDIARIES, ASSOCIATED COMPANIES, AND BRANCHES

An MNL doing business in a foreign country is exposed to foreign currency exchange risks. Pricing action is the best way to recover exchange losses. Next, hedging operations should be conducted, preferably within each country, and the resulting exchange gains or losses should be reported in their respective profit center reports. Local management will thereby be aware of the United States dollar cost of doing business in the foreign country. Responsibility for exchange/risk rests with foreign operating units, but the MNL must monitor and control the overall level of risk.

Certain hedging operations, such as borrowing local currency, are carried out for the benefit of all profit centers in a country, and their costs are distributed among all the centers. Other foreign exchange transactions involve only one profit center and their costs are charged to it.

103

The treasurer delegates most aspects of foreign exchange management to local units. Conflicts between financial policies and operating performance targets should be resolved by division executives and the treasurer.

Banking offices designated in each country are responsible for the statutory accounts and banking relationships of each legal entity. Each banking unit has a financial coordinator who manages exchange risk and ensures adherence to the established level of currency exposure for the country as a whole.

FOREIGN EXCHANGE TRANSLATION AND TRANSACTION GAINS AND LOSSES

Translation gains or losses result when the balance sheet is revalued at the time of a book rate change for either the local currency in which certain assets or liabilities of the profit center are expressed.

Exchange gains or losses resulting from balance sheet revisions at the time of a book rate change are retained in the control reports of the profit center; but translation gains and losses resulting from a change in the book rate of the local currency are normally *not* recorded on the legal books of the local entity.

Transaction gains or losses occur when foreign currencies are bought or sold at rates differing from the current book rates.

Gains and losses resulting from foreign exchange transactions are retained in the the control reports of the profit center and recorded in the legal books of the local entity.

DISTRIBUTION OF EXCHANGE GAINS AND LOSSES

Exchange gains and losses resulting from foreign currency sales or purchases (whether on a spot or forward basis) that are made to settle merchandise indebtedness or obligations not related to borrowings are assumed by the profit center for which the transaction was entered.

If the banking center enters into special foreign exchange

transactions because a single profit center has exceeded its exposure level, causing the country exposure limit to be exceeded, that profit center bears any gain or loss incurred in the transaction.

BOOK RATE CHANGES Book rates of exchange are reviewed before the end of each month, and changes are effective the first day of the new month. Revisions are generally made in the following circumstances:

1 When a currency that customarily has a fixed relationship to the dollar has been officially revalued or devalued.
2 When the spot rate for a currency that floats against the dollar has been consistently above or below the old book rate for a number of days and is a certain or more percentage above or below the old book rate.
3 When a currency has a fixed relationship to a floating currency whose book rate is being changed.

EXPORT INVOICING All sales to customers who are not members of the MNL should be invoiced in local currency. Consequently, all price lists for company products are expressed in the currency of the selling country.

Without the prior approval of the treasurer's office, no unit of the company, whether manufacturing or marketing, may invoice exports in a foreign currency regardless of whether the exports are sales to outsiders or intracompany transfers.

If a manufacturing unit prefers to issue invoices to customers outside the company in currencies other than the local currency, that unit should promptly notify the treasurer's office and request permission to do so.

When a buyer requests billing in a currency other than that of the price list of the seller (usually the seller's local currency) and the request is approved by the treasurer's office, the seller will convert the amount to the currency specified by the buyer at the book exchange rate in effect on the date of the shipment.

BANKING AND BORROWING

**PAYMENTS FOR
IMPORTS OR FOREIGN
CURRENCY LOANS**

Units operating in countries with weak currencies can enter into forward contracts for foreign currencies to meet interest and principal payments on loans as well as for merchandise payments. Units in all countries can buy dollars forward to settle intracompany payables and foreign loans. A unit operating in a country with a strong currency cannot buy forward foreign currencies other than the dollar without the treasurer's permission except to meet obligations to outside suppliers.

The methods of payment for intracompany imports or foreign currency loans can be outlined as follows:

1 *Standard practice*
Unless otherwise authorized, foreign currency required to settle invoices for goods imported from a company supplier, for services furnished by a company entity in another country, or for payments of principal or interest on loans made by another company entity, should be purchased on a "spot" basis at the time remittance is to be made.

2 *Exception if the established exposure limit is likely to be exceeded*
If the representative of the banking center discovers that the established exposure limit for his country is likely to be exceeded he is authorized to purchase United States dollars forward to invoices for goods imported from company entities located in the United States or any other country that invoices in United States dollars. He is also authorized to purchase dollars forward for payments or principal on intracompany loans made in that currency.

3 *Exception for countries with weak currencies*
An exception is made for units that operate in countries undergoing unusually rapid inflation or having other economic or political problems that might well cause the local currency to be devalued against both the United States dollar and other foreign currencies. It is then advisable to pur-

chase foreign currency for delivery on the date the payment in a foreign currency is scheduled to be made. If, in the judgment of local management, it is likely that the value of the local currency will depreciate relative to the United states dollar and other foreign currencies within six months, a contract should, if feasible, be made for the purchase of the foreign currency for delivery at the scheduled dates of the invoice settlement. The decision to purchase foreign currencies forward should, of course, take into account the trade-off between the cost of cover (the "premium," if any, on the forward currency) and the expected cost of devaluation. If there are doubts whether a particular entity should purchase foreign exchange forward or if future contracts are not feasible under local conditions, the treasurer's office should be consulted.

Examples of Forward Purchases

If goods are invoiced by an Italian factory to Country A in Italian lire and the invoices call for payment in 90 days, upon receipt of the invoice the local entity should, if feasible, enter into a forward contract to purchase lire in 90 days.

If goods are invoiced in Swiss francs on 90-day terms by a Swiss subsidiary to Country B and it is expected that payment will be extended for an additional 180 days by promissory note financing, upon receipt of the invoice the local unit should, if feasible, enter into a forward contract for delivery of Swiss francs in 270 days. If future contracts denominated in Swiss francs are not available, the local office may purchase United States dollars for delivery in 270 days and purchase Swiss francs with United States dollars on the date when the promissory note must be repaid.

Foreign Intracompany Loans

Foreign currencies should also be purchased forward for interest payments on intracompany loans when the interest payment is scheduled to be made within six months. Forward contracts should not be entered into for principal payments in currencies other than the United States dollar, however, without authorization from the treasurer's office.

107

Outside Suppliers Foreign currencies required to settle invoices for goods imported from suppliers outside the company or for services furnished by outsiders should, whenever feasible, be purchased at the time the invoice is received for delivery of the exchange on the date of the expected settlement.

Example: If machinery is being purchased from a German supplier with payment to be made in 90 days, deutsche marks should be purchased under a forward contract for delivery in 90 days.

Outside Lenders 1 *Dollar Loans*
If it appears likely that the established exposure limit for the country likely will be exceeded consideration should be given to purchasing forward dollars for scheduled payments of principal and interest on dollar loans made from abroad. Such forward purchases should be made, however, only if the forward premium, if any, is not deemed excessive.

2 *Loans in Other Foreign Currencies*
A forward purchase of a foreign currency, other than the United States dollar, to meet scheduled interest or principal payments on a loan denominated in such currency may be made only with the express permission of the treasurer.

If a unit finds that the purchase of currencies for future delivery is not feasible and the amounts involved are substantial ($100,000 or its equivalent in other currencies), the treasurer should be notified. Similarly, no unit of the company may borrow a foreign currency or enter into a loan agreement that calls for repayment in a foreign currency without the prior approval of the treasurer's office. Needless to say, sale and leaseback contracts also require authorization from the treasurer's office of the MNL.

Remittances to the MNL Headquarters The policy of the MNL usually states that all remittances for royalties, branch profits, management services, interest, or repayment of loans, will be made in local currency. Dividends should not be sold for dollars without special instructions from the shareholder.

Royalties and Licenses

All entities using trade marks, patents, and the like, should pay a royalty or license fee to the MNL if it is allowed under local law.

Relations with Banks in Foreign Locations

Banking relations of MNL foreign subsidiaries and branches must be closely coordinated with the treasurer's office. Decisions about which banks are to be dealt with and the type of facilities to be maintained at each bank rest with the treasurer.

Opening and Closing Bank Accounts

Opening and closing bank accounts and dealings with international banks should be covered by corporate policy and should require the approval of the corporate treasurer's office. Local management has the authority, pursuant to powers of attorney and corporate resolutions, to open and close bank accounts at any bank it chooses. Bank accounts should be maintained with banks that have adequate financial strength to assure the safety of company deposits and with banks that can provide compensating benefits to the company. A new bank account is a collateral benefit appreciated by a bank providing other services, but each additional bank account requires added administrative effort and frequently added financial costs.

Dealing with International Banks

An international bank is any commercial bank with branches or affiliates in more than one country as differentiated from local banks, which operate exclusively in one country. All bank depository accounts should be in local currency; no bank account should be maintained in United States dollars or other foreign currencies without the written permission of the treasurer.

Loans From Banks Outside the United States

Where the general policy of a multinational company provides that loans from local banks or other institutions should be maximized, the corporate policy should also provide for borrowing limits that are specific and appropriate to the volume of business of the local subsidiary or branch. Loans from the follow-

109

ing institutions should require the approval of the treasurer's office of the MNL:

- Loans from international banks
- Loans requiring a parent company guarantee
- Loans in foreign currencies
- Loans requiring that assets be pledged or mortgaged
- Loans requiring changes in capital and debts
- Loans in excess of borrowing limits established by lawful banks

Statement of Loans and Interest Rates

A legal entity of an MNL located in a foreign country should submit a Statement of Borrowings and Interest Rates on a monthly or quarterly basis. The following information is required:

1 The institution providing the credit should be named. Direct loans provided by the company affiliate should also be listed. Separate loans (overdraft, long-term debt, etc.) available from a single lender should be individually listed.
2 The maximum commitment of the lender under the existing credit arrangement and the amount committed should be stated in the currency of repayment. If loans in various Eurocurrencies are permitted, the amount of the commitment should be reported in equivalent local currency. Long-term commitments with periodic repayments should be shown as the original amount, and for revolving credit agreements the maximum drawdown possible should be shown.
3 Identify the currency of repayments.
4 The expiration date of the commitment should be listed if the lender has firmly established one or if it is known from experience that the lender reviews the credit at a particular time each year and confirms its continuing availability. In the case of long-term debt, the expiration date shown should be that of final maturity. For short-term borrowing

(less than one month) available on an offering basis, no expiration date need be shown but it should be described.

5 The amount of the credit should be reported in United States dollars converted at the current book rate.

6 The amount of each outstanding loan as of the close of the month (or any other special reporting requirement) should be specified in the currency of repayment.

7 List notes and loans payable as they will be reported, or intracompany payables as applicable, on the balance sheet for the reporting date after conversion into United States dollars at the current rate.

8 Identify long-term debts outstanding converted to United States dollars. Where a portion of this debt is considered to be current under appropriate accounting principles, the current portion should be listed.

9 The nominal interest rate carried on the face of the debt instrument, the discount rate, or bank charges (in the case of overdrafts and open advances) should also be reported. The rate should be shown as a decimal rounded to the nearest tenth of one percent (i.e., 8.1%).

10 Standard fees and commissions should be as fractions (i.e., 1–1/4%). It is assumed that the compensating balance percentage reported is a percentage of the *outstanding* loan unless otherwise indicated. For instance, it is possible that a balance may be required against the full commitment, and an additional balance required against outstanding loans.

11 If loans in the reporting country are guaranteed by the company, a subsidiary, an affiliate, or a third party, such as a bank, the guarantees should be reported. The guarantee, where applicable, is assumed to be at 100% unless otherwise indicated.

12 If assets are pledged in support of loans, the effective date of the pledge should be reported.

13 The type of asset pledged, whether receivables, inventory, or any other should be described.

14 The book value of the assets (in United States dollars) as

111

carried on the balance sheet at the reporting date should be stated.

15 Additional data—report any unusual terms or conditions related to the credit. Describe in further detail the balance arrangements or repayment schedules for long-term debt. Identify restrictions under the borrowing facility, such as a limitation to bill discounting usage. Indicate whether off-shore loans are hedged or have fixed exchange rates. Where a recourse discounting line for lease or trade receivables is utilized it should be clearly indicated here.

CHAPTER 8

Multinational Management Control

The single principle that characterizes multinational management control is that the managing director of a subsidiary or branch has the same authority and responsibilities as the general manager of a comparable subsidiary or branch in the United States. In the financial management area the MNL establishes financial policy and procedures and sets reporting requirements for its subsidiaries or branches, which are not only comparable to but are the same as the reporting responsibilities of its American counterpart.

MEASURING PERFORMANCE OF FOREIGN OPERATIONS
The MNL establishes the same performance criteria for foreign operations as for its American operations. The reporting requirements established in the financial manual dictate the form and contents of the reports that a managing director of a multinational subsidiary or branch must furnish group or division headquarters in the United States. The reports are identical with those required of American operations.

Measurement of performance of foreign and American operations requires that each activity must meet its operating plan or budget in respect to:

Sales
Operating income

Net income after taxes
Return on capital employed
Balance sheet asset and financing goals.

REPORTING The managing director of an MNL overseas subsidiary or branch, knowing that he has the same rights and authority as his counterpart in the United States, acknowledges at the same time that he has comparable responsibility for reporting results of operations.

The financial manual of the MNL establishes uniform requirements for monthly, quarterly, and annual reports required of overseas as well as United States operations.

The managing director relies on his controller or financial offer to maintain books of accounts on a MNL management control basis as well as a local statutory or legal basis, but *only* if required by MNL policy.

In certain foreign countries the financial officer of an MNL operation must maintain two sets of books. If the MNL financial manual prescribes that month-to-month reporting shall be maintained according to generally accepted accounting principles in the United States, the local financial officer or controller must convert day-to-day transactions entered on the local statutory books of accounts into the pro forma management control reports required for month-end reporting.

COSTS The MNL also expects its subsidiaries and branches to furnish information about costs to headquarters, detailing the manufacturing costs of products fabricated for local sales or export. The cost information shows material costs and labor costs and certain details of the contents of overhead cost.

OPERATING PLAN A multinational company maintains control of its subsidiaries and branches overseas by using the managerial control reports to examine and evaluate their operations. The company expects each subsidiary or branch to prepare an annual operating plan or budget that sets forth expected sales, costs, general sales and administrative expenses, resulting operating income, and net income after taxes. Management control reports furnished to MNL headquarters compare monthly results of operations with the operating plan or budget.

TRANSFER PRICING   An MNL with operations in various countries often has factories in one country manufacturing products to sell in other countries. Fundamental to this operation is the establishment of fair transfer pricing between the factory in the country of origin and the marketing operations in the others. Tax considerations are involved in establishing transfer pricing because certain countries obviously have lower tax rates than others. Major management decisions based on tax considerations alone, without regard to true cost and operating results, can prove to be misguided. Many countries in Europe and also many developing countries have seen through such tax gimmicks and taxhavens. Today's MNL establishes transfer prices that provide a reasonable and justifiable margin to the manufacturing facility in one country and bills the marketing operations in other countries at that transfer price. Prudent management decides to maintain transfer pricing at the lowest possible price in a marketing location so that its subsidiary or branch can meet the local competition in that country.

AUDITING   The foregoing discussion of managerial control over multinational operations in foreign countries establishes first the principle that control of overseas operations is the same as that in the United States. Second, that all operations, American and foreign alike, report monthly, quarterly, and annually in a uniform set of management control reports. Third, that each overseas operation prepares statutory and tax reports pursuant to local requirements. Fourth, that the principles of accounting in each foreign operation conform to accounting principles generally accepted in the United States in preparing the management control reports submitted to MNL headquarters. The principles of accounting required by local law are incorporated in the reports required for statutory and local tax purposes.

The objective of these reports is to ensure performance according to the financial manual published by the MNL headquarters and also to meet statutory requirements of the local country. The MNL may retain certified public accountants to audit the account books of each country. The MNL also establishes its own internal auditing department to conduct financial and operational audits in every operating location, whether in the United States or overseas. The independent public accountants overseas should preferably be associates or members of the same firm of accountants that certifies the MNL's financial statements and expresses opinions about them. The function of the company's internal audit department is to assure uniformity of operating procedures throughout the company, in American as well as foreign branches. They conduct operational audits to insure that the revenue and purchasing cycles, receivables, sales, procurement, and inventory control are handled uniformly throughout.

The internal audit department at MNL headquarters often has functional responsibility over local internal audit departments, which operate in the subsidiaries or branches overseas. The purpose of this functional responsibility is to insure a uniform professional approach to auditing and uniform standards of accounting and auditing throughout the company.

PERFORMANCE CRITERIA

As indicated in the beginning of this chapter, managing directors of overseas operations or branches are expected to achieve performance objectives comparable to their American counterparts. The following criteria measure their performance:

1 *Growth*
   Each operation within a MNL is expected to contribute to the growth of the company. This applies both to total results of the subsidiary or branch and to individual product lines.
2 The net results related to sales, namely the percentage of net income to sales after taxes to sales, should show an increase at least comparable to that of the preceding period, and, more important, a favorable comparison with the operational

plan or budget agreed upon with the chief executive of the MNL at the beginning of the year.

3 The ultimate measure in management is expressed in three letters: ROI—Return on Investment.

The company's net value represents the equity or investment of its stockholders. The MNL management, operating managing directors, and general managers are expected to produce a return on this investment. The return on investment for the MNL can be expressed by determining the return on the capital employed by each segment of the company. It is necessary for managing directors of overseas operations and the general managers of American operations to state in their monthly reports the amounts of capital employed in their respective operations. The net income after taxes is then compared to the return on capital employed. A normal increase in growth, combined with a normal increase in income, will produce a greater return on capital employed only if the amount of capital employed remains constant or is reduced. This places the responsibility on managing directors and general managers not only to increase their growth rate in sales and net income after taxes, but also to sustain at the same time reasonable control over accounts receivable and inventories so that the increase in return over the investment shows comparable improvement.

REPRESENTATIVE FINANCIAL STATEMENTS TO BE PREPARED BY MULTINATIONAL SUBSIDIARIES AND BRANCHES

BALANCE SHEET The balance sheet is the first section of the financial statement. Net assets financed by the MNL include the following external assets:

Cash
Marketable securities

Accounts receivables
Inventories
Prepaid expenses
Plant, property and equipment
Investment in affiliates
Intangible assets
Other assets

The sum of the above total external assets

Less: Other current liabilities
Less: Noncurrent liabilities
Equals: *Capital employed.*

Capital Employed

Less: Current and deferred federal and
national income taxes payable
Equals: *Net amount financed by the MNL.*

These net assets are covered by the total financing:

1 Loans
  Local notes and loans payable
  Long-term debt
2 Investments in and receivables from subsidiaries
  Intracompany receivables from affiliates
  Intracompany payables
3 Stockholders' equity
  Common stock
  Retained earnings
  Apportioned equity

The sum of these loans, investments, intracompany amounts,
and equity equals the MNL total financing of the subsidiary's
or branch's net assets.

INCOME STATEMENT The second section required of an MNL subsidiary is the income statement containing details for the current month, comparing actual amounts, percent of sales, with that of the prior year and with the plan. The income statement also compares the fiscal year to date, the actual percentage of sales, the planned percentage of sales, and the amount favorable or unfavorable with those of the annual plan and the prior year. Representative items on the income statement are as follows:

> *Net Sales*
> Standard cost of sales
> Gross margin at standard
> Manufacturing variances
> Inventory adjustment
> Gross margin at actual cost
> Selling and administrative expenses
> *Operating income*
> Interest expense
> Exchange gains or losses
> Other income or expenses
> Income before taxes
> Provision for income taxes
> *Net income*

SALES SUMMARY The third statement is the sales summary organized by product, comparing the actual sales for the current month and for the year to date with the plan in units as well as dollars.

COST OF SALES The fourth statement contains the details of standard costs of production and manufacturing variances.

    The following data is shown for the current month, actual, percentage, and favorable or unfavorable to plan, and the same for the year to date, actual amounts and favorable or unfavorable to plan:

> Standard cost of purchases

Standard cost of production
Direct material cost
Direct labor cost
Variable expenses
Period cost
Total Standard Cost of Production

Variances:
Purchase price variances
Outside vendors
Other company factory purchases
Total price variances
Material usage variance: Material process changes
Total usage variance

Direct labor variance:
Wage rate and performance
Variable expenses:
Direct labor losses
Indirect labor
Payroll premiums
Employee benefits
Tools and supplies
Maintenance
Scrap or others
Total variable expense

Period cost variance
Spending and volume variance
Total Manufacturing Variances

MANUFACTURING PERIOD AND SERVICE COST

The fifth statement required of a multinational overseas operation is the details of the manufacturing period and service costs. The first section compares the actual costs with the plan for the current month as well as the actual costs with the plan for the year to date. The first section is entitled "Control of indirect factory salaries and wages," and includes:

Payroll premiums
Employee benefits
Canteen expenses
Operating supplies
Toolroom supplies
Maintenance supplies
Telephone, telegraph and postage
Travel and living expenses
Professional and technical services
Other, such as pensions, entertainment, and so on

On the same statement the noncontrollable costs are listed, such as utilities, depreciation, taxes—real estate, taxes—other, rent, building, equipment, insurance, employee transport, indemnities, and any other noncontrollable cost.

INVENTORY AND MANPOWER SUMMARY The sixth and final statement required of an overseas operation is an inventory and a manpower summary. With respect to the inventory, the current monthly balance is compared with the prior month and also with the plan. The inventories are listed as follows:

Finished goods
Work in process—stores
Work in process—floor
Raw material
Supplies—indirect material
Perishable tools
Supplies—other
Total inventory
   Less: Obsolescence reserve
   equals net inventory valuation and rate of turnover.

The final section of this schedule lists manpower, namely total direct labor, total variable number of indirect and period personnel.

EVALUATION OF THE PERFORMANCE OF
FOREIGN SUBSIDIARIES BY MNL MANAGEMENT

MNL companies sometimes invest in foreign subsidiaries as part of a long-term strategy, and at other times in order to solve a very specific and local problem. The immediate decision is often made when an American company cannot serve a foreign market merely by exporting because the cumulative effects of freight, tariff, and other costs are prohibitive. The MNL then decides to invest in a local plant in order to compete with the foreign market. The incentive is still the same—to grow in an industry in that country. They differ, however, in that the manufacturer invests abroad in order to obtain lower costs by employing foreign labor or inexpensive foreign materials and he expects his products to remain more competitive than local manufacturers.

Having made the decision to invest overseas, the underlying assumption is that the subsidiary or branch will be evaluated according to the company's normal criterion of return on investment. The fundamentals of evaluation are the same even though there is great variation in expected profitability of overseas operations. The key factors are the product price, the product volume, and the cost of raw materials. In addition, the MNL may expect profits from components, shipped from the United States, that are included in manufacturing the product overseas. When an MNL decides to manufacture products overseas it must make a fundamental manufacturing decision, namely that the foreign subsidiary must be judged according to precisely the same criteria as the domestic subsidiary. Without exception this judgment takes the form of return of investment as the basic measure of performance. Multinational companies also provide for the same planning and budgetary procedures in their foreign operations as they do in domestic ones; these procedures in some form or other consist of two documents:

1 An operating plan or budget that contains income statements, balance sheets, and cash flow projections. Most com-

panies require these income statements every month, but some companies require balance sheets and cash flow projections only every quarter. Where cash flow is significant or a prerequisite to the financial plan of an MNL, invariably the month-to-month balance sheets are required, indicating control of receivables and inventories. The cash flow document follows and the MNL expects from its foreign subsidiaries the complete package of income statement, balance sheet, and cash flow projections.

2 A capital budget listing individual projects or capital investments that the overseas subsidiary contemplates for the coming year.

The operating plans or budgets should reflect the return on investment of the overseas enterprise and should be comparable to similar MNL operations. It is obvious that the return on investment in certain overseas enterprises, particularly in developing countries, may require a modified goal to measure their performance. The performance objectives can be tightened in subsequent years to keep up with potential growth and expansion.

SUMMARY There are four essentials for multinational financial control:

1 The performance of multinational foreign operations is measured by the same criteria as their national counterparts.

2 The multinational company prepares and issues to all its subsidiaries and branches a uniform financial manual containing policies and procedures for the valuation of its assets and the requirements for monthly, quarterly, or annual reports.

3 The managing director of a foreign subsidiary or branch is responsible for reporting the results of its operations. He expects of his financial officer or controller the same reliability in preparing monthly management control reports as is required to keep the books of accounts pursuant to local statutes and tax regulations.

4 The local managing director is expected to meet certain performance criteria, namely return on capital employed, expected growth rate in sales, and net income after taxes according to an operating plan that is approved by management at the beginning of the year.

FINANCIAL PLANNING

THE OPERATING PLAN The financial planning and control of a multinational company start with the development of an operating plan. The end product of the forecasts and decisions of operating executives are distilled into a forecast of profit or loss. In translating the plans of operating activities into their ultimate effects on the earnings of the company, the chief financial officer and his staff assist management by initiating reappraisals of many programs, forecasts, and decisions.

An orderly process for gathering the required forecasts and other data from department heads and presenting the results as an operating plan enables managers at every level to actively participate in the analysis, review, and approval of company programs. The managers are better able to manage because they are aware of overall plans and of their responsibilities in achieving the company's planned profit objectives.

The raw materials needed to develop an operating plan can be outlined according to six general categories of management:

1 *Sales*
Volume of business by product lines
Pricing policies
Delivery and completion schedules
2 *Engineering*
Design changes in present product lines
New products
New services
Research and development

3 *Manufacturing*
  Plant capacity and productivity
    Production schedules
    Manpower requirements
    Supervisory staffing
    Inventories
    Cost performance

4 *Purchasing*
  Procurement schedules
    Material requirements
    Prices

5 *Personnel*
  Policy and rates
    Labor market
    Training and education

6 *Finance*
  Cash availability and requirements
    Investment in facilities and inventories
    Capital asset appropriations and expenditures
    Costs and budgets
    Rate of return on capital assets employed
    Rates of turnover of assets

DEVELOPING THE OPERATING PLAN

The operating plan expresses in money the results of the plans that the various divisions and departments of the organization have made on the basis of programs to be accomplished and the anticipated volume of business.

A break-even chart, prerequisite to an operating plan, indicates the minimum volume of business that must be maintained in order to make a profit. It is evident that only costs of direct labor and materials vary directly with the volume of sales. The remaining costs, even those classified as variable, ordinarily do not decline at the same rate as sales volume. Accordingly, when business drops below the point where income from sales is sufficient to meet fixed and semivariable costs, a loss results. On the other hand, since these expenses do not increase at the same rate as sales, greater profit can be achieved with greater volume of business.

The basic steps in developing an operating plan are as follows:

1 Establish as specifically as possible a set of assumptions relative to sales volume and prices.

2 Establish a set of assumptions relative to manufacturing capacity and anticipated production.

3 Assign to each segment of the organization responsibility for carrying out its share of the tasks required to accomplish the objectives involved in each assumption.

4 Express the sales assumptions as a forecast of sales by the type of business and major product classes. Incorporate in the forecast anticipated changes in prices, product lines, new markets (domestic or overseas), and any other changes that would affect the anticipated volume of sales.

5 Express the manufacturing assumptions as the value of production capacity, material, labor and overhead costs, and rates of overhead required to adequately determine the cost of production and sales.

6 Calculate the resulting values of materials as cost of sales, cost of finished production, work put into process, and purchases for stock, and estimate their effects (increase or decrease) on inventories.

7 Calculate the direct labor cost in the cost of slaes, finished production, and work in process. Correlate the resulting direct labor cost with the value of payrolls estimated to be earned by the productive direct labor force during the periods considered.

8 Calculate total manufacturing and engineering expenses, department by department, as personnel, staff and indirect payrolls, supplemental payroll costs, indirect materials, supplies, services, internal rents, interest, and other expenses. Resulting amounts must then be compared and reconciled with overhead that is estimated to be absorbed in the

cost of manufacture at prescribed rates of overhead absorption.

9 Determine estimated or budgeted selling and administrative expenses, department by department, as personnel and other costs. These amounts must also be analyzed according to programs or functions in such activities as data processing, communications, office supply, and any other services performed by one group for the benefit of other groups and subject to either direct charges or proration of such expenses.

10 Accumulate the data from each of the above categories in the form of a statement of earnings so that the resulting effect can be established in terms of anticipated profit or loss. Review and analyze the results, revise where necessary, and submit them to the appropriate management committee for approval. With such approval, the results become the operating plan of the company.

Figure 7 presents a suggested time schedule for preparing the annual operating plan. Additional analysis should be made of the facilities and inventory planning programs in order to evaluate the extent to which return on capital employed could be improved by increasing the turnover of assets. More favorable results can be achieved if sales increase without a comparable increase in facilities, receivables, and inventories, or if sales remain constant but investment in facilities or inventories can be reduced.

THE POSITION OF FINANCE IN PRODUCTION PLANNING Decisions on production capacity have impact on more than the production department and the cost of manufacturing overhead charges to products. The entire pricing structure of the sales organization is guided to a large extent by the effect that capacity factors have on quoted factory prices.

The finance office should strongly influence decisions regarding production capacity, principally because the ultimate profitability of operations depends on the balance between

Organization Activity	April–May	June–July	August–September	October–November	December
Executive	After annual meeting of board of directors, develop broad plans and objectives.	Review and discuss with company executives.	Assign responsibility for plans and programs to management.		Review. Analyze results. Approve Profit Plan.
Sales			Determine assumptions relative to sales. Develop marketing plans. Prepare forecast of sales by product lines.	Review and revise sales forecasts.	
Engineering		Review plans. Discuss changes. Compare plans with last year's performance.	Prepare research and development plans.	Forecast direct order engineering work load. Forecast engineering indirect and type costs.	Review and revise as required.
Manufacturing			Determine assumptions relative to manufacturing. Develop manufacturing plans. Develop facilities and machinery requirements.	Establish production capacity. Prepare manpower schedules. Forecast production of products and procurement of materials.	
Finance			Analyze assumptions for sales and manufacturing for their effect on overhead rates, product cost calculations, and pricing.	Forecast selling, administration personnel, and costs. Prepare forecast of sales, costs and expenses, gross operating profit, etc.	Prepared recommended Profit Plan.

Figure 7 Profit Plan Time Schedule

sales prices and costs. The finance office can be completely objective because its prime responsibility is for the economic results of the company as a whole, and not for sales, engineering, or production.

Volume influences many important policy decisions, including decisions about the following:

1 *Facilities*
   (a) Utilization and administration of existing facilities
   (b) Requirements for new facilities and machinery
   (c) Return on capital employed

2 *Cash*
   (a) Requirements
   (b) Funds generated from profits
   (c) Funds generated from depreciation
   (d) Borrowing, if necessary

3 *Prices*
   (a) National market
   (b) Foreign markets
   (c) New products
   (d) New services to clients

4 *Anticipated Earnings and Profits*
   (a) Profitability of various product lines
   (b) Ability of product lines to earn the minimum return on capital employed
   (c) Ability of product lines to earn profits commensurate with the efforts expended and ingenuity demonstrated by management.

A fundamental criterion of productive capacity is the ability of plants to produce, each with its given complement of workers and machines. Even though the capacity of many factories may be greater than estimated, it is advisable to consider additional factors. Such as which products will be in demand in the future. A projection of this market and its potential sales volume should be weighed carefully against existing manufacturing facilities to ascertain whether productive capacity actually exists in the product lines that the company expects to sell in the coming years. If the results of such analyses are not compatible, the productive capacity figures first reached may have to be adjusted to make them more realistic.

The outlook in the labor market must also be considered. For example, if the labor market in a given locality is saturated, productive capacity cannot be measured solely by the number and kinds of machinery with which a plant is equipped. Capacity estimates must be modified to take into account the problems of labor supply that the company may face in the future. Because of the tremendous impact of productive capacity on pricing and market position, procedures for establishing such figures should be carefully reexamined. In addition to the fundamental consideration of productivity of workers and machines, special conditions often arise from the special requirements of customers.

The MNL should attempt to establish an objective production capacity base for each line of products. Capacity bases set only for manufacturing plants may prove unrealistic and may not necessarily reflect true product costs. The availability of supporting services (especially in engineering) to develop and meet customer requirements must be considered in order to select the most desirable and profitable level of operation for each product line. The ability of the entire production, engineering, and sales system to support each product line effectively sets limits and should ultimately determine what base will produce the most profitable product mix.

The objective is to establish a standard volume base that considers all these factors. The analysis of such factors in relation to setting figures for production capacity should be performed by the finance staff. In the centralized finance organization proposed here, the talents and the available information on the subject in the sales statistics department are joined with their counterparts in cost and budget control to develop productive capacity objectives that the chief financial officer can recommend to management. The resulting figures should be the optimum from the viewpoints of profits, sales, engineering, and production. These figures should be based not only on current capacity and circumstances, but also on such considerations as the long-range market outlook. This type of financial analysis may also lead to a realignment of manufacturing facilities and production units in order to place each component where it can serve its purpose most effectively.

The most significant reason for the chief finance officer to be concerned with the subject of production capacity is its impact on profitability of product lines, make or buy decisions, pricing, and budgets. In subsequent chapters the relationship between capacity and product costing is discussed, as are volume, and prices and the profitability of operations.

THE POSITION OF THE FINANCE OFFICE IN MATERIALS PROCUREMENT
(See Figure 8)

The finance department is vitally concerned with the use of funds for purchasing materials and manufacturing goods for stock. Its concern is not with the details of stock control and the order requirements for individual raw materials, parts, or products, but with the total value of the investment in inventories and the effect of purchases on cash flow. These problems are subject to appraisal at the highest level of management. The finance staff should address itself particularly to this subject because the greatest current expenditures are for purchases of materials and the manufacture of goods for stock.

Analysis of the total inventory requires, first, a comparison of the value of stock on hand (by major product groups) with anticipated new business (the backlog of orders on hand plus forecasts of future orders). Next, a comparison must be made with actual demand experience in the past 12 months to ascertain the effective rate of turnover. Finally, a comparison is required of the trend of inventory balances by major product lines with the trend of orders received during the same period.

The procurement situation can be analyzed by comparing trends in major product lines, weighing both the purchases of materials required to make each line of products and the production of finished products in each group against new business (incoming orders from customers during the same period).

131

Tools for management control	Functions of Controller Relative to column 1	Functions of Vice-President— Materials management
1. Control of inventories–Policies and procedures	Assists material management in the development of control procedures and concurs on all policies and procedures developed by material management staff. Develops ratios and other financial control procedures requisite to effectively control the monetary level of inventories.	Exercises primary responsibility for the development of improved inventory control policies and procedures. Reviews policy to determine its sufficiency and objectivity and make provision for improved policy where necessary.
2. Inventory control–reporting, analysis, report evaluation	Exercises primary responsibility for the development and installation of an effective reporting system that will adequately record inventory levels and movements and will produce the desired information for the control of inventories. a. Develop and install a system for reporting inventory levels of productive and nonproductive inventories. b. Prepare inventory reports and submit to management. c. Consolidate inventory reports and submit analyses to management. d. Evaluate inventory reports and develop recommendations for management action.	Assists finance in the development and installation of an inventory reporting system and concurs on system developed. Determines policy in regard to need for short interval or long-term stockpiling. Functionally supervises plant, regional, and field inventory control functions. Evaluates inventory reports, determines reasons for deviations from accepted normal inventory levels and submits recommendations to management for action.
3. Annual physical inventories—policies and procedures	Maintains primary responsibility with materials management staff for the development of improved procedures for taking the annual physical inventory. Develops the financial procedures required for recording the monetary valuation of inventories. Prepares responsibilities of finance personnel in taking the inventory.	Maintains joint responsibility with controller's staff for the development of improved procedures for taking the annual physical inventory. Develops the materials management procedures required for recording the statistical data concerning inventories. Prepares responsibilities of materials management personnel in taking the inventory.

Figure 8 Continued.

4. Annual physical inventories—administration	Administers taking the annual physical inventory. a. Prepares the annual inventory report and comments on report and submits to management. Responsible for the preparation of consolidated annual corporate inventory reports. Prepares comments on the report and analyzes it to determine the financial implications of inventory levels	Functionally supervises the materials management activities at the divisions in taking inventories. Evaluates the level of inventory and prepares recommendations for management action.
5. Periodic inventory cycle checks—policies and procedures	Exercises joint responsibility for development of procedures for taking periodic cycle checks of inventory. Adjusts book inventories on the basis of cycle checks taken by Materials Management.	Exercises primary responsibility for the development of procedures for taking inventory cycle checks. Makes inventory cycle checks and prepares reports for management.
6. Service parts inventory level control—policies and procedures	Has the primary responsibility for developing an effective reporting system to provide desired financial information. a. Develop a system of reporting sales, transfers, floats, and other factors bearing on the economy of services parts operations. b. Prepare reports on service parts inventory activities. Analyzes financial implications of services, parts, production, and inventory levels. Evaluates financial implications of inventory levels and submit recommendations to management for action.	Assists in developing reporting an effective system to provide desired financial information. Develops policy and procedures for the control of service parts inventory levels. Has functional responsibility for inventory control methods at regional level. Analyzes effect of regional practices and inventory levels on servicing operations throughout the company. Evaluates efficiency of regions in inventory control.
7. Excess and obsolete inventory disposal—Policies and procedures	Assists materials management in the development of improved procedures for disposition of excess and obsolete inventories and concurs in methods proposed by materials management.	Has primary responsibility for developing policies and procedures for the disposition of excess and obsolete material.

Figure 8. Inventory Control

Such an analysis can reveal whether the company is buying only to replace what it sells or whether it is building up inventory at a greater rate than new business warrants.

The potential for an additional source of cash flow money by utilizing stocks on hand to fill new customers' orders is also significant. The realization of cash by effective and orderly liquidation of excessive inventory stock is a tangible example of effective inventory management.

Financial analysis should be made of procurement and inventories in relation to new business (sales orders) by major product classes. These reports should be timely, so that critical or questionable trends can be pointed out to production and purchasing divisions in time to effect corrective action.

THE POSITION OF THE FINANCE OFFICE IN FACILITIES PLANNING AND CAPITAL BUDGETING

The return on capital employed in operations is one objective means of evaluating the achievements of the company. Internal interest and rents builds into the company's cost system a provision for at least a minimum return on such investment, but the continuing success and expansion of the company's activities depends on earning more than this minimum.

Facilities Planning

Because the cost of factory buildings and machinery is so important in this approach to evaluating profits, facilities planning should be especially emphasized by finance management. Deciding how much money to invest in manufacturing facilities involves more than determining which machinery to buy in order to produce more efficiently; rather, it is a financial problem: how much investment in any given facility is profitable when measured in terms of return on capital employed and when compared with alternative uses for corporate money. Future markets for products and the local labor market, discussed earlier in relation to production capacity, are only two aspects of the production capacity problem, which also affects facilities planning, the utilization of funds, and cash flow. The financial objective is to plan the acquisition of new facilities and machinery so that maximum utilization of facilities is achieved. The finance department must make sure that investments are not made in locations that cannot absorb additional capacity. It must also be able to determine, for instance, whether production is expanding facilities to build product A when the trend of sales indicates that the company is selling more of product B. The finance department must also consider how technological developments influence the use of funds for facilities.

The responsibilities of the finance staff in the area of facilities planning can be described in five basis steps:

1 Initiate control by establishing procedures for authorizing funds so that departments requesting or using company facilities must submit forecasts of their requirements in advance of each fiscal period. After analysis of the material presented in support of the request, and after approval by an appropriate executive committee, the authorizations are incorporated in financial forecasts.

2 Maintain control over the acquisition and purchase of each facility and machine. Procedures should be issued that govern the initiation of the request, the form and contents of the cost analysis or support for the need for the item, and the appropriate approvals prior to authorization of the purchase.

3 Report on the progress of the acquisition of each facility and the payments made. Current information should be prepared by type of facility and machinery indicating acquisitions approved, purchase commitments made, expenditures to date, anticipated payments by periods, and (where appropriate) the amount of money appropriated but not yet committed.

4 Analyze the results of facilities planning in relation to the company's investment practices, investment reserves, depreciation, and related tax matters.

5 Establish a capital budget on the basis of planned appropriations and facilities programs.

Capital Budgets Fundamental to capital budgeting is a procedure for the preparation, review, and approval of requests for capital appropriations and also for disposal of property. At least these four steps should be included in such a procedure.

1 Requests made by operating departments are supported by detailed estimates of costs and returns.

2 Amounts requested and supporting detail must be broken down to permit adequate control over subsequent commitments and expenditures. In other words, the cost of purchasing machinery must be distinguished both from the costs of labor and material required for installation and from auxiliary equipment.

3 Requests for appropriations must be identified as planned items in the advance forecasts of requirements or as a substitute for a planned item.

4 Requests must be approved at designated levels of management prior to commitment and purchase (or disposal).

Finance staff personnel should be in a position to assist administrative staffs in the operating departments with planning, analyzing, and preparing requests for appropriations. They are also responsible for the financial review and analysis of the requests and for making appropriate recommendations. Evaluating the purposes, benefits, risks, financial effects, and available options are part of the review.

Essential in effective capital budgeting are the control features inherent in analysis of the "justification" for investments. Every request for additional facilities must be scrutinized in the light of total corporate needs, present as well as long-term. Continuous analysis of the justification of requests for capital expenditures enables top management to keep informed of its needs and of the financial implications of each outlay of capital funds.

Control of actual commitments and expenditures is the final step in capital budgeting; it insures that expenditures are held within the estimates made on the original request for appropriation. Procedures for initiating commitment, purchasing, and completing installation of facilities should provide for proper coding of each transaction so that each commitment can be verified.

Accounting records must be maintained to reflect, on a current basis, cumulative data and uncommitted balances available for each appropriation. The supporting records must be so set up that they can be promptly summarized and reported upon as to the status of appropriations, commitments, and expenditures. It is essential to provide within the record-keeping procedure the means of identifying overruns promptly and of reporting on completed projects as soon as possible after completion of the work.

Capital budgeting procedures for disposal of facilities (whether property, buildings, or machinery) must be as thorough as for acquisition and appropriation. Requests for disposal initiated by operating departments should indicate the reason, the implications of costs and expenses, the status of value and depreciation and the intended means of disposal. The requests should be subjected to financial analysis and executive review and approval. Accounting records should also provide for proper coding and identification with the request so that the property records can be closed out and the results of the actual disposal transaction can be compared with the estimates contained in the request for disposal.

OPERATING BUDGETS

BUDGETS Budgets are the blueprints of operating planning expressed in dollars. Budgeting is essentially planning and controlling operations. Budgeting starts with the organizing and planning of operations, and is identical to the method of determining specifications in a quality control program. The next step is to determine the requirements of manpower, materials, and other expenditures, and then to manage make and sell. The final step in the process is control, which involves reporting performance, analyzing variations, and returning the results to appropriate levels of management, particularly those who can take corrective action. This final step, taking corrective action, closes the loop of budgeting control. The following discussion of budgeting in multinational management concentrates on those features of the budgeting process that must be emphasized to the general managers and controllers of overseas operations. Many of the features are grounded in sound economics and have already been applied in foreign manufacturing. The multinational company must ensure that budgeting techniques are true to fundamental economics of the manufacturing process, techniques that have to be built into the budget and accounting system of the multinational company.

Recommendation 1   Flexible budget techniques must be built into the annual budget. A flexible budget system provides plant management with the tools to control performance at different levels of production. It accomplishes this by making allowances in the budget for manufacturing expenses should the rate of expenditure change with the volume of production. It is fundamental for managers to reduce expenses and cut overhead costs when production declines. In a flexible budget system, these objectives to reduce costs are established in advance, incorporated in management plans for operations, and become the basis for measuring future performance. The operating budgets, which are compared later with actual performance, are realistic targets at any volume level within the planned range of activities for the coming budget year.

Recommendation 2   Fixed overhead costs should be defined precisely and interpreted strictly in flexible budgeting. Fixed overhead costs are those costs that are necessary (a) to provide a planned amount of production capacity; (b) to maintain the plant organization and physical facilities during a three month shutdown period; (c) to permit the plant to resume production operations after the shutdown without undue delay.

Fixed overhead costs are distinguished from variable costs, which are subject to plant management plans to adapt to fluctuations in the volume of production.

This strict interpretation of fixed overhead costs has a number of effects. In this approach to budgeting, the concept of ability to pay becomes an added consideration in making budget allowances. When the volume of sales and production declines the company can no longer pay for certain staff and services. In planning for any production decline, the variable rates more accurately measure and give greater weight to considerations of volume. The companion control feature is that no allowances can be made in the budget of a cost center unless they are justified by a level of plant activity necessary to support such expenditures.

Recommendation 3 Budget responsibilities of the plant managers should be delegated to the level of supervision directly responsible for incurring costs.

Manning tables should be used in preparing budgets for indirect labor in order to provide supervisors and foremen with the most effective tools for carrying out their budget responsibilities. A training program should be established for the middle-management level of supervisors and foremen so that they can fully understand the interaction of manning tables, fixed cost, and variable cost.

The objective of a manning table is to plan manpower requirements within an anticipated range of production activity. The collaboration of the plant manager, controller, department head, and even foreman results in a well thought-out schedule for manpower requests that is valid for a number of conditions and volume levels. After critical evaluation, cost center by cost center, these manning tables become the basis of the budget for the coming year.

Recommendation 4 Budget authorization bases for variable expenses should be founded on quantitative production data in order to make them better understood and more readily applicable in budget reporting. Quantitative data are part of the common language of shop supervisors and foremen and are better understood than direct labor cost dollars.

Recommendation 5 The budget should be subjected to objective tests and evaluation at the plants before it is approved. Budget studies at various levels of production provide management with a clear picture of the effect the overhead of plants will have on plant profits under various operating conditions. Such studies establish guidelines that are useful in weighing different plans for the future. They make the overhead budget more realistic because it has been evaluated at operating levels other than at the profit planning volumes of the coming years. Budget evaluation studies at various volume levels also reveal inconsistencies in profit planning, standard cost, and budgeting.

Recommendation 6 Reporting of budget performance should provide plant managers and department heads with monthly summaries and unit supervisors and foremen with brief, weekly action-type reports.

Recommendation 7 The budget for plant engineering and maintenance should be designed to highlight the special control needs and responsibilities in this kind of service activity.

Recommendation 8 Budget control should offer a systematic program for analysis of variances and corrective action to eliminate the conditions responsible for excessive costs.

LONG-TERM PROFIT GROWTH PLANNING

A profit growth plan starts with a general commentary letter summarizing the division's competitive position in the foreign country in which it operates, significant performance goals to be realized according to planned objectives, and the extent to which the division's profits, operating performance, and competitive position could be improved if the plan is realized. The purpose of the letter is to provide a summary in narrative form of the division's goals and plans for the period of planning profit growth.

The first section explains the division's current operating problems, market conditions, and its competitive position with regard to sales volume, products, and selling prices. It provides information required to understand and appreciate the significance of performance improvements to be realized by the growth plan. This commentary analyzes the division's competitive strengths and weaknesses compared to those of its principal competitors and of the company. The statistical information for each principal competitor should include its sales, estimated net income, return on investment, and, above all, its share of the market.

The division's competitive market position, product leadership cost leadership, and profit position are essential. The next section indicates planned goals, distinguishing between profit increases expected to result from market growth and those expected to result from improved performance. This section also identifies and describes the amount and source of increased profits expected to result from planned improvements such as new products, capturing a larger share of the market, and reductions of costs and expenses. The final section of the commentary summarizes anticipated results of the growth plan, discussing how attaining the plan's major goals will improve the division's market position, product leadership, cost leadership, and profit standing.

Selected schedules should follow the commentary letter. Schedule 1, the statement of income, describes actual performance during the past two or three years and the profit growth plan projected for the next three to five years. At the bottom the schedule lists the key assets employed in order to indicate the return on capital employed.

Schedule 2 is a profit improvement commentary describing the action the division plans to take to realize the improvements described in the body of the letter. It should answer questions such as what is new and different about the planned improvement; how will the planned improvement be accomplished; and whether new markets or new products will contribute to increased sales.

141

Schedule 3 discusses economic changes, for example, the extent to which annual sales are affected by increases in selling prices or changes in pricing policy. Planned advertising programs and their effect on selling prices are also described. The economic change summary also discusses the effect of increased wages, salaries, purchase prices, or other economic increases. In addition, it details the amount of direct material purchases, supply purchases, hourly wage rates, salary increases, and fringe benefits. Methods to accomplish planned cost reduction in manufacturing expenses, either direct or indirect, are also included in this section.

Schedule 4 summarizes the profit planning in each product line. This schedule indicates the dollar sales effect of changes in volume, sales, and selling prices and the methods to realize the anticipated increases in selling prices by product lines.

Schedule 5 reviews the planning of the product and the product line market. It includes the share of market percentages for each projected year, existing product increases, improved products, new products, total market planning, market growth increases, market penetration, and new markets.

Schedule 6 consists of a summary of cost reduction planning, and includes improvements in annual operating expenses that the division plans to accomplish in the projected profit growth years.

Schedule 7 summarizes the planning capital expenditures for the projected growth years. This commentary includes the facilities of its principal competitors in each major product market, and the most modern production equipment available at the lowest cost. It answers the questions: who is the cost leader, that is, the lowest cost producer in the industry; how do the division's present manufacturing facilities compare with the cost leader's; would acquisition of more modern equipment put the division in a position of cost leadership in the industry.

The final schedule in the profit growth plan is the cash generation summary, indicating gross profits, taxes, net income, depreciation, and amortization.

CAPITAL BUDGETING FOR THE MULTINATIONAL

The process of making investment decisions is basically the same for both domestic and multinational operations: to make the most profitable investments after considering the options and the risks involved. There are two additional considerations:

1   *Opportunity Cost*
    The opportunity cost is the risk-free rate of return on a company's capital resources. Any investment possibility is measured against this minimum reinvestment rate. If the return on an investment equals the opportunity rate, the deciding factor is either the risk or the degree of certainty of achieving a specific return. Opportunity cost is a guideline used to measure the consequences of an investment decision.

2   *Present Value Approach*
    Every firm has a cost of acquiring capital. In order to sustain a company's financial position, every investment of capital resources must yield a return at least equal to its cost of capital. One measure of the consequences of an investment decision is net present value. According to this method, the cash flows from an investment decision are discounted back to period 0 at the cost of capital and compared to the original required investment. The total present value of the cash flows is profitable to the firm if it is greater than the investment.

THE MULTINATIONAL ENVIRONMENT   Operating in an international environment poses some special problems in formulating investment guidelines. The following principally affect investment decisions:

1   *Investment Climate*
    Expected future demand for the product.
    Consumption patterns.

143

Industry growth.

Import and export practices.

Promotion and distribution channels.

Competition at the local level.

Governmental taxes, special duties, tariffs, and price regulations.

Forecast of future exchange rates and actual monetary value of eventual returns to the parent company.

Future economic climate.

2 *Remittance factor*

The return on an investment is measured by the cash flow realized on the investment amount. The remittance policies of the countries involved are critical to accomplishing this return. The following should be examined:

Limitations on remittance of earnings.

Remittability of technical fees.

Royalties.

Withholding taxes on dividends.

Past history of remittances.

3 *Cash Flows*

Cash flow from an investment can be used to repay local debt obligations, to reinvest in the host country or in another country, or to remit to the home country. Cash flow used as a source of funds for operations is measured in terms of the return realized from those operations. Cash flow reinvested or remitted to the home country must be added in order to determine the total return on the investment. Another means of measuring cash flow is to look only to the "net available inflows," those project cash flows that can be be freely converted into currencies and transferred elsewhere.

4 *Risk*

In the multinational field there are environmental, financial, and business risks. Environmental risk is the national climate in which the investment will operate: the stability of the present government, the government's attitude to-

wards foreign business control, and the attitude of organized labor. Financial risk measures the ability to realize
return on the investment in real monetary values: future
foreign exchange rates; remittance attitudes of the country,
taxes, and withholding on dividends. Business risk measures the impact of future competition and the likelihood of
meeting projected cash flows.

Subjective probability is one means of quantifying risk, as
follows:

Step 1. Assign probability factors for achieving the projected
cash flows for each risk factor involved.

Step 2. Multiply the projected cash flows by each probability
factor to determine the expected value of the inflow. This expected value is the average net present value of future out-
comes.

Step 3. Analyze the investment in terms of expected return.
The investment that yields the highest rate of return at the
minimum reinvestment rate of the parent company will be the
best investment for the firm.

APPENDIX: A CASE STUDY

A multinational plans to open operations in South America.
Preliminary studies disclosed two feasible choices: to establish
operations in Country A or in Country B.

Country A
Environment
A strong central government
Attitude toward increased national ownership
History of stunted expansion of local companies

Economic Conditions

Long run inflation with no coordinated plan of remedy

Present policies

(a) "watchdog" price policy
(b) changing exchange rates
(c) restrictive overseas borrowing
(d) no increased taxation
(e) long-run surplus position in foreign trade

Business Conditions

Strong restrictive trade laws

Discourages foreign investment

No competition

Tax Rates and Duties

Local income–40%

Export duties–25%

Other Factors

Remittance regulations–40% after local income tax

Country B

Environment

New government—top two leaders are businessmen

Policies

(a) Redistribution of national income
(b) Controlled foreign investment

Economic Conditions

Increasing inflation

Strict price control

Level exchange rates

Increases in key taxes to improve fiscal deficit

Long-run surplus position in foreign trade

High interest rates but free foreign borrowings

Business Conditions
Open to foreign investment
No local competition
Tax Rates and Duties
Local income–35%
Export duties–30%
Remittance Regulations
5% of sales, 30% after tax income

A ten-year cash flow forecast was prepared for each alternative. The investment required over a three-year period by the parent company is the same for both alternatives. Country A sales are expected to increase 3% a year, whereas country B sales will be constant because of strict price controls.

Reinvestment of the cash flows remitted to the parent company will be at 15% and the company's cost of capital will be at 10%. The value at the end of the ten-year period represents the average annual net inflow available to the parent company amortized at 8%. Adjustments to account for risk were then evaluated to weigh the average probabilities of achieving the net inflows for each risk category.

Finally, the internal rate of return was calculated for each investment using the discounted cash flow method and assuming reinvestment at the calculated internal rate of return.

CONCLUSION   The results indicated that both investments exceed the cost of capital of 10%. Both net present values are positive but the present value of investment A is greater than that of investment B. The internal rates of return for the projects employing the discounted cash flow approach are 16.2% for alternative A and 15.4% for alternative B. Assuming a reinvestment rate of 15%, the modified discounted cash flow rate of return is 15.7% for alternative A and 15.2% for alternative B. In each evaluation alternative A exceeds the return on investment B, reflecting B's greater risk. Country A is the recommended investment.

Risk Factors For Alternative Investments A and B

	Risk Constant	Weight	Weighted Probability
Alternative A			
Environmental risk	.8	.4	.32
Financial risk	.5	.2	.10
Business risk	.6	.4	.24
Total		1.0	.66
Alternative B			
Environmental risk	.5	.4	.20
Financial risk	.7	.2	.14
Business risk	.5	.4	.20
Total		1.0	.54

CHAPTER 9

Management Information System

OBJECTIVES OF THE MNL FINANCIAL MANAGEMENT INFORMATION SYSTEM

The management information system is an integral part of an MNL financial management program. The director of finance has the responsibility for developing, in conjunction with other departments, an integrated system that will meet the information needs of all concerned. The system provides for the dissemination of all information necessary to manage the company's affairs in addition to that provided in financial reports. A systems and procedures group has the responsibility for coordinating and working out the system in detail, thereby assuring continuity with current procedures that are well-understood by management.

The company-wide system is concerned with all information that is significant in the general management of the company and that passes from one department to another. Figure 9 shows a broad view of the information flow. Much of this information is quantitative, but certain analytical and statistical studies in monetary terms are a necessary part of the system. Information required only within individual departments and generated for them, is usually already covered in that department's internal procedures; however, this information must be integrated with the management information system and provide basic source data for it.

In developing a management information system certain

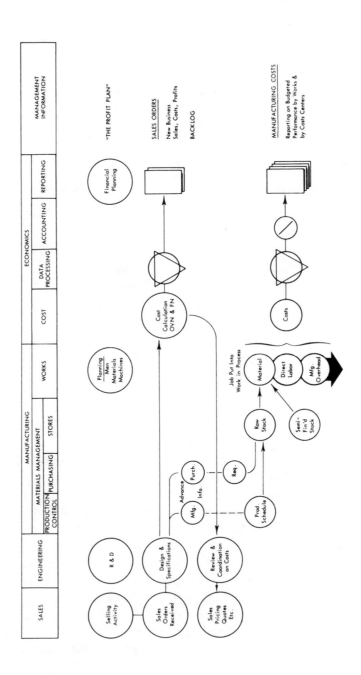

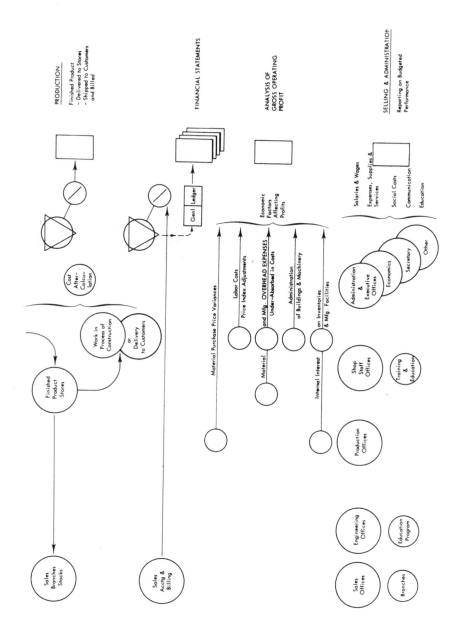

Figure 9. MNL Management information system.

151

broad objectives have to be established. Every step in the system from initial input (each occurrence or transaction) to ultimate output (the record or report to management) must meet the tests of reason and need. The results depend to a large extent on the strict subjection of each step to the fundamental questions of who, what, where, when, and why. With respect to mechanization, the test should be equally objective—can the step or operation be performed best by a person or by a machine or other automated device.

The following goals are typical of an MNL's approach to a management information system:

• *Integration.* Complete integration from the initial data recording through the final reporting. A uniform company-wide coding system is used in manual, mechanized, and computerized applications.

• *Timeliness.* In reporting information, timeliness is achieved through efficient use of facilities and personnel and, where necessary, by early cutoff or closing of transactions and records, provided the effects are not material.

• *Condensation.* Results are summarized only by persons in those levels of organization responsible for corrective action and, where appropriate, only according to major product lines with relevant factors expressed in the common denominator of money.

• *Exception.* Where original data are voluminous or detailed, reports are restricted to factual information about conditions requiring corrective action.

• *Uniformity.* A manual of standard operating procedures with forms, flow charts, and instructions assures uniform practices throughout the company.

Discussions of representative types of information in the areas of finance, sales production, materials management, selling, administration, and economic matters follow in succeeding parts of this chapter.

FINANCIAL INFORMATION The reports discussed in the previous chapters are part of the information system. Financial statements and graphic analyses are for the most part monthly or quarterly reports. To complement these, an interim semimonthly summary of financial data is suggested.

The semimonthly summary, intended only for the managing director of president and the vice presidents of the company, gives them on one sheet of paper, or on one card, a quick insight into the company's interim business results. The objective is to provide the executives with current financial data that they can use between the time they receive one financial management report and the next.

The following is representative of the information for cumulative month-to-date reporting:

In addition to the above many executives have compiled for their own use all the essential information about their company in what is called a "Brain Book." Figure 10 outlines the type of data usually included in what can be loosely described as a "bakers dozen" of key information items.

SALES INFORMATION Information relative to sales orders and deliveries arranged by major product lines is presented monthly in a series of graphic analyses. Comparisons of actual with budgeted amounts and indications of profit margins are also shown on the graphs. Data relative to the production index and backlog would round out this informative set of charts.

Sales information also includes selling and administrative expenses. Supplemental data for sales branches and sales offices are also prepared, showing comparisons of actual performance with budgeted expenses. Additional graphs provide analytical data on certain sales matters that affect profits, such as sales volume, share of markets, product mix, and changes in the selling price.

PRODUCTION INFORMATION Needs for production information vary according to the plant and type of manufacturing activity. Certain representative types of information are summarized in the following outline:

153

Weekly or SemiMonthly Summary Report

	Total	Commercial	Industrial	Branches	Other
New business–orders received					
Sales–delivered and billed					
Backlog of orders					
Production delivered to stores Manufacturing activity– Direct labor Material put into process					
Materials purchases					
Personnel—direct —indirect					
Order index					
Production index					
Estimated gross operating profit					
Sales					
Cost of sales					
Provision for manufacturing Cost factors Provision for economic factors					
Net					
Working capital–cash Receivables–payables inventories					

BRAIN BOOK	TOTAL INT'L OPERATIONS	Canada	Mexico	Europe
1 *Net Sales*				
Planned sales				
Amt. better/(worse) than plan				
% " " " "				
Net sales in U.S. $				
2 *Net Income*				
Planned income				
Amt. better/(worse) than plan				
% " " " "				
New income in U.S. $				
3 *Investment*–local currency				
–U.S. $				
4 *Financial Analysis*				
Earnings per sales dollar				
(% net income to net sales)				
Capital turnover (sales/investment)				
Return on investment				
5 *Cost of Sales per Sales Dollar*				
Direct materials				
Direct labor				
Overhead				
Other costs				
Total actual				
Total planned				
6 *New Orders Booked to Date*				
Planned orders to date				
Order index				
Company price index				
7 *Procurement*				
Purchase orders placed to date				
Percentage to orders booked				
8 *Production Rate*				
Planned rate				
9 *Work Force*				
Production direct				
Production indirect				

Salaried supervision
Salaried office and other
　　Totals

10　*Hours Worked per Man Work*
Overtime hours worked
Average hourly rate $/Hr

11　*Total Payroll*
Labor cost per sales dollar
Sales per employee—local currency
　　　　　　　—U.S. $
Investment per employee—local currency
　　　　　　　—U.S. $

12　*Operating Expense per Sales Dollar*
Salaries and wages—administration
(incl. suppl., selling advt.,
payroll expense)—other
　　TOTAL

Telephone and communications
Rentals
Supplies and stationery
Office expenses
Service charges

　Total actual

　Total planned

13　*Plant, Building, Machinery, and*
　　Equipment—Occupancy Costs
Depreciation
Insurance
Taxes
Light, heat, and power
Maintenance
Service, etc.
　　TOTAL

Area in use—sq. meters

Cost per sq. meters—local currency
　　　　　　—U.S. $

14　*New Plant and Equipment Expenditures*
Planned expenditures

New plant expenditures–U.S. $

Figure 10. Brain Book.

1 Finished products delivered to customers and stores grouped by product lines.
2 Backlog of orders grouped by product lines.
3 Manufacturing activity
  Material put into process
  Direct labor operations arranged by works and production groups
  Production indexes
  Comparison with backlog indexes
4 Quality control
  Quality index
  Rejected products returned by customers
  Rejected products due to design faults
  Rejected products due to materials or metallurgical failure
  Rejected products due to poor workmanship
  Material cost of rejected products related to material cost of production
5 Personnel and manpower statistics
  Direct labor arranged by plant and production groups
  Indirect labor
  Foremen and supervisory staffs
  Shop office staff   Related in percentages
  Maintenance work force   to direct labor and
  Inspectors and quality control   manpower budgets
  Production office staffs
6 Maintenance and repair
  Maintenance work orders
    Completed
    In process
    Received
    Backlog
  Comparison of the actual cost of maintenance work orders with estimates
  Preventive maintenance
    Cost
    Percentage of total work
  Maintenance materials (costs versus estimates in budget)
    Repair parts

Replacement parts

Maintenance supplies

Report on outside maintenance services

7 Analysis of the cost of production delays in the shop

MATERIALS MANAGEMENT INFORMATION

The most significant information in the area of materials management concerns the relation of procurement and inventories to the amount of new business received in incoming orders. Financial reports show the status of inventories in summary form grouped by product classes and in more detail grouped by types of product.

The following represents the kind of information that should be submitted by materials management in either graphic or printed form:

1 Value of purchase orders placed in relation to sales orders
2 Inventory levels related to sales orders grouped by product types
3 Backlog of orders related to inventory levels, indicating the imbalance in stocks
4 Analysis of variances in the purchase price of materials and price index factors
5 Comparison of the MNL purchasing experience with published industry-wide price indexes
6 Analysis of the decisions to make or buy grouped by types of product and kinds of manufacturing operations
7 Analysis of the cost of production delays in terms of materials management costs
8 Analysis of vendor performance with respect to delivery schedules
9 Analysis of manufacturing performance in relation to production schedules
10 Analysis of customer delivery performance

SELLING AND ADMINISTRATIVE EXPENSES

The essential information in the area of selling and administrative expenses is related to cost and budgetary control. Budget comparisons discussed earlier are supplemented with data comparing personnel on the payroll with manpower schedules.

Attention is directed particularly to special administrative activities and services. The training and education program should be analyzed and reported with respect to both engineering and manufacturing as well as general and administrative expenses.

The following administrative activities should also be reported:

Telephone, telegraph, and other communications
Office supplies
Printing and reproduction services

Cost and expense are compared with budget objectives, but appropriate charges are made throughout the company for services. Budget reports also indicate information regarding volume of transactions, calls, supplies, printing, and engraving, and so forth.

INFORMATION ON ECONOMIC FACTORS

The impact of economic factors on profits significantly affects the success or failure of the MNL. No information system is complete without supplementing the basic financial figures with detailed statistics and analysis. The following lists items for which continuing statistical information should be maintained:

1 *Price Indexes*
   For the industry as a whole and for the MNL in particular
2 *Depreciation*
   Analysis of the replacement cost versus the book depreciation of buildings and machinery
   Report of the cumulative value of funds provided in the cost of production for replacing facilities
3 *Administration of Buildings and Machinery*
   Depreciation
   Interest
   Insurance
   Property taxes
   Light, heat, and power

Maintenance costs

Services

Comparison of the total of these administrative costs with rents charged to business using the facilities.

4 *Internal interest*

Analysis of the effects of external as well as internal interest on the prices of various product lines.

5 *Analysis of the Return on Investment*

By product lines

By manufacturing facilities

6 *Analysis of Capital Investment*

Fund requirements versus funds provided by profits and depreciation.

DESIGNING AN INTEGRATED MANAGEMENT INFORMATION SYSTEM

The system of financial management information depends on system of electronic data processing, which in turn depends upon clerical procedures, programming, and operating hardware. The combined clerical and mechanical operations involve the recording, transmission, manipulation, and storage of information for accounting, operating, planning, and management control. Various analytical and decision-making functions also depend on the information provided by the data-processing system.

The general objectives of systems of management information and integrated electronic data processing are:

• Provide management reports promptly.

• Strengthen management control through reports on performance and budget control.

• Maintain adequate internal control over the company's assets.

• Reduce the amount of detail reviewed by management and staff.

• Present information in a well-understood form.

• Provide information not presently available.

• Provide "tools" to assist in developing or evaluating plans for more productive utilization of the company's resources.

160

• Provide adequate audit trails as to the accountability for assets and financial reports.

• Maintain flexible reporting cycles.

• Provide the facilities to permit the timely and accurate preparation of reports.

• Maintain sufficient flexibility of systems design to meet changing requirements.

• Reduce the cost of data processing.

• Eliminate duplication of efforts and costs by integrating functions.

LIMITATIONS OF SYSTEMS STUDIES AT CERTAIN MNL'S

The following are examples of conditions that limit success in some systems of management information and data processing:

1 Overlap, duplication, and lack of integration in functions converted to electronic data processing (EDP) equipment. In processing orders, for example, responsibility and control are split among sales, production, and finance.
2 Some EDP systems are designed to meet only the requirements that were previously satisfied by the manual systems, which inefficiently utilizes the new equipment and does not satisfy information needs dictated by new organizations or new management controls.
3 Some systems and procedure groups are understaffed.
4 The EDP programming effort and installation plan proceed at a pace out of step with systems design and development plans. Unless the timing and contents of systems, programming, and installation schedules are coordinated expensive and time-consuming pitfalls are likely to be encountered.

ACCOUNTING AND COST SYSTEMS

An accounting system may be described as a chemical process from which financial statements are distilled. The schematic drawings, Figures 11 and 12, depict the essential steps in an accounting system designed to produce financial statements for management: a balance sheet, an income statement, and the details of revenue, costs, and expenses according to the principal divisions or operations of the company. Figure 11 is the procedures chart for preparing financial statements. As indicated, the principal sources of information in an accounting system are first, the payroll time sheets from employees whether the source of revenue is products manufactured for sale or services performed for billing to clients. The second source is the paycheck prepared for the employee. The third is the cash disbursements checks and check register. The fourth is the cash receipts, that is, cash or checks received from customers or clients. The fifth is invoices from vendors and the sixth is general journal vouchers prepared each month to maintain the books of accounts on an accrual basis. As indicated they include entries for accrued liabilities, prepaid insurance, amortization, depreciation, miscellaneous adjustments, and transfers necessary to keep records according to different segments of the business. Accountants' working papers, which are required to support the financial statements and other reports, supplement the other sources of information. These working papers are also required to control and support statutory reports, such as tax returns, employee withholding taxes, employee insurance reports, and reports related to payments to consultants, contractors, legal fees, and audit fees. Other working papers are needed to control and report on accounts that have to be reconciled monthly, quarterly, or periodically. Finally, there are working papers to analyze accounts for auditing or internal control.

The chart in Figure 11 shows the key succeeding steps in the accounting process. For example, a labor summary of the payroll time sheet distribution is prepared that becomes the general journal voucher known as the payroll distribution. This entry also includes a distribution of the burden or overhead that has to be added to the direct labor payroll in order to accumulate total costs on the general ledger. Direct costs other than payroll are recorded in a voucher register prepared principally from invoices from vendors but also from the general journal vouchers.

The summary of materials, services, and other charges plus fees or markup represent revenue that, in a series of closing entries, are recorded on the general ledger as revenue, cost of revenue, operating expenses, other income, other expenses, variance accounts, and the net difference between revenue costs and expenses. The procedures chart on the right side clearly indicates that in addition to summary distributions made in the general ledger, it is necessary to maintain subsidiary ledgers for advances received from clients or customers as well as accounts receivables. Supporting ledgers are also required for fixed assets, buildings, and equipment, prepaid expenses are credits, prepaid insurance, subscriptions, supplies, rents, and deposits, miscellaneous accruals; and accounts payable, contract purchases, and so on.

The end result is shown on the extreme right, the financial statements prepared for management: a comparative balance sheet, a comparative statement of income for the total company, and a summary comparison of actual and planned performance by the principal operating seqments of the business.

The second procedures chart, Figure 12, represents the method by which revenue costs and expenses are related to cost reports and services billed to clients. This representation of a cost system, while portraying principally revenue derived from services rendered, is not different from a firm whose revenue is derived from products manufactured and sold to customers. The sources of the information depicted on the left side are the same. Time sheets from employees are prepared whether for engineers in a consulting firm or for workers in a manufacturing plant. Time sheets multiplied by applicable pay rates results in the direct costs, either salaries or hourly payrolls, directly chargeable to projects. Invoices from vendors and the journal vouchers, which are described in greater detail on the first chart, have to be processed and approved. Vouchers for materials, supplies, services, and travel are charged directly to projects wherever possible. Certain payrolls and vouchers,

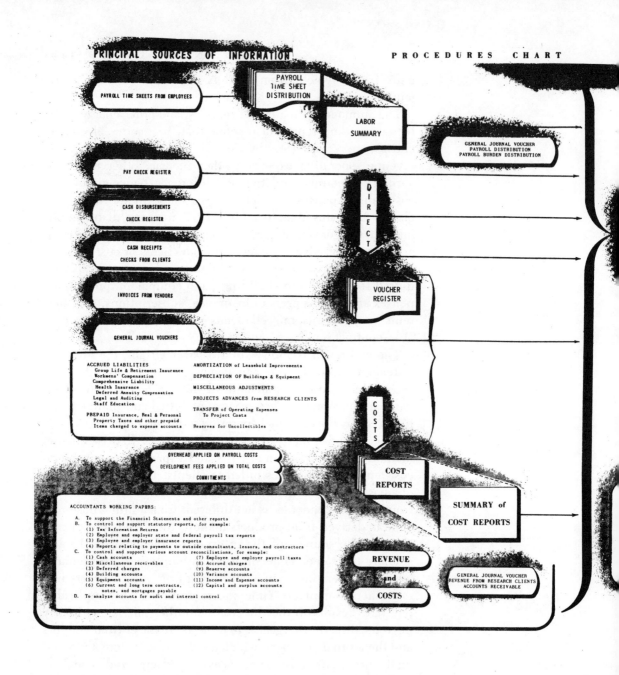

Figure 11. Accounting system.

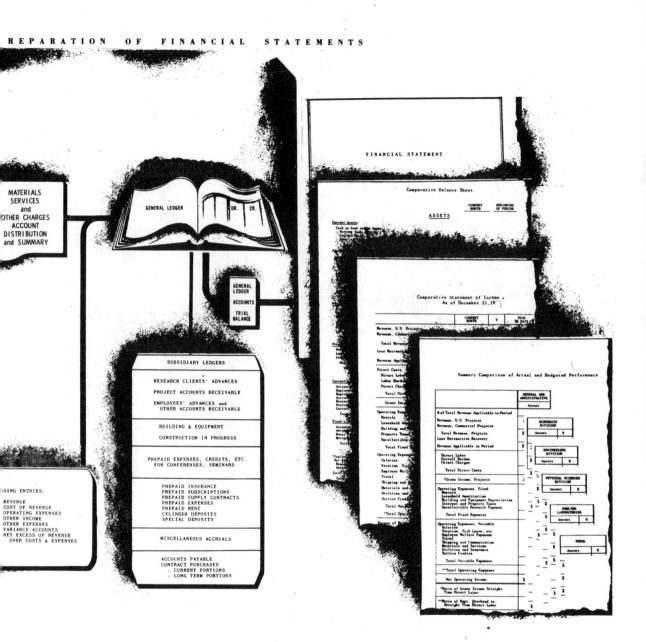

MATERIALS
SERVICES
and
OTHER CHARGES
ACCOUNT
DISTRIBUTION
and SUMMARY

GENERAL LEDGER   DR.   CR.

GENERAL
LEDGER

ACCOUNTS

TRIAL
BALANCE

FINANCIAL STATEMENT

Comparative Balance Sheet

ASSETS

SUBSIDIARY LEDGERS

RESEARCH CLIENTS' ADVANCES

PROJECT ACCOUNTS RECEIVABLE

EMPLOYEES' ADVANCES and
OTHER ACCOUNTS RECEIVABLE

BUILDING & EQUIPMENT

CONSTRUCTION IN PROGRESS

PREPAID EXPENSES, CREDITS, ETC.
FOR CONFERENSES, SEMINARS

PREPAID INSURANCE
PREPAID SUBSCRIPTIONS
PREPAID SUPPLY CONTRACTS
PREPAID EXPENSES
PREPAID RENT
CYLINDER DEPOSITS
SPECIAL DEPOSITS

MISCELLANEOUS ACCRUALS

ACCOUNTS PAYABLE
CONTRACT PURCHASES
- CURRENT PORTIONS
- LONG TERM PORTIONS

Comparative Statement of Income
As of December 31, 19

Summary Comparison of Actual and Budgeted Performance

SING ENTRIES:

REVENUE
COST OF REVENUE
OPERATING EXPENSES
OTHER INCOME
OTHER EXPENSES
VARIANCE ACCOUNTS
NET EXCESS OF REVENUE
OVER COSTS & EXPENSES

165

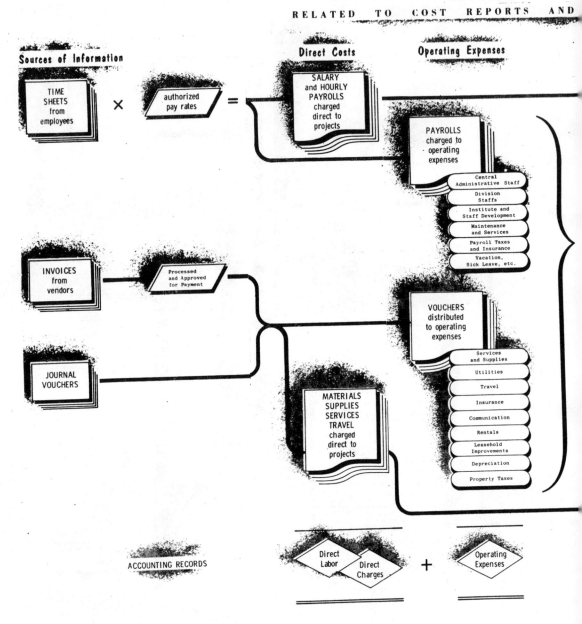

Figure 12. Cost system.

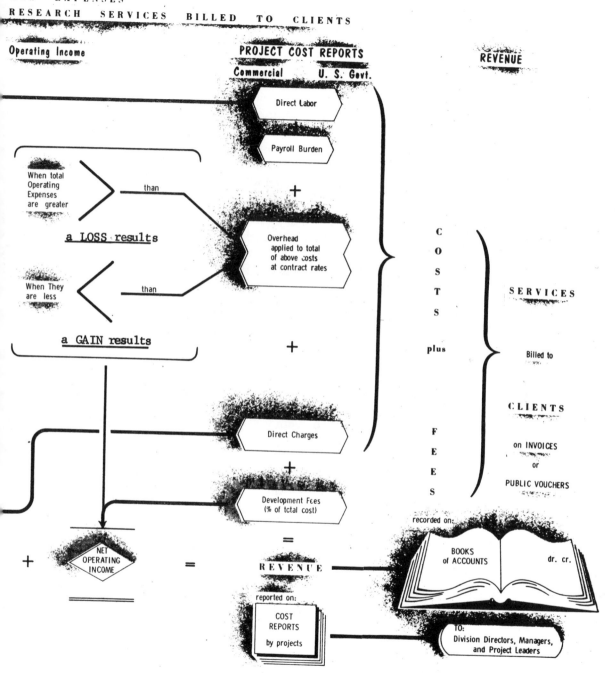

Operating Income

PROJECT COST REPORTS

Commercial   U. S. Govt.

REVENUE

Direct Labor

Payroll Burden

When total Operating Expenses are greater

than

a LOSS results

+

Overhead applied to total of above costs at contract rates

When They are less

than

a GAIN results

C O S T S

plus

F E E S

S E R V I C E S

Billed to

C L I E N T S

on INVOICES

or

PUBLIC VOUCHERS

+

Direct Charges

+

Development Fees (% of total cost)

recorded on:

BOOKS of ACCOUNTS   dr. cr.

+   NET OPERATING INCOME   =   R E V E N U E

reported on:

COST REPORTS by projects

TO: Division Directors, Managers, and Project Leaders

167

however, cannot be so charged. These payrolls represent administrative staff salaries, division staff salaries, maintenance and services, payroll taxes, insurance, vacations and so on. Vouchers attributed to operating expenses consist of services, supplies, utilities, travel, insurance, communication costs, rentals, leasehold improvements, depreciation, and property taxes.

Before operating income can be determined, operating expenses must be applied or allocated as logically as possible to the direct cost incurred. The usual method applies overhead proportionally to the direct labor cost incurred. The right side of the chart in Figure 12 indicates that the direct labor category on project cost reports must have two factors added:

1 A payroll burden percentage
2 An overhead rate applied to the total of the direct labor and payroll costs at contract or predetermined rates. A fundamental principle of cost accounting provides that before the gross margin can be determined the total operating expenses actually incurred in a given period have to be compared with the overhead applied in that period. When total actual operating expenses are greater than the applied amount, a loss results. When the total is less than the overhead amounts applied at the standard rate, a gain results. This overhead cost affects the net operating income. The right side of the chart shows summarily that the direct labor plus payroll burden, plus overhead, plus the direct charges from materials and services, plus the fee or markup represents total revenue. Running across the bottom of the chart there is a summary of the contents of the accounting records, namely, direct labor, direct charges, plus operating expenses, which when compared with revenue represent net operating income. The total of these costs plus fees or a markup where products are sold represents sales or the services billed to clients and they are recorded as such in the books of accounts. Supporting the books of accounts are cost reports that are prepared in detail, that is, for each project undertaken for each client.

The results are summarized monthly and provided to division directors, managers, and project leaders. In sum, this is a cost system, a system that operates within the accounting system necessary to prepare financial statements for management.

ASSOCIATED COMPANIES—GUIDE TO CONTROL AND FINANCE MANAGEMENT

The MNL sets forth in its administrative manual the basic requirements for control and finance applicable to its wholly owned companies and operating divisions. The reports and procedures specified therein meet the needs of the MNL management. There are other reports that are fundamental and practices that every management should follow. The following outlines representative reports and practices that an MNL would recommend to the management of its associated companies:

1 *Financial Reports*
   Prepare monthly the following reports:
   Statement of income
   Sales, costs, and gross profits grouped by principal product categories
   Operating expenses
   Cash report
2 Prepare a balance sheet quarterly.
3 Prepare monthly a letter of comment for the associated company board to transmit to its MNL stockholders.
4 Prepare annually a profit plan consisting of the following schedules:
   Forecast statement of income
   Sales, costs, and gross profits grouped by principal product categories
   Operating expenses

Cash forecast by months
Statement of income by months
Balance sheets at the beginning and end of the year

These schedules are prefaced by a general commentary, a marketing plan, a manufacturing plan, and an operating or administrative plan.

5 Prepare annually a capital expenditure budget indicating the planned investment expenditures, the effects of investments on cash and profits, and the return on investment. Provide a breakdown of the budget in a simplified form using the following categories:
Cost reduction projects
Projects for new products
Profits improvement projects
Necessity projects

Appropriation requests approved in accordance with the company's bylaws must be prepared before any project can be undertaken and funds expended or committed. Sale or disposal of all capitalized property should also be properly authorized.

6 An audit by independent certified public accountants should be made annually.

7 An associated company administration manual should be compiled, containing statements of the company's policies and practices in each of the following areas:
Office of the president
Control and finance
Legal and corporate affairs
Manufacturing services
Marketing services
Personnel administration
Public relations
Research

8 Representative subject matter for the control and finance section includes:

(a) Internal control standards
     Bank accounts
     Cash receipts and deposits
     Disbursement authority and signatures
     Bank statement reconciliation
     Accounts payable
     Payrolls
     Petty cash
     Securities
     Accounts receivable
(b) Inventory valuation policy
(c) Property, plant, and equipment
(d) Depreciation
(e) Insurance
(f) Chart of accounts
(g) Principles governing determination of income
(h) Manufacturing cost system
(i) Records retention policy

9 Representative subject matter for the general corporate section includes:
Organization of the company
Delegation of authority to executives
Research
Patents, trademarks, and copyrights
Real estate, leases, and so on
Procurement policies
Conflict of interest
Contributions
Memberships
Industrial relations
Salary and hourly pay policies
Employment policies
Vacation and holidays
Expense reports

LETTER OF COMMENT

The financial reports recommended to be prepared monthly in the foregoing section, items 1 and 2, are basic types of reports and need no further description of their form or contents, which are adapted to the particular needs of each MNL. The letter of comment recommended in item 3, however, provides an opportunity for original thoughts in reporting to management. This letter, prepared for the associate company board and its stockholders, comprehensively views the company's operations for the current period and forecasts things to come.

The report on international operations; Figures 13, 14, 15, and 16, represents an innovative approach to a letter of Comment. The first page, Figure 13, summarizes the results of the year to date along with a forecast for the entire year. It shows the big picture—a long-term look at the company—and comments on the statement of income, industry economics, and marketing. The second page, Figure 14, analyzes the net income and gross profit variances of sales during the last month, particularly the effects of volume, price realization, cost performance, and products mix. The second part of Figure 14 analyzes last month's operating expenses and variances from planned operations. The third page (and additional pages as necessary), Figure 15, analyzes gross profit variances by product lines determining the reasons why gross profits were better or worse than planned according to cause, volume, price realization, or cost performance. A sample calculation of the formula for this analysis is provided in Figure 17. The final page of the Letter of Comment, Figure 16, contains an operations forecast with comments on the short-term outlook for sales and income in comparison with the budget. Also indicated are comments on orders, backlog, production, and inventories as they relate to the operations forecast.

The letter of comment consists basically of only four pages: additional pages are added only if there are four or more product lines to be analyzed. The letter of comment is signed by the president or managing director, with the details having been prepared by his financial officer or controller.

ANALYSIS OF OPERATING RESULTS

The letter of comment is prepared by the managing director or president of a subsidiary or associate company for the information of the stockholders, and particularly for the information of that segment of the stockholders known as the multinational company. The letter of comment emphasizes a foreword and backward look at the results of operations, but more specifically the analysis of gross margin according to price, volume, and cost performance, and the effect of mixed product sales on the gross margin. This section describes a supplement to the letter of comment, an analysis of operating results. Schedule I, Figure 18, is a complete statement of income prepared for a number of months, that is, the year to date. The analysis is prepared for gross sales, cost of sales, standard gross profit, a series of manufacturing cost variances, other costs, operating expenses, and the resulting income before taxes.

The purpose of the analysis of operating results is to indicate in each category those variances from planned profit that result from an increase or decrease in the volume of sales, as against those profit variances that were better or worse than planned because of actual performance during the period. The determination of the profit variance due to volume is the result of calculating the profit plan at actual volume and comparing that plan with the profit plan at budget volume. For example, if gross sales were actually 25% greater than the budgeted volume one would expect the cost of sales at standard and planned manufacturing cost variances, other costs, and operating expenses to be proportionately higher. To calculate the variance in detail, take the actual gross sales, insert it in column 3 of Figure 18 and multiply that figure by the percentage of gross sales indicated in the fifth column under profit plan budget volume. The difference in each respective cost and expense category between the third and fourth columns is the increase or decrease in variances due to volume.

Profit variances due to performance are arrived at by comparing the actual gross sales, the actual standard cost of sales, manufacturing cost variances, other costs, and operating ex-

LETTER OF COMMENT

INTERNATIONAL OPERATIONS

Date of Letter 19____

National Name of ____ Company

Official Corporate Name

STATEMENT OF INCOME

____ months ended
Last Mo. end 19____

	YEAR TO DATE					TOTAL YEAR 19			
	(2) ACTUAL		PROFIT PLAN			(1) FORECAST		PROFIT PLAN	
	AMOUNT	%	AMOUNT	%		AMOUNT	%	AMOUNT	%
Gross Sales									
Returns, Allow. & Disc.									
NET SALES									
Cost of Goods Sold									
GROSS PROFIT									
Admin. & Gen. Expense									
Selling Expense									
Adv. & Sales Prom.									
Res. & Development									
Service Charge									
Operating Expense									
Operating Income									
Other Charges (Net)									
PRE-TAX INCOME									
Prov. for Inc. Tax									
NET INCOME	(2)					(1)			

INVESTMENT			
RETURN ON INVESTMENT	(3) %	(2) %	(1) %

(4) COMMENT ON STATEMENT OF INCOME - YEAR TO DATE AND FORECAST OF TOTAL YEAR
(5) INDUSTRY ECONOMICS & MARKETING FACTORS

This page shows the big picture---the long-term look at your company.

1. First and foremost, your latest forecast for the total year is compared with profit plan.

2. Actual results to date are likewise reported in comparison with plan.

3. Return on investment is calculated on an annualized basis, according to the Corporate formula.

4. Confine your comments here only to the aforementioned data.

5. What industry economics and marketing factors affect total year results? Discuss here impact of price changes, competitors' actions, potential changes in national economy or other factors affecting the company's long-term results.

Figure 13. Letter of Comment.

LAST MONTH'S NET SALES, NET INCOME AND ANALYSIS OF GROSS PROFIT VARIANCES – TOTAL COMPANY

SUMMARY	ACTUAL	PLAN	VARIANCE	ANALYSIS OF GROSS PROFIT VARIANCE		VOLUME (Units Sold)	ACTUAL	PLAN
Net Sales				Volume		Quantity		
Gross Profit				Price Realization		Price		
% of Gross Profit to Net Sales				Cost Performance	(1)	Actual Volume @ Planned Prices		
				Product Mix	(2)			
				TOTAL				

COMMENTS ON GROSS PROFIT ANALYSIS

This section summarizes total company results -- the details by product groups or lines are found on the next page. Comments here, therefore, need highlight only the most important factors which influenced gross profit improvement (or lack thereof).

Note: That Cost Performance variance (1) is the total of the product line variances from Page 3.

Product Mix (2) is the difference between Cost Performance of the total company and this amount (1).

LAST MONTH'S OPERATING EXPENSES AND ANALYSIS OF VARIANCES — TOTAL COMPANY

OPERATING EXPENSES	ACTUAL	% NET SALES	PLAN	% NET SALES	VARIANCES VOLUME	VARIANCES PERFORMANCE
Administrative & General Expense					(4)	(3)
Selling Expense						
Advertising & Sales Promotion						
Research & Development						
Service Charge						
TOTAL						

COMMENT ON OPERATING EXPENSE

This section tells the reasons why last month's operating expenses were better or worse than profit plan. The variances will be classified ordinarily as performance (3). Variance due to volume (4) can be identified only if the change in volume was quite significant, and the company can determine proper allowances for those expenses which are not influenced by change in volume.

Figure 14. Letter of Comment.

LAST MONTH'S NET SALES, NET INCOME AND ANALYSIS OF GROSS PROFIT VARIANCES — BY PRODUCT LINES

PRODUCT LINE	ACTUAL	PLAN	VARIANCE	ANALYSIS - GROSS PROFIT VARIANCE			VOLUME (Units Sold)	ACTUAL	PLAN
Net Sales				Volume			Quantity		
Gross Profit				Price Realization			Price		
% of Gross Profit to Net Sales				Cost Performance			Actual Vol.@ Plan. Prices		
				TOTAL			TOTAL		

COMMENTS ON PRODUCT LINE ANALYSIS

Prepare the data for and comment upon gross profits contributed by each significant profit line. Group in "other" the product lines which are not large enough to have impact on total company results.

Use extra sheets if you have 4 or more product lines.

PRODUCT LINE	ACTUAL	PLAN	VARIANCE	ANALYSIS - GROSS PROFIT VARIANCE			VOLUME (Units Sold)	ACTUAL	PLAN
Net Sales	a	b		Volume	x		Quantity	f	
Gross Profit	c	d		Price Realization	y		Price		g
% of Gross Profit to Net Sales		e		Cost Performance	z		Actual Vol.@ Plan. Prices	h	
				TOTAL			TOTAL		

COMMENTS ON PRODUCT LINE ANALYSIS

This is the formula for Analysis - Gross Profit Variance:

1. Calculate what actual volume of sales would have been at planned prices, that is - - - - - h = f x g

2. Volume variance - x is the difference between gross profit on actual volume at planned prices and the planned gross profit. - - - x = (h x e) - d

3. Price realization - y is the difference between actual sales and actual volume at planned prices - y = a - h

PRODUCT LINE	ACTUAL	PLAN	VARIANCE
Net Sales			
Gross Profit			
% of Gross Profit to Net Sales			

COMMENTS ON PRODUCT LINE ANALYSIS

ANALYSIS-GROSS PROFIT VARIANCE	VOLUME (Units Sold)	ACTUAL	PLAN
Volume	Quantity		
Price Realization	Price		
Cost Performance	Actual Vol.@ Plan. Prices		
TOTAL			

Continued:

4. Cost Performance - z is the difference between cost of sales of actual volume at planned prices and actual cost of sales. - - - z = h (1.00 - e) - (a - c)

Figure 15. Letter of Comment.

Date of Letter 19 _____   National name of _____ Company

OPERATIONS FORECAST

ACTUAL LAST MONTH		THIS MONTH	Next three months - -
NET SALES			
	Budget		
	Last Forecast		
	This Forecast		
NET INCOME			
	Budget		
	Last Forecast		
	This Forecast		

COMMENT ON OPERATIONS FORECAST & SHORT TERM OUTLOOK

The comments here should be confined to your forecast for this and the next three months. The emphasis here is only on the short-term outlook as it affects these operations.

**COMMENT ON ORDERS, BACKLOG, PRODUCTION AND INVENTORIES
IN RELATION TO OPERATIONS FORECAST**

Again confining remarks to the short-term outlook, indicate how orders

and backlog will influence these results. Your planned production rate,

manpower, etc. in relation to capacity and the status of inventories

will contribute to better understanding of the operations forecast.

President or Managing Director   _Date_

Figure 16. Letter of Comment.

	Actual	Plan	Volume		Volume Quantity Price	Actual	Plan
Sales[a]	109,200	100,000[b]	9200			105,000[f]	100,000
Gross Profit[c]	36,300	40,000[d]	(3700)		Price	$1.04	$1.00[g]
Percentage of gross profit to net sales	33%	40%					

Actual volume at planned prices

$$h = 105^f \times \$1.00^g = \$105,000$$

Volume variance

$$X = (105,000^h \times 40\%^e) = 42,000$$
$$-d = -40,000$$
$$ 2,000$$

Price realization

$$105,000 \times 1.00 = 105,000^h = 4200$$

Cost performance

$$Z = 105,000^h \times 100\ -40\ 60\% = \$63,000$$
$$109,200^a - 36,300^c = (\$72,900)\quad (9900)$$

Summary

Analysis—gross profit variance

Volume = x = 2000

Price realization = y − 4200

Cost performance = z = (9900)

$$Y = 105,000 \times 1.04 = 109,200$$
$$\text{To}\quad (3700)$$

Figure 17. Letter of Comment.

Analysis of Operating Results
  Statement of Income
Year to Date through _____

Date _____

Division _____

SCHEDULE 1

Figure 17. Letter of Comment.

	Actual			Profit plan at actual volume	Profit plan at budget volume				Profit variances		
	Amount	%	gross	sales	Amount	%	gross	sales	Volume	Performance	Total
Gross Sales											
Sales returns and allowances	—			—	—			—	—	—	—
Net sales	—			—	—			—	—	—	—
Cost of sales at standard	—			—	—			—	—	—	—
Standard gross profit	—			—	—			—	—	—	—
Manufacturing cost variances											
Material price variances											
Material usage variances											
Spoilage variances											
Rework variances											
Labor rate variances											
Labor performance variances											
Spending variances											
Overhead volume variances											
Other cost variances											
Total	—			—	—			—	—	—	—
Other Costs											
Inventory adjustments											
Outbound freight											
Shipping expense											
Service and repair expense											
Other operating costs											
Total	—			—	—			—	—	—	—
Actual gross profit	—			—	—			—	—	—	—
Operating expense											
Administrative and general											
Selling expense											
Advertising and sales promotion											
Research and development											
Administrative service charge											
Total	—			—	—			—	—	—	—
Other charges—net	—			—	—			—	—	—	—
Pretax income	—			—	—			—	—	—	—

Figure 18. Analysis of operating results.

penses with the gross sales calculated at the percentages of profit planned gross sales in column 5. Accordingly, the difference between column 1 and the actual amount of sales cost and expenses and column 3 represents performance factors in manufacturing cost variances, other costs, and operating expenses.

The analysis of operating results is a very effective management tool in bringing to the fore the cost variances due to spoilage, rework, labor rates, and so on, which may have been greater during this period than had been anticipated in the profit plan.

CRITICAL PLANT REPORT—COST OF GOODS SOLD, OPERATING PERFORMANCE

There are times when a manufacturing plant of an associated company produces results that are clearly out of hand in the opinion of the management and its board. When this occurs more incisive, additional analysis of the component parts of costs is warranted. A critical plant report provides a means of analyzing the cost of goods sold in order to identify those elements of cost that produced the adverse operating performance. The analysis is prepared first for the current period and then for the number of months through the end of the period year to date. The objective is to determine which of the operating variances were better or worse when planned because of the volume of production and which variances were adverse because of performance. Figure 19, the critical plant report, indicates the method of calculating the variances in volume and performance. Basically the costs for the current period at the volume of planned profits are compared to the current period's profit plan at actual volume in order to determine the operating variances due to volume. The profit plan of the current period at actual volume compared to the operating results of the current period at actual volume determines the variances in operating performance. This formula resembles that analyzed in the previous section; however, the important differ-

COST OF GOODS SOLD OPERATING PERFORMANCE

CRITICAL PLANT REPORT

PLANT _____
DIVISION _____

DATE _____
PERIOD. _____

	Current Period Profit Plan @ Plan Volume	Current Period Profit Plan @ Actual Volume	Current Period Operating Results @ Actual Volume	Operating Variance Analysis Volume	Operating Variance Analysis Perform-ance	Operating Variance Analysis Total	Year-to-Date Profit Plan @ Plan Volume	Year-to-Date Profit Plan @ Actual Volume	Year-to-Date Operating Results @ Actual Volume	Operating Variance Analysis Volume	Operating Variance Analysis Perform-ance	Operating Variance Analysis Total
1. MANUFACTURING COST												
2. Direct Labor					XXX						XXX	
3. Direct Material					XXX						XXX	
4. Manufacturing Overhead Absorbed					XXX						XXX	
5. Engineering Drawing Costs					XXX						XXX	
6. Direct Charges					XXX						XXX	
7. Rework Cost Allowance					XXX						XXX	
8. Spoilage Cost Allowance					XXX						XXX	
9. Other					XXX						XXX	
10.												
11. (Increase)/Decrease in Inventories												
12. Work in Process					XXX						XXX	
13. Finished Goods					XXX						XXX	
14.												
15.												
16. MANUFACTURING COST OF GOODS SOLD					XXX						XXX	
17.												
18. COST OF RESALE GOODS SOLD					XXX						XXX	
19.												
20. MANUFACTURING COST VARIANCES												
21. Material Price Variance												
22. Material Usage Variance												
23. Labor Variance – Rate												
24. – Performance												
25. Rework Variance												
26. Spoilage Variance												
27. Spending Variance – Current Budget												
28. Spending Variance – Profit Plan												
29. Volume Variance												
30. Other												
31.												
32. INVENTORY ADJUSTMENTS												
33. Physical Inventory Adjustments												
34. Obsolete & Slow-moving Adjustment												
35. Revision of Standard Costs												
36. Other												
37.												
38.												
39. DISTRIBUTION COSTS												
40. Outbound Freight												
41. Shipping Expense												
42. Warehouse Expense												
43. Other												
44.												
45.												
46. OTHER OPERATING COSTS												
47. Cash Discounts on Purchases												
48. Revenue from Sale of Scrap												
49. Major Rehabilit'n, Modernizat'n, & Reser.												
50. Other												
51.												
52.												
53. TOTAL COST OF GOODS SOLD												

① ② ③ ④ ⑤ ⑥

Current Period Profit Plan at Plan Volume

Enter the plant's calendarized amounts for the month reported from the worksheets supporting Annual Profit Plan Schedule 18.

Current Period Operating Results at Actual Volume

Enter Income Statement Schedule B-3 amounts for the month reported.

Operating Variance Analysis Volume

Enter the difference between the Column 1 and 2 amounts. If the Column 2 amount is greater than the Column 1 amount, enter in parentheses.

Operating Variance Analysis Performance

Enter the difference between the Column 2 and 3 amounts in accordance with Column 4 instructions for the proper use of parentheses.

Operating Variance Analysis Total

Enter the net of the Column 4 and 5 amounts. Column 6 entries should be the difference between the Column 1 and 3 amounts.

Figure 19. Critical plant report.

185

ence is that the critical plant report analyzes cost performance according to each element of the cost of goods sold. Lines 1 through 54 of the sample report in Figure 19 indicate the amount of detail included; for example, variances in manufacturing costs are broken down into direct labor, material, engineering, rework, spoilage, and costs. The costs of resale goods are analyzed separately. Variances in manufacturing costs are analyzed in detail according to price, usage, labor rates and performance, spending variances, and so on.

The effect of inventory adjustments on the cost of goods is often significant. For this reason the amount of physical inventory adjustments, both obsolete and slow-moving, and revisions in standard costs are analyzed to ascertain whether the actual results were significantly greater than the planned costs of these adjustments. The remaining part of the report indicates the variances in distribution costs, outbound freight, shipping and warehousing expenses, cash discounts on purchases, revenue from the sales of scrap, and even the costs of rehabilitation, modernization, or plant rearrangement.

The critical plant report is not a routine report and should not normally be prepared in any given plant. It is, as the title indicates, a critical plant report which is prepared when the operating performance of the cost of goods sold of a multinational subsidiary or associated company is out of hand.

MANAGEMENT LETTERS

Some multinational companies are not oriented toward the analytical approach described in the two previous sections as exemplifed by the letter of comment and the analysis of operating results, which provide detailed analysis of volume, price, and cost performance. Other multinational managements prefer that a management letter be prepared in narrative form, emphasizing a clear description of the factors that affect the financial results of the subsidiary or associated company. This type of a management letter discusses environmental and external factors occurring in the industry or in the economy of a country as well as the internal factors influenced by management decision, either at the local or multinational level. A management letter of this type commenting on interim results for a given period places appropriate emphasis on the firm's share of the market, the position of the product with respect to cyclical changes in customer demand, and the steps that management has taken to counteract the effect of cyclical factors. These decisions might be in marketing and pricing policy or they might involve changing the method of distribution, that is, selling directly through the firm's own stores or distributing through dealers or even canvassers.

The narrative of the cost of sales and the gross margin describes supply and price conditions prevailing in the country, the opportunity for purchasing on volume, major changes in the sources of supply, contracts with major suppliers, the costs of shipping, in-freight, duties, and the effect of the market share on price.

Labor costs are described relating the costs and variances to the volume of production and to the conditions and availability of labor in the area. No management letter is complete without describing union contracts, wage rates, and the changes expected in labor contracts. Overhead cost is described indicating adverse effects of declining volume of production as well the cost of depreciation when new capital equipment has been introduced in manufacturing.

After describing the effects of costs on the gross margin, the letter discusses selling expenses, advertising, and general and administrative expenses. It indicates the cost and types of selling methods, the effect of the market share on selling expenses, the efforts made in local advertising, and the conditions affecting administrative costs, including the use and availability of computers or computer services from outside bureaus.

The balance sheet of the management letter opens with a description of the current state of the company's cash position, anticipated revenue from collection of receivables, and the availability of financing on a short-term and long-term basis.

The condition of accounts receivable, collectibility of accounts, aging and liquidity, credit policy of the firm compared to the competition's, and the effect of relaxing or constraining price controls and credit controls on the accounts are fully described.

The amount of inventories on hand is compared with planned levels and the resulting increases or decreases are explained with respect to customer demand for particular products, purchasing policies, the price conditions in the market, and similar matters. Where the subsidiary or associated companies have made short-term investments in marketable securities or bank paper, the local market conditions are described along with the investment policies that proved to be an advantage or a disadvantage in handling marketable securities or short-term paper. The letter discusses the condition of the liabilities, accounts payable, and the ability of the firm to meet credit terms, along with conditions of the location's credit market and the ability to provide liquid funds on a short-term basis to meet obligations as they become due.

Finally, the letter closes with a description of the state of the firm's fixed assets, new machinery and equipment that has been purchased or is expected to be purchased, the depreciation policy, and the effect of new machinery and equipment on product costs.

LEGAL BOOK REPORTING

Many American multinational companies have difficulty with financial statements prepared according to foreign legal books or to accounting principles in the United States. To resolve differences and provide a means for periodic reconciliation a sample set of forms is provided in Figures 20, 21, 22, 23, 24, and 25, which are titled, respectively,

• Total Entity Consolidating Control Report Income Statement in United States Dollars

Figure 20. Legal book reporting reconciliation with consolidating control reporting.

TOTAL ENTITY CONSOLIDATING CONTROL REPORT BALANCE SHEET IN U.S. DOLLARS

AS OF _____

CHECK ONE
SUB
BRANCH

CHECK ONE
ACTUAL
OPERATING PLAN
FORECAST

PROFIT CENTERS

CONSOLIDATING JOURNAL ENTRIES

TOTAL ENTITY

LINE	ASSETS
1	Cash and Marketable Securities
2	Accounts Receivable Discounted
3	Other Accounts and Notes Receivable
4	Unearned Carrying Charges
5	Deferred Lease Revenue
6	Allowance for Losses
7	Accounts and Notes Receivable—Net
8	Inventories
9	Prepaid Expenses
10	TOTAL CURRENT ASSETS
11	Property, Plant and Equipment—Gross
12	Accumulated Depreciation and Amortization
13	Property, Plant and Equipment—Net
14	Investments in Affiliates—Equity
15	Investment in Affiliates—Cost
16	Receivables from Affiliates
17	Investments in Subsidiaries
18	Intra. Receivables
19	Intangible Assets
20	Other Assets
21	
22	TOTAL ASSETS

23	Notes and Loans Payable
24	Obligations Under Capital Leases – Current
25	Guarantor Liabilities – Receivables Discounted
26	Current Taxes Payable
27	Deferred Taxes Payable
28	Other Current Liabilities
29	TOTAL CURRENT LIABILITIES
	Non-Current Liabilities:
30	Obligations under Capital Leases – Long Term
31	Long Term Debt
32	Equalization Account
33	Intra- Payables
34	Reserves
	Shareholders' Equity:
35	Preferred Stock
36	Common Stock
37	Capital Surplus
38	Retained Earnings
39	Apportioned Equity
40	TOTAL SHAREHOLDERS' EQUITY
41	TOTAL LIABILITIES AND SHAREHOLDERS' EQUITY

Figure 21. Legal book reporting reconciliation with consolidating control reporting.

191

**RECONCILIATION OF TOTAL ENTITY CONTROL REPORT
INCOME STATEMENT TO LOCAL LEGAL BOOK
INCOME STATEMENTS PERIOD ENDED:** _____

Local Currency: THOUSANDS ☐ MILLIONS ☐ OTHER ☐

LOCATION NAME ____ LOCATION CODE ____

CHECK ONE: SUB ☐ BRANCH ☐   DATE PREPARED ____

PREPARED BY ____

CHECK ONE: ACTUAL ☐ OPERATING PLAN ☐ FORECAST ☐

LINE #	ACCOUNT	CONTROL REPORTS		ADJUSTMENTS		SUB TOTAL	RECLASSIFICATIONS		LOCAL LEGAL BOOK STATEMENTS
		DOLLAR *	LOCAL CURRENCY	DR.	CR.		DR.	CR.	
1	NET SALES								
2	COST OF SALES (Detail Information Optional)								
3									
4									
5									
6									
7									
8	GROSS MARGIN								
9	S&A EXPENSE								
10	R&D EXPENSE								
11	OPERATING INCOME								
12	INTEREST EXPENSE								
13	EXCHANGE GAIN/(LOSS) – TRANSACTION								
14	– TRANSLATION								
15	– FASB #8								
16	OTHER INCOME/(EXPENSE)								
17	INCOME BEFORE TAX								
18	PROVISION FOR TAX								
19	NET INCOME								

Figure 22. Legal book reporting reconciliation with consolidating control reporting.

- Total Entity Consolidating Control Report Balance Sheet in United States Dollars
- Reconciliation of Total Entity Control Report Income Statement to Local Legal Book Income Statements
- Reconciliation of Total Entity Control Report Balance Sheet to Local Legal Book Balance Sheet
- Analysis of Adjustments used in the Reconciliation of Control Reports to Local Legal Book Statements
- Analysis of Reclassifications used in the Reconciliation of Control Reports to Local Legal Book Statements
- Total Entity Local Book Detail of Retained Earnings

Total entity forms are completed by entities that have more than one profit center. Any transactions between profit centers making up the entity must be eliminated in consolidation so as to arrive at a consolidated total entity statement. Data in the total entity column in Figures 13 and 14 should be carried forward to the first column on the reconciliation forms.

The United States dollar control report balance sheet of each profit center should be recorded on the entity form. All intra-entity balances among profit centers must be eliminated on consolidation so as to arrive at a consolidated total entity balance sheet.

Figures 22 and 23 provide the reconciliation from the total entity control report financial statements to local legal book statements. The results of control reports of local currency for the total entity are to be inserted in the second column. These results must be consistent with dollar results and computed on the same basis, that is generally accepted accounting principles (GAAP).

The remainder of the reconciliation forms (Figure 24) is designed to explain accounting differences between control report and local legal book statements. Two major types of differences exist—adjustments and reclassifications:

Adjustments refer to those entries that are needed to explain the differences between GAAP and local legal accounting prin-

RECONCILIATION OF TOTAL ENTITY CONTROL REPORT
BALANCE SHEET TO LOCAL LEGAL BOOK
BALANCE SHEET AS OF: _____

Local Currency
THOUSANDS ☐
MILLIONS ☐
OTHER ☐

LOCATION NAME
LOCATION CODE

CHECK ONE
SUB ☐
BRANCH ☐

DATE PREPARED

PREPARED BY

CHECK ONE
ACTUAL ☐
OPERATING PLAN ☐
FORECAST ☐

LINE #	ASSETS	CONTROL REPORTS		ADJUSTMENTS		SUB TOTAL	RECLASSIFICATIONS		LOCAL LEGAL BOOK STATEMENTS
		DOLLAR *	LOCAL CURRENCY	DR.	CR.		DR.	CR.	
1	Cash and Marketable Securities								
2	Accounts Receivable Discounted								
3	Other Accounts and Notes Receivable								
4	Unearned Carrying Charges								
5	Deferred Lease Revenue								
6	Allowance for Losses								
7	Accounts and Notes Receivable—Net								
8	Inventories								
9	Prepaid Expenses								
10	TOTAL CURRENT ASSETS								
11	Property, Plant and Equipment—Gross								
12	Accumulated Depreciation and Amortization								
13	Property, Plant and Equipment—Net								
14	Investments in Affiliates—Equity								
15	Investments in Affiliates—Cost								
16	Receivables from Affiliates								
17	Investments in Subsidiaries								
18	Intra- Receivables								
19	Intangible Assets								
20	Other Assets								
21									
22	TOTAL ASSETS								

| | LIABILITIES & SHAREHOLDERS' EQUITY | CONTROL REPORTS | | ADJUSTMENTS | | SUB TOTAL | RECLASSIFICATIONS | | LOCAL LEGAL BOOK STATEMENTS |
		DOLLAR	LOCAL CURRENCY	DR	CR.		DR	CR.	
23	Notes & Loans Payable								
24	Obligations Under Capital Leases — Current								
25	Guarantor Liabilities—Receivable Discounted								
26	Current Taxes Payable								
27	Deferred Taxes Payable								
28	Other Current Liabilities								
29	TOTAL CURRENT LIABILITIES								
30	Non-Current Liabilities: Obligations Under Capital Leases — Long Term								
31	Long Term Debt								
32	Equalization Account								
33	Inter- Payables								
34	Reserves								
35	Shareholders' Equity: Preferred Stock								
36	Common Stock								
37	Capital Surplus								
38	Retained Earnings								
39	Appentioned Equity								
40	TOTAL SHAREHOLDERS' EQUITY								
41	TOTAL LIABILITIES & EQUITY								

Figure 23. Legal book reporting reconciliation with consolidating control reporting.

ciples that affect income or balance sheet valuations, such differing principles for inventory and fixed asset valuations. Detailed explanations are shown in Figure 24.

Reclassifications reflect those differences between GAAP and local legal books accounting principles that affect only the presentation of accounts and do not affect reported results. Detailed explanations are shown also in Figure 24.

On the reconciliation forms the far right hand column, "Local Legal Book Statements," should agree with the final audited financial statements for the entire year, differing only in format. If the format of audited financial statements differs significantly from the format shown on these forms, a detailed explanation should be appended to the audited statements to inform the MNL.

The last form, Figure 25 analyzes the change in the retained earnings in the local legal books of the total entity during the year. Specific portions of retained earnings should be indicated in the proper column. Appropriated earnings are defined as appropriation of accumulated net income carried as reserves on books because of government regulations or resolutions of the entity's board of directors. Unappropriated retained earnings are those not appropriated or declared as dividends.

"January 1, 19   Balances" is the starting point on the form, although any change from the end of the prior year must be explained, as must any addition other than net income. Deductions include dividends paid by the entity and other adjustments made directly to retained earnings. The current balance plus the appropriated retained earnings should equal the balance of retained earnings shown on the reconciliation balance sheet. Each entity should also provide an analysis of retained earnings between remittable and nonremittable funds as well as to indicate taxed and untaxed portions.

Reconciliations of actual results and back-up work papers are reviewed by the internal auditors and, at the end of the year, by external auditors as part of their normal procedures.

The reporting requirements for each entity is determined according to need at the MNL financial office. Some entities

LEGAL BOOK REPORTING
ANALYSIS OF RECLASSIFICATIONS USED IN THE
RECONCILIATION OF CONTROL REPORTS TO LOCAL LEGAL BOOK
STATEMENTS

Local Currency | LOCATION NAME

PREPARED BY

THOUSANDS
MILLIONS
OTHER

LOCATION CODE

CHECK ONE
SUB
BRANCH

DATE PREPARED

ANALYSIS OF RECLASSIFICATIONS
(INDICATE ACCOUNTS EFFECTED AND DESCRIBE)

LINE NUMBER											
Income Statement	Balance Sheet										

CHECK ONE
ACTUAL
OPERATING PLAN
FORECAST

PERIOD ENDED
DR. CR.

PERIOD ENDED
DR. CR.

PERIOD ENDED
DR. CR.

PERIOD ENDED
DR. CR.

ANALYSIS OF ADJUSTMENTS USED
IN THE RECONCILIATION OF
CONTROL REPORTS TO LOCAL LEGAL BOOK
STATEMENTS

Local Currency | LOCATION NAME

PREPARED BY

THOUSANDS
MILLIONS
OTHER

LOCATION CODE

CHECK ONE
SUB
BRANCH

DATE PREPARED

ANALYSIS OF ADJUSTMENTS
(INDICATE ACCOUNTS EFFECTED AND DESCRIBE)

LINE NUMBER											
Income Statement	Balance Sheet										

CHECK ONE
ACTUAL
OPERATING PLAN
FORECAST

PERIOD ENDED
DR. CR.

PERIOD ENDED
DR. CR.

PERIOD ENDED
DR. CR.

PERIOD ENDED
DR. CR.

Figure 24. Legal book reporting reconciliation with consolidating control reporting.

TOTAL ENTITY
LOCAL LEGAL BOOK
DETAIL OF RETAINED EARNINGS
AS OF
_____

NAME

CODE

PREPARED BY

CHECK ONE
SUB ☐
BRANCH ☐

CHECK ONE
ACTUAL ☐
OPERATING PLAN ☐
FORECAST ☐

DATE PREPARED

LOCAL CURRENCY

LOCAL CURRENCY
IN THOUSANDS ☐ MILLIONS ☐ OTHER ☐

	RETAINED EARNINGS APPROPRIATED			RETAINED EARNINGS UNAPPROPRIATED
	ACCOUNT NO.:	ACCOUNT NO.:	ACCOUNT NO.:	
			TOTAL ACCOUNT	
BALANCE: JANUARY 1, 19 ____				
ADDITIONS:				
NET INCOME				
OTHER (EXPLAIN)				
TOTAL ADDITIONS				

DEDUCTIONS:

DIVIDENDS

OTHER (EXPLAIN)

TOTAL DEDUCTIONS

CURRENT BALANCE

RETAINED EARNINGS APPROPRIATED

TOTAL RETAINED EARNINGS

ANALYSIS OF RETAINED EARNINGS: A. REMITTABLE

NON-REMITTABLE

TOTAL

B. TAXED

UNTAXED

TOTAL

Figure 25. Legal book reporting reconciliation with consolidating control reporting.

199

submit quarterly year to date actual results and an up dated projection of the income statement of the total year and the year-end balance sheet. Other entities submit only a 9 months year to date actual results and a projection of the total year income statement and the year-end balance sheet.

CHAPTER 10

Reporting On Foreign Operations

CONSOLIDATED FINANCIAL STATEMENTS

The publication of American Institute of Certified Public Accountants, *Accounting Trends and Techniques,* reported in 1974 that the majority of companies with foreign subsidiaries published consolidated financial statements, with the exception of finance, leasing, and insurance subsidiaries, or those operating under duress in certain countries.

In Canada, the handbook of the Canadian Institute of Chartered Accountants, *Long-Term Intercorporate Investments,* dated January 1973, states, "Where a company has one or more subsidiaries, that company's financial statement should be prepared on a consolidated basis except in the rare instances where this is not the more informative presentation."

United Kingdom: The Companies Act, 1948, London, Section 150, remains unchanged by the Companies Act of 1967. "(1) Where at the end of its fiscal year a company has subsidiaries, accounts of statements (in this Act referred to as group accounts) dealing with the state of affairs and profit and loss of the company and the subsidiaries shall . . . be laid before the company in general meeting when the company's own balance sheet and profit and loss account are so laid."

In 1973, the Accountants' International Study Group concluded that "in all but rare instances, financial statements of companies with subsidiaries should be prepared on a consolidated basis because they are likely to be the most informative presentation. When consolidated statements are presented together with parent company or other individual company statements, the consolidated statement should be considered to be the primary financial statement."

The International Accounting Standards Committee was founded on 29 June 1973 by institutes of certified, chartered, and registered accountants of Australia, Canada, France, Germany, Japan, Mexico, the Netherlands, the United Kingdom, Ireland, and the United States. In 1976 the Committee published *International Accounting Standard 3–Consolidated Financial Statements,* which became operative for periods beginning on or after January 1, 1977.

Standard 3 covers the presentation of consolidated financial statements for a group of companies under the control of one parent company. Consolidated financial statements provide information about the financial position and results of operations of the group of companies. It also provides that the equity method of accounting be used for the presentation of long-term investments in the consolidated financial statements.

In substance, *International Accounting Standard 3* provides that a parent company should issue consolidated financial statements, which consolidate all subsidiaries, foreign and domestic. Uniform accounting policies should be followed by companies in the consolidation. Should different accounting policies be used, the proportion of assets and liabilities to which different accounting policies have been applied should be disclosed.

The *equity method* of accounting for investments, used for investments in associated companies and in subsidiaries that are not consolidated, should be included in the consolidated financial statements under the equity method of accounting.

A subsidiary should be excluded from consolidation if control is temporary, or if it operates under conditions in which severe long-term restrictions on the transfer of funds impair control by the parent company over the subsidiary's assets and operations. A subsidiary may also be excluded from consolidation if its activities are so dissimilar from those of the other companies in the group that better information for the parent company's shareholders and other users of the statements would be provided by presenting separate financial statements.

CONSOLIDATION PROCEDURES

In the consolidated financial statements, the accounts of the parent company and its subsidiaries are combined line by line by adding together items of assets, liabilities, revenue, and expenses. The following are eliminated in consolidation:

1 Intercompany balances and intercompany transactions, including intercompany sales, intercompany charges, and intercompany dividends.
2 The cost to the parent of its investment in each subsidiary and the parent company's portion of share capital, preacquisition reserves, and preacquisition profits and losses of each subsidiary.
3 Unrealized profits resulting from intercompany transactions that are included in the carrying value of assets, such as inventories and fixed assets. The portion of unrealized profits arising in the current period is charged against consolidated income after giving appropriate consideration to minority interests.

FINANCIAL STATEMENT PRESENTATION

The minority interest in the equity of consolidated companies is classified in the consolidated balance sheet as a separate item and not as part of shareholders' equity. The minority interest in the profits or losses of such companies is shown separately in the consolidated income statement.

INVESTMENTS IN ASSOCIATED COMPANIES AND UNCONSOLIDATED SUBSIDIARIES

There are two principal methods of accounting for investments in associated companies and in unconsolidated subsidiaries: the *cost method* and the *equity method.*

The Cost Method

Under the cost method, an investor records an investment in the shares of an investee at cost; income is recognized only to the extent that dividends are distributed from net accumulated profits of the investee arising subsequent to the date of acquisition by the investor. Dividends received in excess of such subsequent profits are considered a recovery of investment and are recorded as reductions of the cost of the investment.

The Equity Method Under the equity method, the carrying amount of an investment in the shares of an investee is increased or decreased to recognize the investor's share in the profits or losses of the investee after the date of acquisition. Adjustments in the carrying amount of the investment may also be necessary to account for alterations in the investor's proportionate interest in the investee as a consequence of changes in the investee's share of capital. Dividends received from an investee reduce the carrying amount of the investment.

Many of the procedures appropriate for the application of the equity method of accounting are similar to those that are applicable in the consolidation of investments in subsidiaries. The investor's share of profits or losses is adjusted to eliminate unrealized profits and losses included in the carrying amounts of assets acquired by either the investor or the investee through intercompany transactions, after appropriate recognition of outside interests.[1]

Definitions The following terms are used for the purpose of this Statement.

An *investor* is a company that holds an interest in the voting power of another company (the investee).

An *investee* is a company in whose voting power an interest is held by another company (the investor).

A *subsidiary* is a company which is controlled by another company (known as the parent company).

A *parent company* is a company that has one or more subsidiaries.

Consolidated financial statements are statements which pre-

---

[1]The foregoing material on *International Accounting Standard 3* and the definitions that follow have been extracted from the definitive text of the *Standard* published by the International Accounting Standards Committee, 3 St. Helen's Place. London, EC3A 6DN, England, June 1976.

sent the assets, liabilities, shareholders' accounts, revenue, and expenses of a parent company and its subsidiaries as those of a single enterprise.

Control is ownership, directly, or indirectly through subsidiaries, of more than one half of the voting power[1] of a company.

A *group* is a parent company and all its subsidiaries.

Minority interest is that part of the net results of operations, or of net assets, of a subsidiary attributable to shares owned other than by the parent company or another subsidiary.

Equity capital is the issued share capital of a company which is neither limited nor preferred in its participation in distributions of the profits of a company or in the ultimate distribution of its assets.

An *associated company* is an investee company that is not a subsidiary and in respect of which

1 The investor's interest in the voting power of the investee is substantial, and
2 The investor has the power to exercise significant influence over the financial and operating policies of the investee, and
3 The investor intends to retain its interest as a long-term investment.

Significant influence is participation in the financial and operating policy decisions of the investee but not control of those policies. An investor may exercise significant influence in several ways, usually by representation on the board of directors but also by participation in policy making processes, material intercompany transactions, interchange of managerial personnel, or dependency on technical information. If the investor holds less than 20% of the voting power of the investee, it should be presumed that the investor does not have the power to exercise significant influence, unless such power can be clearly demonstrated.

The *equity method* is a method of accounting by an investor for certain types of long-term investments in associated companies and for certain unconsolidated subsidiaries. Under the equity method, the investment account of the investor is adjusted in the consolidated financial statements for the change in the investor's share of net assets of the investee. The income statement reflects the investor's share of the results of operations of the investee.

THE UNITED NATIONS AND TRANSNATIONAL CORPORATIONS

In 1976, the Commission on Transnational Corporations (a subsidiary body of the Economic and Social Council) and the Centre on Transnational Corporations (a part of the United Nations Secretariat) were created by governments to serve as the focal point within the United Nations for a full range of issues concerning transnational corporations. In the fall of 1976 the Ad Hoc Group of Experts on International Standards of Accounting and Reporting met to discuss requirements for disclosure, many of which are common to national as well as transnational companies. The objective was to apply the same standards of accounting and reporting to all enterprises whether privately or state-owned in all member states of the United Nations.

The *International Standards of Accounting and Reporting for Transnational Corporations* recommended the following:

• Minimum requirements for general purpose reporting apply to transnational corporations that meet on a consolidated basis at least two of the following criteria: total assets of over $50 million (U.S.); net sales of over $100 million (U.S.); number of employees averages over 2500 during the period.

• Segment reporting by industry and geographical area is an integral part of the standard.

• Non financial information in general purpose reports is required to be disclosed in respect to labor and employment, production, investment programs, organizational structure, and environmental measures.

In 1978, the Commission on Transnational Corporations, in its fourth session, noted the report of the Group of Experts on International Standards of Accounting and Reporting and recommended that the ad hoc group of intergovernmental experts consult international accounting bodies and elicit views of other interested parties on specific issues. This project is ongoing and carried out in conjunction with the Commission's efforts to establish a comprehensive information system. The purpose of the system is:

• To further understanding of the political, legal, economic, and social effects of transnational corporations.

• To promote their contribution to national development goals in world economic growth.

• To strengthen the negotiating position of host countries, in particular the developing countries, in their dealings with transnational corporations.

THE EUROPEAN ECONOMIC COMMUNITY FOURTH DIRECTIVE

The Fourth EEC Directive on Company Law adopted on July 25, 1978 by the Council of Ministers applies to the annual accounts of all limited companies in the nine Common Market countries: Belgium, Denmark, France, Germany, Ireland, Italy, Luxemburg, the Netherlands, and the United Kingdom. The directive changes the presentation of company accounts and the type of information included in them. The national legislation of each EEC country will be changed to conform with the directive, with certain options and alternatives provided to the end that a fairly uniform set of Companies Acts will be in effect by 1982. The concept of the EEC is a common market for goods, services, labor, and capital, but beyond that, fair competition for all. The same information disclosed in one company's accounts can be found in the accounts of its competitors.

The fourth directive is designed to cover the annual accounts of individual companies, their accounting principles, form of presentation, publication, and audit by persons authorized by law. The proposed seventh directive which covers consolidated accounts of groups of companies as well as reporting requirements for affiliated undertakings.

REPORTING ON FOREIGN OPERATIONS IN THE EEC

The annual accounts are the balance sheet, the profit and loss account, and the notes on the accounts. The objective is to give a true and fair view of the company's assets and liabilities, financial position, and profits or losses. Valuation of accounts follow five basic criteria: historical cost, going concern, prudence, accruals, and consistency. Provision is made for inflation accounting instead of historical cost where member states so elect. Comparative financial statements are required but a statement of changes in financial position is not required to be presented as part of the annual accounts.

With respect to valuation requirements, the directive prescribes historical cost based on purchase price or production cost. Tangible fixed assets and inventories (stocks) may be valued at replacement value; these and other financial assets may be assessed by other methods "which take into account current values." The method of evaluation used must be disclosed in the notes on the accounts and any decrease in reserves must be shown separately in the profit and loss account.

The following lists other selected provisions of the directive:

• Adjustment of current assets if the market is lower than cost.

• Provision for impairment of fixed assets where a permanent depreciation in value has occurred.

• Inclusion of indirect manufacturing cost in the valuation of inventories.

• Reconciliation of evaluation based on taxes with evaluation based on historical cost accounting through disclosure.

• Acceptance of the LIFO method of inventory valuation.

• Recognition of subsequent events in the annual report.

• Provisions for contingent liabilities and other charges may not exceed the necessary amount.

With respect to disclosure, the directive further requires that notes on the accounts give a true and fair view. Selected minimum requirements are:

• Description of accounting policies and valuation methods.
• Departures from historical cost accounting.
• Holdings in other undertakings, that is, investment of 20% or more, in the capital of other companies and whether the equity method of accounting is used.
• Goodwill and research and development.
• Amount of financial risk.
• Sales (turnover) arranged by product line categories and geographical market.
• Financial operations, extraordinary items, and taxes attributable to operations.
• For items included in the annual accounts that are or were originally expressed in foreign currency, the bases of conversion used to express them in local currency must be disclosed.[1]

STATEMENT OF FINANCIAL ACCOUNTING STANDARD NO. 8

ACCOUNTING FOR THE TRANSLATION OF FOREIGN CURRENCY TRANSACTIONS AND FOREIGN CURRENCY FINANCIAL STATEMENTS

In the United States the Financial Accounting Standards Board issued FASB 8 in October, 1975. The second paragraph of the introduction defines its objectives:

This statement establishes standards of financial accounting and reporting for foreign currency transactions in financial statements of a reporting enterprise. It also establishes standards of financial accounting and reporting for translating foreign currency financial statements incorporated in the financial statements of an enterprise by consolida-

[1] Article 43.1.1 of the Fourth Council Directive of 25 July 1978.

209

tion, combination, or the equity method of accounting. Translation of financial statements from one currency to another for purposes other than consolidation, combination, or the equity method is beyond the scope of this statement.

A key point of the introduction is contained in the section entitled "Foreign Statements":

The objective of translation requires that the assets, liabilities, revenue and expenses in foreign statements be translated and accounted for in the same manner as assets, liabilities, revenue and expenses that result from foreign currency transactions of the enterprise. Foreign currency transactions of an enterprise involve amounts denominated or measured in foreign currency, but the assets, liabilities, revenue, and expenses from foreign currency transactions are additionally measured and recorded in dollars, and in conformity with United States generally accepted accounting principles. . . .In contrast, assets, liabilities, revenue, and expenses, in foreign statements are initially measured and recorded in foreign currency and may not be in conformity with United States generally accepted accounting principles. Since translation cannot transform the results obtained under dissimilar foreign accounting practices, into acceptable measurements under United States accounting principles, special procedures are necessary to insure that the translator's statements are in conformity with United States generally accepted accounting principles.

FASB 8 addressed the problem of an American company having to account for imports and exports denominated in a foreign currency of an American company that later had to repay borrowed funds in a foreign currency. Paragraph 3 defines the extent of its coverage regarding foreign currency transactions: "an enterprise (a) buys or sells on credit goods or services who prices are stated in foreign currency, (b) borrows or lends funds and the amounts payable or receivable are denominated in foreign currency, (c) is a party to an unperformed forward exchange contract, or (d) for other reasons, acquires assets or incurs liabilities denominated in foreign currency. Regarding foreign operations it states that "an enterprise conducts activities through a foreign operation whose assets, liabilities, revenue, and expenses are measured in foreign currency."

Since 1975, FASB 8 has had significant impact on every company doing business overseas. The following describes the more significant changes that affect how multinational companies report profits:

• Inventories. Multinationals are required to translate inventories on their balance sheet at acquisition cost, that is, historical rates. Profits or losses resulting from foreign exchange fluctations are recognized in the period the inventory is sold, but not in the period of the balance sheet date and not when the exchange rate changes.

• Long-term foreign currency debt. This debt is translated at the current rate. It is assumed that the current rate existing at the balance sheet date will be the same 5, 10, or 20 years later depending on the outcome of the long-term debt.

• Foreign exchange contracts. Profits or losses on forward contracts must be accounted for on an accrual basis, that is, recognized at their market value. (There is an exception when these contracts can be related to identifiable commitments.)

• Accounting for foreign exchange gains or losses. Foreign exchange profits or losses that result from the translation of assets and liabilities are denominated in foreign currencies have to be included in a foreign currency in determining net income for the period during which the rate changes. It is not possible to apply these gains or losses to reserves of foreign exchange fluctuations, which must be recognized in the current income statements.

FASB 8 is a comprehensive document of 101 pages and selected paragraphs from its Appendix A warrant reproduction here. Appendix A, "Translation of Certain Accounts" (paragraphs 38–52) explains and illustrates certain applications of the procedures set forth in paragraphs 11–13. It also describes and illustrates ways to ensure that amounts in translated statements conform to United States generally accepted accounting principles in those situations indicated in paragraph 14. See Figure 26, which represents key paragraphs (pages 19, 20, and 21) of FASB 8.

Figure 26   FASB No. 8—selected paragraphs.

TRANSLATION OF CERTAIN ACCOUNTS

38. Paragraphs 11 and 12 distinguish those balance sheet accounts in foreign statements that shall be translated at either current or historical rates. The table on the following page indicates the rates at which certain common balance sheet accounts in foreign statements shall be translated. In addition, the following paragraphs discuss certain additional; aspects of translating foreign statements. Two topics included in the discussion—appling the rule of cost or market, whichever is lower, to inventory and applying *ABP Opinion No. 11* to deferred income taxes—requiring procedures not described in paragraphs 11 and 12 (see paragraph 14).

Holdings of Debt Securities

39. Debt securities held that are essentially equivalent to notes receivable shall be translated at the current rate. An example is a bond that is intended to be held to maturity and is carried at an amount that is the present value of future interest and principal payments based on the effective rate of interest at the date of purchase (that is, at maturity amount plus or minus an unamortized premium or discount). A debt security held that is not essentially equivalent to a note receivable shall be translated (a) at the current rate if carried at current market price or (b) at the historical rate if carried at cost.

Translation After a Business Combination[16]

40. The method an enterprise uses to account for the acquisition of a foreign operation affects certain aspects of translation. If a business combination with a foreign operation is accounted for by the *pooling-of-interests method,* the assets and liabilities of the foreign operation shall be translated as if the foreign operation had always been a subsidiary of the enterprise. Therefore, assets and liabilities that are translated at historical rates shall be translated at the rates in effect at the date the foreign operation recognized the specific transactions or events.

41. If a business combination with a foreign operation is accounted for by the *purchase method,* assets and liabilities that are translated at historical rates shall be translated at the rates in effect when the enterprise acquired its interest in the assets or liabilities. Thus, assets and liabilities of a foreign operation at the date of its acquisition shall be adjusted to their fair values in local currency

[16]*APB Opinion No. 16,* "Business Combinations," prescribes generally accepted accounting principles for business combinations. Paragraphs 87–92 are particularly pertinent.

and then translated at the rate in effect at the date of acquisition. A difference between the translated net assets and the dollar cost of acquisition by the enterprise is *goodwill* or *an excess of acquired net assets over cost* as those terms are used in *APB Opinion No. 16.* Translation at the date of acquisition, as described, establishes the dollar measures of the assets acquired and liabilities assumed as the date of acquisition that are translated at historical rates in subsequent balance sheets.

Translation of an Investment Accounted for by the Equity Method[17]

42. The foreign statements of an investee that are accounted for by the equity method first shall be translated into dollars in conformity with the requirements of this Statement; then the equity method shall be applied.

Minority Interests

43. The minority interest reported in an enterprise's consolidated financial statements shall be based on the financial statements of the subsidiary in which there is a minority interest after they have been translated according to the requirements of this Statement.

Figure 26   Continued.

Rates Used to Translate Assets and Liabilities

	Translation Rates	
Assets	Current	Historical
Cash on hand and demand and time deposits	X	
Marketable equity securities:		
Carried at cost		X
Carried at current market price	X	
Accounts and notes receivable and related unearned discount	X	
Allowance for doubtful accounts and notes receivable	X	
Inventories:		
Carried at cost		X

[17]*APB Opinion No. 18,* "The Equity Method of Accounting for Investments in Common Stock," prescribes generally accepted accounting principles for the equity method.

Carried at current replacement price or current selling price	X	
Carried at net realizable value	X	
Carried at contract price (produced under (fixed price contracts)	X	
Prepaid insurance, advertising, and rent		X
Refundable deposits	X	
Advances to unconsolidated subsidiaries	X	
Property, plant, and equipment		X
Accumulated depreciation of property, plant, and equipment		X
Cash surrender value of life insurance	X	
Patents, trademarks, licenses, and formulas		X
Goodwill		X
Other intangible assets		X
Liabilities		
Accounts and notes payable and overdrafts	X	
Accrued expenses payable	X	
Accrued losses on firm purchase commitments	X	
Refundable deposits	X	
Deferred income		X
Bonds payable or other long-term debt	X	
Unamortized premium or discount on bonds or Notes payable	X	
Convertible bonds payable	X	
Accrued pension obligations	X	
Obligations under warranties	X	

POSTSCRIPT AND UPDATE ON FASB 8 On February 21, 1979, Robert Metz in "Market Place," in the *New York Times,* predicted that the FASB may soon make certain revisions and that some of the following changes will be accepted:

• Corporations will have to tell more about the impact of currency changes, such as their effect on sales, cost of sales, gross margins, and income tax rates.

• The board will go back to the old method of deferring unrealized currency gains and losses.

• Currency translation gains and losses will be reflected as an extraordinary item in the income statement so that earnings per share from continuing operations will not be affected.

• The board will allow corporations to translate inventory valuations at the current rate of exchange.

It is generally thought that the FASB has been impressed with corporate complaints and that there will be major changes for the better. These changes are presently under study by the FASB as part of their ongoing review of the opinions that have been expressed.

FINANCIAL REPORTING FOR SEGMENTS OF A BUSINESS ENTERPRISE

FASB Statement No. 14 requires that annual financial statements provide the following information:

- Operations in different industries
- Foreign operations
- Export sales sales
- Major customers

The statement requires multinational companies to separately close domestic and foreign operations, which in turn have to be broken down by country or groups of countries, aggregating about 10% of consolidated revenues or assets. Foreign operations include revenue from either unaffiliated customer sales or intracompany sales outside the United States or other home country. Foreign operations do not include other investments of unconsolidated subsidiaries.

Operations in foreign countries are grouped into geographical areas that are proximate, have economic affinity, similar business environments, and interrelated operations.

Significant foreign operations are reportable industry segments if *either* of the following conditions is met:

1 Foreign operations' revenue from sales to unaffiliated customers is 10% or more of consolidated revenue.
2 Foreign operations' identifiable assets are 10% or more of consolidated assets.

COMBINED RESULTS The information to be disclosed for domestic operations, significant foreign operations, and remaining foreign operations covers revenue, profitability, and identifiable assets.

REVENUE Revenue by area is disclosed in the same manner as reportable industry segments, that is, by separate disclosure of sales to unaffiliated customers and intracompany sales and transfers. The basis of accounting for intracompany sales and transfers and the type and effect of any change in methods are also disclosed.

PROFITABILITY Operating profit or loss, net income, or other measure of profitability between operating profit and net income is disclosed by area.

IDENTIFIABLE ASSETS These are disclosed in the same manner as reportable industry segments.

OTHER FOREIGN REPORTING CONSIDERATIONS A number of considerations affect a multinational's ability to make reasonable disclosures of the scope, risk, and profitability of foreign operations:

• Distinction between foreign operations and export sales, including sales of domestic products through foreign marketing channels.

• Manufacturing processes or similar activities performed outside the United States.

• Foreign operating revenue dependent on sales in countries other than that of a foreign segment's branch, for example, sales to the Middle East from Europe.

• Domestic sales to an independent broker who exports products.

METHOD OF PRESENTATION   Disclosures of industry segments, foreign operations, export sales, and major customers can be in any of three forms:[1]

1. In the financial statements with appropriate notes.
2. Entirely within the footnotes.
3. In a separate schedule within an annual report that is not part of the financial statements.

Segment and geographic area revenues, operating profits, and identifiable assets are reconciled to related amounts in the consolidated financial statements. Operating profit is reconciled to income before taxes from continuing operations (before gain or loss on discontinued operations, extraordinary items, and cumulative effect of a change in accounting principles). Identifiable assets are assets held for corporate uses and the type of such assets (cash and marketable securities) comform with the consolidated balance sheet.

INTERCOMPANY TRANSACTIONS   The American Institute of Certified Public Accountants (AICPA) Committee on Accounting Procedures, *Accounting Research Bulletin, ARB No. 51,* "Consolidated Financial Statements" (1959), paragraphs 6, 14, 17, and 90 provides that intercompany profit or loss on assets remaining within a consolidated group should be eliminated, usually based on gross profit or loss. Exception is made for regulated industries permitting capitalization of intercompany profit equivalent to a reasonable return on investment ordinarily capitalized under established industry practice. Paragraph 6 also prescribes complete elimination of intercompany profit from the asset whether or not a minority interest is present, and continues: "The elimination of the intercompany profit or loss may be

[1]Financial Accounting Standards Board, Statement of Financial Accounting Standard No. 14, Financial Reporting for Segments of a Business Enterprise," 1976, Paragraph 28.

allocated proportionately between the majority and minority interest."

AICPA, Accounting Principles Board, *Opinions of the Accounting Principles Board, APB Opinion No. 16,* "Business Combinations" (1970), paragraph 56 provides that where a combination is accounted for as a pooling of interest, the effects of the intercompany transactions for periods presented and on retained earnings at the beginning of the period presented should be eliminated to the extent possible. Paragraphs 56, 87, and 89 describe the methods to be used in valuing assets acquired and liabilities assumed in an acquisition accounted for as a purchase. It does not cover treatment of profits recognized on preacqusition trasactions between the parties.

APB Opinion No. 18, "The Equity Method of Accounting for Investments in Common Stock" (1971), paragraph 19a states: "Intercompany profits and losses should be eliminated until realized by the investor or investee as if the subsidiary, corporate joint-venture or investee company were consolidated."

AICPA, "Accounting Interpretations of *APB Opinion No. 18;* Intercompany Profit Elimination under Equity Method," *Journal of Accountancy* (1971) provides that except for a transaction that is not at arm's length, it would be appropriate for an investor to eliminate intercompany profit, on either upstream or downstream transactions, in relation to the investor's common stock interest in the investee. International Accountants Standards Committee, IAS No. 3, "Consolidated Financial Statements," London (June 1976), paragraph 12, states, "Unrealized profits resulting from intercompany transactions which are included in the carrying value of assets, such as inventories and fixed assets, are eliminated. The portion of the unrealized profits arising in the current period is charged against consolidated income after giving appropirate consideration to minority interest."

REPORTING PURCHASE OF FOREIGN COMPANIES

The AICPA Accounting Principles Board *APB Opinion No. 16,* "Business Combinations" (1970), paragraph 68 states, "a portion of the total cost is. . . assigned to each individual asset acquired on the basis of its fair value. A difference between the sum of the assigned costs of the tangible and identifiable intangible assets acquired less liabilities assumed and the cost of the group is evidence of the unspecified intangible values."

Paragraph 87 develops this method in assigning costs of an acquired company to individual assets and liabilities. It states:

First, all identifiable assets acquired, either individually or by type, and liabilities assumed in a business combination, whether or not shown in the financial statements of the acquired company, should be assigned a portion of the cost of the acquired company, normally equal to their fair values at date of acquisition.

Second, the excess of the cost of the acquired company over the sum of the amounts assigned to identifiable assets acquired less liabilities assumed should be recorded as goodwill. The sum of the market or appraisal values of identifiable assets acquired less liabilities assumed may sometimes exceed the cost of the acquired company. If so the values otherwise assignable to noncurrent assets acquired (except long-term investments in marketable securities) should be reduced by a proportionate part of the excess to determine the assigned values. A deferred credit for an excess of assigned values of identifiable assets over costs of an acquired company (sometimes called negative goodwill) should not be recorded unless those assets are reduced to zero value.

International Accounting Standards Committee, *IAS 3,* "Consolidated Financial Statements," London (June 1976), paragraphs 13 and 16 states,

At the date of acquisition, the cost of a parent company's investment in a subsidiary is allocated, if possible, to the subsidiary's individual identifiable assets and liabilities on the basis of their values, and the allocated amounts serve as the basis on which the subsidiaries' assets and liabilities are reported in the parent company's consolidated financial statements subsequent to the acquisition. Any difference between the cost of the parent company's investment and the parent company's share in the amounts allocated to individual identifiable assets and liabilities is shown in the consolidated balance sheet appropriately described.

The results of operations of a subsidiary for the financial reporting period in which the subsidiary is acquired are included in the consolidated income statement only from the date of its acquisition.

GOODWILL   *APB Opinion 17,* "Intangible Assets" (1970), paragraphs 27 to 31 state,

The recorded cost of intangible assets should be amortized by systematic charges to income over the periods estimated to be benefited. . . . The period of amortization should not . . . . exceed 40 years. . . . The straight-line method of amortization—equal annual amounts—should be applied unless a company demonstrates that another systematic method is more appropriate. A company should evaluate the periods of amortization continually to determine whether later events and circumstances warrant revised estimates of useful lives.

The Canadian Institution of Chartered Accountants, *Business Combination CICA Handbook,* Section 1580, Toronto (April 19, 1974) writes,

The accounting procedures followed in Canada for determining goodwill are fundamentally the same as those followed in the United States. In Section 1580.44 states: The excess of the cost of the purchase of the acquiring company's interest in identifiable assets and acquired liabilities assumed should be reflected as goodwill. Similar to *APB Opinion No. 17,* Section 1580.58 requires the amortization of goodwill by the straight line method over the estimated life over such goodwill but not to exceed 40 years.

The Accountants International Study Group, *Accounting for Goodwill* (1975), paragraph 25 states, "Goodwill should be accounted for as an intangible asset which has a limited life and should be amortized to income on a systematic basis over its estimated useful life."

JOINT VENTURES   *APB Opinion No. 18,* "The Equity Method of Accounting for Investments in Common Stock" (1971) paragraphs 3D and 16 writes: ". . . investors should account for investments in common stock of corporate joint ventures by the equity method . . . ."

According to *APB Opinion No. 23,* "Opinion Accounting for Income Tax, Special Areas" (1972), paragraph 17: "The board concludes that the principles applicable to undistributed earnings of subsidiaries . . . also apply to tax effects . . . attributable to earnings of corporate joint ventures that are essentially permant in duration."

POOLING OF INTEREST AICPA Accounting Principles for *APB Opinion No. 16,* "Business Combinations" (1970), paragraphs 42–49 says the following about pooling interest:

The opinion specifies 12 conditions, all of which must be met, if a business combination is to be accounted for by the pooling of interest method. Since the conditions specified in Paragraph 47B requires an exchange of common stock for substantially all of the voting common stock of another company, with substantially defined as 90 percent or more, this single condition makes the use of the purchase method mandatory for a great many intercorporate combinations.

Paragraph 43 requires that acquisitions of some or all stock by minority stockholders of a subsidiary (not a business combination) be accounted for by the purchase method. The purchase and pooling of interests method are "not alternatives in the accounting for the same business combinations." A single method should be applied to an entire combination; the practice now known as part purchase, part pooling is not acceptable.

TWO EXAMPLES OF MNL REPORTING

Evidence of the trend towards uniformity in reporting foreign operations can be found by comparing two annual reports, from 1978, of the Singer Company and Siemens A.G.

SINGER The Singer Company's annual report, 1978, and SEC Form 10k contain in their notes to financial statements the following summary of accounting policies under the heading, "Principles of Consolidation,"

The accompanying financial statements include the accounts of all subsidiaries other than the Company's wholly owned finance subsidiaries and the Singer Housing Company and consolidated subsidiaries, which are reported in the financial statements as investments carried on the equity basis. Other investments in which the company exercises significant management influence are also reported on the equity basis and accordingly, the Company's share of their results of operations is included in income. All other investments are carried at cost. All significant intercompany transactions are eliminated in consolidation.

The report of 1978 omits the following statement of accounting policies with respect to foreign operations, which appeared in its report of 1977.

The Company's accounting policy for the translation of foreign currency transactions and financial statements complies with the requirements prescribed with Statement No. 8 of the Financial Accounting Standards Board which became effective January 1, 1976. Financial statements for years prior to the effective date have not been restated as the adoption of this policy had no material effect on the results of the operations for those years. Exchange adjustments, including amounts relating to forward exchange contracts, are charges or credited to income when a stipulated change in currency valuation occurs.

Since FASB 8 has now become a part of generally accepted accounting principles for American companies, reference to it is no longer needed in the annual report.

SIEMENS Siemens, a German company, ranks among the foremost electrical engineering companies with sales totaling over $15 billion. It has manufacturing plants in Germany and throughout the world, including the United States. Siemens is one of the largest companies in this branch of the industry with over 300,000 employees. The following are excerpts from notes to the 1978 worldwide consolidated financial statements of Siemens A.G., titled, "How We Consolidate." In addition to Siemens A.G. we have included in the worldwide financial statements virtually all of the companies in the Federal Republic of Germany and abroad in which Siemens holds a direct or indirect interest of more than 50 percent, a total of 28 domestic and 107 foreign companies.

We have prepared the statements of both the domestic and foreign consolidated companies according to uniform principles of evaluation and classification as set forth in the German Corporation Act. The consolidation of our investment in subsidiaries is affected in accordance with a method which closely resembes that used in the United States. In the Consolidated Statements we have eliminated inter company profits; sales; expenses and income within the group; and all receivables and liabilities between consolidated companies. Interim statements have been used where companies have a fiscal year that differs from that of Siemens A. G.

How we Translate into Deutschmarks

Our foreign companies' property, plant, and equipment, investments in subsidiaries and associated companies and equipment leased to customers are translated at the exchange rates prevailing at the date of their acquisition or production, other assets and liabilities at the year-end middle rate.

Income and expenses shown in the statement are translated at the average rates for the fiscal year, except for depreciation on property, plant, and equipment and equipment leased to customers, for which we use the rate prevailing at the time of acquisition or production.

Where the balance resulting from the transaction of foreign finacial statement is negative, we charge it against the year's income; we transfer a positive balance to a provision for exchange risk. A gain was recorded in the year under review.

The foregoing notes are signed by the managing board of Siemens A.G. It should be noted that the worldwide consolidated statements, balance sheet, and income statements are signed first by the managing board and then by the company's independent auditors who state the following: "According to our audit, conducted with all due professional diligence, the consolidated financial statements and the report relating thereto comply with all statutory requirements."[1]

---

[1]The annual report of Siemens, published in German, is also available in English translation.

CHAPTER 11

Taxes And The Multinational

"Times change." This phrase is nowhere more apt than in international taxation of the multinational company. Many foreign countries have changed their tax systems in recent years or, if not, their definitions of taxable earnings. Income from foreign sources is difficult to categorize and rules change for the determination of income on sales, leases, licensing, and dividends. Some say that the American tax law has become the most complicated tax law of any country at any time. To fully develop the subject of taxes for multinationals in the United States and in foreign countries obviously would require a book in itself. The purpose of this chapter is, first, to summarize selected conditions confronting a multinational in dealing with taxes; second, to outline some basics in the American foreign tax credit law, and finally, to synopsize certain key indicators that MNL management should be aware of in developing tax plans and strategies.

Except for a constantly shrinking number of tax-haven countries, taxes mean 40 to 50% of every penny earned throughout the world. The trend toward worldwide taxation is definitely on the increase. Taxation varies from one country to another; there are different tax systems and tax rates. Finally, there are definitions, definitions that vary more in their contents than in the translation of their respective languages. The key definitions are the determination of taxable income, the delineation of which expenses are deductible and which are not, and the number and types of items that can be credited against taxes payable. There are differences in withholding taxes and in the bases upon which taxes are withheld. In some countries tax laws have not changed but their administration has become more stringent; the taxes called for by law have to be paid, whereas previously they might have been avoided because of lax enforcement.

BASIC TAX SYSTEMS   The classical or separate corporate tax system does not distinguish between taxes on profits that are retained in the business and those which are distributed as dividends. The system in the United States is the classical system, which is often described as an economic double taxation because shareholders receiving dividends after taxes have been paid on corporate profits are again subject to taxes on almost all these dividends.

The partial integration system has two subsections: (A) The split rate system provides that taxes are less when profits are distributed. Germany, for example, taxes distributed profits at 36%; the recipient shareholders pay the normal progressive income taxes on those dividends. On the other hand, if a German company does not distribute its profits, they are taxed at approximately a 56% rate. (B) The imputation system applies similar rates whether profits are retained or distributed, but the shareholder receives credits for the corporate taxes that have been paid on distributed profits. This system is found in the United Kingdom, France, and Italy.

Finally, there is a so-called full assimilation system of corporate tax, which completely integrates undistributed profits retained in the business with those distributed to stockholders. A number of such systems have been proposed but I know of none that is actually in effect.

Although the concept of income for tax purposes is fairly consistent in countries around the world, the definition of taxable income varies from country to country as a result of differences in accounting; depreciation, for example, is often calculated differently in different countries. In addition to the double declining methods, certain countries allow a depreciation deduction of up to 100% for the cost of machinery and equipment in the year of purchase. In the United States, investment tax credits provide an economic incentive to acquire machinery and equipment.

Most countries have adopted the worldwide principle of taxing income arising outside their borders when that income is received by a company incorporated in the country or that has its seat of management there. Worldwide taxing countries usually provide credits for income taxes paid abroad on income from foreign sources, but this has not proved sufficient to avoid double taxation or disputes over tax jurisdiction. Switzerland and Hong Kong are representative of countries that follow the territorial principle; companies located in these countries do not pay taxes on dividends or other income earned outside the territory.

TAX PROBLEMS The problem an American MNL faces in the field of taxation involves more than the amount of tax that has to be paid overseas, as well as in the United States, and the amount of foreign tax credit that can be claimed. In addition, there is the problem of determining earnings for financial reporting. APB Opinion No. 23 requires an MNL to make an American tax provision in its accounts to the extent of excess of American tax over foreign tax if it intends to repatriate the earnings on current basis. On the other hand, an MNL that plans to reinvest its profits overseas for an indefinite time does not have to provide for American tax on these profits.

APB Opinion No. 23, "Accounting for Income Taxes–Special Areas," contains the following key provisions:

The Board concludes that including undistributed earnings of a subsidiary in the pretax accounting income of a parent company, either through consolidation or accounting for the investment by the equity method, may result in a timing difference, in a difference that may not reverse until indefinite future periods, or in a combination of both types of differences, depending on the intent and actions of the parent company.

Timing difference. The Board believes it should be presumed that all undistributed earnings of a subsidiary will be transferred to the parent company. Accordingly, the undistributed earnings of a subsidiary included in consolidated income (or in income of the parent company) should be accounted for as a timing difference, except to the extent that some or all of the undistributed earnings meet the criteria in (the paragraph entitled "indefinite reversal criteria").

Indefinite reversal criteria. The presumption that all undistributed earnings will be transferred to the parent company may be overcome, and no income taxes should be accrued by the parent company, if sufficient evidence shows that the subsidiary has invested or will invest the undistributed earnings indefinitely or that the earnings will be remitted in a tax-free liquidation.

APB Opinion No. 23 adds the following on income tax allocation accounting:

Income taxes of the parent company applicable to a timing difference in undistributed earnings of a subsidiary are necessarily based on estimates and assumptions. For example, the tax effect may be determined by assuming that unremitted earnings were distributed in the current period and that the parent company received the benefit of all available tax-planning alternatives and available tax credits and deductions. The income tax expense of the parent company should also include taxes that would have been withheld if the undistributed earnings had been remitted as dividends.

UNITED STATES FOREIGN TAX CREDITS

American companies are initially taxed twice on overseas earnings: by the foreign government and by their own government. The income tax laws of the United States treat all earnings of American corporations, individual citizens, and resident aliens as income subject to taxation. This includes income from American sources as well as foreign sources. Since 1913 when the present income tax system started, all earned income has been taxed equally without regard to the nation of origin.

Although the United States taxes income from foreign sources, the timing of the taxation varies. Thus, dividends, royalties, interest, and so on from foreign subsidiaries of American companies are not subject to United States taxation until they are received in the United States. (There is one exception to this rule involving subsidiaries in tax-haven countries that trade with affiliated companies, of which more will be said later on.) By contrast, the United States taxes on a current basis each year earnings of American companies that do business abroad through branches rather than locally incorporated subsidiaries. Such branch earnings are subject to American taxes when earned, whether or not remitted to the United States.

Income originating from outside the United States is also subject to local taxation, thus setting up the basis for the phrase "double taxation." This inequity is avoided by a system of credits and deductions of foreign taxes that have been paid, which is commonly called "foreign tax credits." Without a foreign tax credit every American multinational operating overseas would be at a competitive disadvantage; American exports would practically be eliminated and the balance of payments in the United States would suffer immeasurably. Foreign tax credits are available to all American companies operating overseas. Foreign taxes are not credited against taxes on any income earned in the United States.

Foreign tax credits only permit foreign income taxes to be offset against American taxes levied on income earned abroad. It is the opinion of many American companies that other industrial foreign nations give not similar but better treatment to their multinationals. The foreign tax credit, in summary, is an effective means of avoiding double taxation. Without foreign tax credits America's economics surrounding foreign investment by an MNL would be changed significantly.

OPTIONS   What would happen if there were no foreign tax credit?

The first option is diagrammed thus. If total earnings by an MNL include

Foreign operations	$100,000
Taxes by a foreign country at 40%	(40,000)
United States taxes at 46%	(46,000)
Net income after taxes	$ 14,000

The effective tax rate would be 86%.

The second option would be taxation of foreign income after deduction of foreign income taxes. For example, if income earned by an American corporation overseas is $100,000 and foreign taxes are at 40% or $40,000, the balance of American income after deducting the amount of foreign taxes already paid would be $60,000. If the United States tax is 46% of $60,000 or $27,600, the income after taxes would be $32,400. The effective tax rate would have improved to 67.6%, but it still would be in excess of the rate paid by American corporations operating only in the United States.

The third option allows that income earned by an American company with foreign operations is $100,000, foreign taxes are at 40% or $40,000, the United States taxes at 46% of $100,000 less the credit allowed for the foreign tax of $40,000. The actual tax paid in the United States is $6000. The total of the taxes paid abroad of $40,000, plus the $6000 paid in the United States, equals $46,000. The balance, or the income after taxes, is $54,000. The effective tax rate has been reduced to 46%, the same rate paid by American corporations.

PROVISIONS OF THE INTERNAL REVENUE CODE

Basic provisions of the Internal Revenue Code allow taxpayers to elect to take a credit for qualified foreign taxes that have already been paid. The Code permits American companies and individual stockholders to take a credit for foreign taxes paid by its subsidiary operations outside the United States. Credit is permitted against the domestic tax on dividends received from foreign subsidiaries. Another section of the Code provides limitations of the amount of tax credit that may be taken against

American income taxes. This section prevents credits taken in excess of the current domestic rate. Another section, which is limited exclusively to foreign trading companies and foreign companies with substantial amounts of investment income, allows American corporations to take the credit for taxes on income deemed to have been received. These deemed credits are allowed as if the distribution from the foreign subsidiaries had actually been made.

Other sections of the Code limit the credits or adjust them for special conditions. There are many revenue rulings, tax court decisions, treasury regulations, and tax treaties that affect the specific applications of foreign tax credits. The law in this area and the regulations are always subject to change, but the basic concept remains; the object is to insure that a multinational company is not penalized in the payment of its taxes in comparison to another corporation operating solely in the United States. These sections of the regulations are only touched upon for the obvious reason that their specific application can only be made after consultation with competent tax attorneys and accountants.

The Internal Revenue Code basically limits the total foreign tax credit to the amount equal to the American tax on similar earnings. Without such an overall limitation the credit for foreign taxes would not only offset the American tax on foreign operations but also the tax on domestic earnings. This limitation restricts the amount of foreign tax credit to a proportion of the total American tax equal to the ratio of foreign taxable income to total taxable income. A full credit is obtained for taxes paid overseas as long as (1) the combined overseas effective rate for the year is less than or equal to the American rate, and (2) there is no domestic loss for the year. Foreign tax credits in excess of the limitation may then be carried back two years and forward five years.

Figure 27 shows the calculation of the foreign tax credit limitation in four representative situations.

Figure 27. Calculation of foreign tax credit limitation.

$$\frac{\text{Taxable foreign source income}}{\text{Total income (foreign and domestic)}} \times \text{U.S. tax on total income} = \text{Foreign Tax Credit Limitation}$$

1. Foreign source income 1000; Foreign tax 600;
   Domestic loss 2000; Total loss 1000

   $$\frac{\$1000}{(1,000)} \times \text{Zero} = \text{Zero; Excess foreign tax credit 600}$$

   Result: There is no foreign tax credit allowed because the net loss means no United States tax.

2. Foreign source income 1000; Foreign tax 600;
   Domestic breakeven; Total income 1000

   $$\frac{\$1000}{1000} \times 460 = 460; \text{Excess foreign tax credit 140}$$

   Result: a. When the income is only from foreign sources, the United States tax is cancelled.
   Result: b. Since the foreign rate is higher than the United States rate, an excess foreign tax credit remains.

3A. Foreign source income 1000; Foreign tax 600;
    Domestic source income 3000; Total income 4000

   $$\frac{\$1000}{4000} \times 1840 = 460; \text{Excess foreign tax credit 140}$$

3B. Foreign source income 1000; Foreign tax 600;
    Domestic source income 5000; Total income 6000

   $$\frac{\$1000}{6000} \times 2760 = 460; \text{Excess foreign tax credit 140}$$

   Result: The tax credit limitation is the same in 3A and 3B because foreign tax credits do not change United States tax on United States source income.

4. Foreign source income 1000; Foreign tax 400;
   Domestic source income 5000; Total income 6000

   $$\frac{\$1000}{600} \times 2760 = 460 \quad \text{United States tax before tax credit}$$

   400 Foreign tax credit
   60 United States tax which must be paid unless it can be reduced by excess foreign tax credits from other years.

Situations 1, 2, and 3 produce excess foreign tax credit that can be carried forward or back. The tax strategy for an MNL with excess foreign tax credits is to plan its future operations so as to increase income from foreign sources that is taxed at a low rate; any domestic losses will then be eliminated. Selected ways of increasing income from such foreign sources are as follows:

• Increase royalties.
• Borrow from the MNL rather than local banks.
• Increase export sales.
• Increase management fees.
• Increase the income of subsidiaries, branches, or associated companies now in a loss position.

INTERNATIONAL TAX PLANNING

If taxes and the multinationals are the subject of one textbook, international tax planning is the subject of a second textbook. The following is a synopsis of what a multinational company can do in the area of tax planning. Basically, it represents an inventory to be taken: an inventory of the persons competent in taxes, and an inventory of the scope and the kind of taxes that have to be paid overseas as well as in the home country; it describes the structure of a planning and review program designed to evaluate the maximum and minimum flows of income between the multinationals and associated companies, to and from host countries, and to the home country.

The planning program starts with an inventory of people, that is, the personnel in the tax departments of the MNL company worldwide, who have expertise in the tax regulations in the host countries as well as in the home country of the multinational. The second step in the inventory is to determine the kind of taxes or quasi-taxes, such as those in the following list, that are likely to be encountered in the home country or in each foreign country where the MNL has subsidiaries, branches, or associated companies:

• Federal income taxes
• State or local income taxes

• Value added or turnover taxes
• Sales taxes
• Customs duties or import duties
• Exchange control regulations and assessments

The third element of the review involves an inventory of those various flows of money that have influence on the tax structure of the company:

• Dividends
• Royalties
• Management fees
• Technical service fees
• Interest expenses
• Insurance premiums

The fourth phase of the inventory is a chart indicating all of the countries in which the MNL operates and a condensation of the base tax rates for statutory purposes and for other related taxes. A supplement to the tax rate schedule would compare the accounting methods of treating various elements of income and expenses, for example, statutory requirements with respect to the basics of inventory, cost of market, or replacement cost.

• Depreciation—straight line, accelerated double declining balance, or even 100% in the year of purchase
• Tax period
• Acceptable cash or accrual methods
• Method of handling installment receivable accounting
• Completed contract of percentage of completion recognition of income

The fifth phase of the inventory summarizes tax incentives that are available in selective host countries in which the MNL operates, for example, relief from taxes in underdeveloped or depressed areas, credits for export, and credits or adjustments of import duties for machinery and equipment used in industrializing depressed areas. The summary is supplemented by a description of the responsibilities of the MNL subsidiary, branch, or affiliate in each host country regarding exchange control, customs duties, value added or turnover taxes, sales taxes, property taxes, and franchise taxes.

The sixth element in the inventory required for tax planning is a description of the policies and procedures that have been established by the MNL for the following types of transactions:

- Loans
- Equity and capitalization in each host country
- Transfer pricing policies and cost bases
- Transfer of technology
- Service contracts and warranties

Finally, there should be a complete description of any tax treaties that exist between the home country of the MNL and any of its host countries.

CHANGES   Certain recent changes in the American tax law have made it more difficult for an MNL to apply its foreign taxes as credits against its American tax liabilities.

The 1977 Treasury Regulations list many kinds of deductions of expenses, such as research and development, that have to be allocated to foreign source gross income in determining foreign taxable income for purposes of foreign tax limitation. Interest and a portion of management's time or functions, which the corporation carries on as an investor in a related foreign country, are also allowed as expense deductions. Where an expense previously allocated against domestic income must now be allocated against foreign source income, the effect is to reduce the foreign tax credit limitation, making it more difficult to utilize foreign tax credits. At the same time, this shift in the allocation of expenses increases domestic income, which in turn increases American tax payments. This explains the popularity of these regulations with the Internal Revenue Service.

Finally, the IRS is insuring that foreign taxes claimed as credits by MNLs are substantiated and documented. The steps to take in order to counteract the foregoing combination of increased amounts of foreign taxes and the strengthening of the American foreign tax credit limitations have become the focus of tax planning.

Other changes affecting tax planning are occasioned by the reduction or elimination by foreign countries of certain devices that MNLs have used in the past to repatriate profits to the United States from foreign subsidiaries without paying withholding taxes levied on dividends. Among the vanishing breed are the following:

• *Management or technical services fees.* Many foreign countries are investigating these fees and disallow them unless they can be documented. The few MNLs that can charge such fees are those who have been doing business in certain countries for long periods of time and have established precedent for the management fees.

• *Royalties.* Royalties have often been charged to foreign subsidiaries for patents that have either expired or have lost their usefulness or uniqueness.

• *Transfer pricing.* Any attempt to provide other than reasonable, arm's-length mark-up on cost may result in higher value added taxes, higher custom duties, and so on. A number of high-tax foreign countries are scrutinizing intercompany profits, expecially when they result in zero profits or in percentages of profits that are far lower than those earned in affiliated low-tax country companies or than that reported by the American MNL in its annual report.

Section 482 of the Internal Revenue Code is addressed to the subject of transfer pricing:

In any case of two or more organizations, trades, or businesses (whether or not incorporated, whether or not organized in the United States, whether or not affiliated) owned or controlled directly or indirectly by the same interests, the Secretary or his delegate may distribute, apportion or allocate gross income, deductions, credits, or allowances, between or among such organizations, trades or businesses, if he determines that such distribution, a portion, or allocation is necessary in order to prevent evasion of taxes or clearly to reflect the income of such organizations, trades or businesses.

The Regulations under Section 482 of the Code also provide a guide to the following types of intercompany transactions:

1 Intercompany loans and advances.
2 Performance of services by one affiliate or another.
3 Use of tangible property of one affiliate by another.
4 Use or transfer of intangible property.
5 Intercompany sales of personal property.

Tax Havens. American tax legislation limits the use of tax-haven subsidiaries as a means of reducing taxes. If a tax haven does not meet the test of arm's-length dealing or if its income is imputed to be that of the parent, the IRS may, in effect, impute dividend income to the American parent company.

OTHER TAX CONSIDERATIONS Tax planning involves the study of new allowances and changes in the laws of many foreign countries. Tax relief for inflation is provided in the United Kingdom, for example, by permitting companies to establish tax deductible reserves for their inventories. The American definition of the Last in First Out (LIFO) inventory is usually not allowed in foreign countries. Brazil makes special allowances under the general title of indexing, which has an effect similar to that of the LIFO method of costing inventories.

Germany has a split tax rate that requires careful study of the timing of dividends. In other words, dividends are taxed by means of withholding. The failure to pay a dividend, that is, retaining all earnings in the company, results in higher taxes. A number of countries provide tax reduction incentives and even cash grants for operations established in depressed areas or industries.

The United States consolidated tax return is not often found in European countries. On the other hand, certain countries provide relief or a common basis of taxes for groups of companies in a given industry. In Germany, there is *Organschaft* under which certain companies are pooled for tax purposes in order to offset profits and losses of one against the other. Australia also has devices for leveling out the profits for a group of companies in order to avoid tax loss in any one. Spain and the United Kingdom have group relief for resident companies so that losses sustained by one United Kingdom affiliate can be applied against the profits of others.

The foreign taxes payable by American MNL's are notably affected by foreign exchange gains and losses. IRS regulations allow unrealized exchange gains and losses in determining earnings for American subsidiaries in certain situations. There is a great disparity, however, in the tax treatment of foreign exchange gains and losses in foreign countries.

When an American company wishes to form a new foreign subsidiary overseas, or otherwise transfer assets outside the United States, the law requires a tax be paid on any unrealized appreciation in value of the asset on the transfer date. This prevents American companies from transferring appreciated assets overseas tax-free and selling them overseas to avoid taxation in the United States. When the shares of an affiliated subsidiary are sold or the company is liquidated, the IRS generally requires any gain to be taxed as ordinary dividend income rather than as capital gains. Foreign tax credits, however, may be used to cancel American taxes in such cases.

THE MNL SURVEY AND EVALUATION OF ITS INTERNATIONAL TAX POSITION

A report of an MNL on its tax position worldwide first lists all its activities outside the home country indicating by corporate name, its subsidiaries, foreign branches, affiliated companies, and joint ventures and partnerships; second, it briefly describes the activities conducted by each of these.

Four fundamental questions arise. First, has any new foreign subsidiary been formed by transferring assets or stocks acquired during a recent year? Second, has any reorganization of a foreign subsidiary occurred during a recent year? Third, has any sale or liquidation of a foreign subsidiary taken place in the last year or two? Finally, has any sale of patents or intangible assets to a foreign corporation controlled by the MNL been reported?

INTERCOMPANY TRANSACTIONS BETWEEN RELATED PARTIES

A section of the American Internal Revenue Code is concerned with items of income deductions, credits, and other allowances that are related to the control existing between the American company and other American corporations doing business abroad. Among the types of transactions that should be defined are intercompany loans, advances, and services. The MNL should determine whether the interest charge can be described as arm's-length, and whether the intercompany sales of merchandise and other property are conducted at arm's-length. Finally, the MNL taxpayer should calculate the profit on each product line sold to third parties.

The review should state whether a foreign corporation qualifies as a "controlled foreign corporation," that is, one of which more than 50% of the total voting power is owned by American shareholders. If so, and if the foreign corporation buys products from a second country and sells these products to a third country, and deals with an affiliate in the process, the income will constitute foreign base company sales income of the controlled foreign corporation. American shareholders are taxed on their pro rata share of such income and increase in earnings invested in United States property on the theory that repatriation of such retained earnings is substantially the same as a dividend.

The final section of the report should thoroughly describe the foreign tax credit situation of the MNL. It should state whether the corporation claims the benefits of a Domestic International Sales Corporation (DISC), and whether the MNL taxpayer has formed a DISC and met the requirements for valid election, gross receipts test, and gross assets test. Finally, the report should justify any export sales not being run through the DISC and conclude with information about foreign captive insurance companies or banking entities owned by the MNL.

DOMESTIC INTERNATIONAL SALES CORPORATION (DISC)

A Domestic International Sales Corporation was introduced in the Revenue Act of 1971 in order to induce American companies to increase exports and thereby improve the balance of payments. Under the Revenue Act of 1971, the profits of a DISC corporation were not taxed to the DISC but instead taxed to the shareholders when distributed. The actual provisions of the Act meant that 50% of a DISC's taxable income was deferred and the other half was considered to be taxable as a dividend distributed to the shareholder.

The Tax Reform Act of 1976 changed the DISC arrangements so that a DISC could export American goods to related or unrelated persons. A DISC may lease or sublease products to persons for use outside the United States. A DISC may also perform construction, engineering, or architectural services for projects in foreign countries. An American corporation will qualify for a DISC in any taxable year if it is not engaged in manufacturing and meets these four requirements:

1 Gross receipts test: At least 95% of its gross receipts for the taxable year are composed of "qualified export receipts."
2 Assets test: At least 95% of its assets at the close of the taxable year are "qualified export assets."
3 Capitalization requirement: A DISC must have at least $2500 of capital on each day of the taxable year and it must have only one class of stock.

4 Election requirement: A corporation will be treated as a DISC only if it holds an election during the 90-day period immediately before the beginning of the taxable year or the 90-day period after incorporation.

QUALIFIED EXPORT RECEIPTS

Receipts defined as qualified export receipts are the following:

- Sale of export property.
- Lease or rental of export property for use of the lessee outside the United States.
- Services related and subsidiary to the above types of transactions.
- Sale of qualified export assets.
- Interest on obligations that are qualified export assets.
- Receipts from engineering or architectural services on construction projects abroad.
- Management services provided for unrelated DISCs to aid them in producing export receipts.

QUALIFIED EXPORT ASSETS

1 Export property, manufactured, produced, grown, or extracted in the United States and held for sale or lease abroad. This type of property can be considered as the property that is usually recorded on the balance sheet as inventory.
2 Assets used in the sale, rental, storage, handling, transportation, packaging, assemblage, or servicing of export property, or in the performance of engineering, architectural, or managerial services.
3 Accounts receivable and evidence of indebtness arising from export transactions.
4 Money and short-term investments, such as bank deposits, needed for working capital requirements of the DISC.
5 Loans arising in connection with a "producer's loan."
6 Stock or securities of related foreign corporations.
7 Obligations issued, guaranteed, or insured by the Export-Import Bank or the Foreign Credit Insurance Association.
8 Obligations of an American corporation organized only for

the purpose of financing sales of export property under agreement of the Eximbank, where the loans are guaranteed by that bank.

9 Amounts deposited in banks at the end of the taxable year that are in excess of the needs of the working capital of the corporation, which are invested in qualified export assets within a specified period of time after the end of the taxable year.

THE TAX REFORM ACT OF 1976

The Tax Reform Act of 1976 changed the following foreign tax credit restrictions:

• *Recapture of Foreign Losses.* The American tax savings derived by taxpayers from the reduction of an "overall foreign loss" from American source income is recaptured in subsequent years when the taxpayer earns foreign source income. This provision, introduced in the Oil Income Tax Reduction Act of 1975, was thus extended to all industries.

• *Dividends from Less-Developed Countries.* Dividends received from corporations in less-developed countries are taxed in the same manner as dividends from other foreign corporations.

• *Captial Gains Source Rules.* The sale of capital assets abroad results in foreign source income. The new provisions require adjustments in the limitations calculations of the foreign tax credit to reflect the lower rate of the American tax on capital gains. Other technical amendments reduce the benefits formerly available.

• *Foreign Gas and Oil Extraction Income.* For foreign tax credit purposes, foreign taxes paid on profits from foreign gas and oil extraction had been limited to a percentage of such income. The percentage for 1977 onward was figured at 50% under the Tax Reduction Act for 1975.

• *Underwriting Income.* The Act changed the long-standing source rule for underwriting income whereby the geographic source was determined on the basis of where an insurance contract was negotiated. The source of underwriting income is now determined on the basis of where the risk is located. Amounts received by domestic or foreign insurance of United States risks are American source income.

CHAPTER 12

Internal Accounting Controls And Internal Auditing

Management is planning, organizing, controlling, innovating, and working through people. Management control is making it work the way you wanted it to work in the first place—the way you planned it. Management control systems are the means an MNL uses to make it work according to plan. Accounting systems are essential pragmatic means of accomplishing management control expressed in the language of business: profits and losses, balance sheets, and assets and liabilities.

Financial management is in one sense the quarterback position; the chief financial officer calls the plays:

- The assets needed to carry out the management plans.
- The structure and composition of these assets.
- The sources of capital funds needed to finance the assets.

In systems control, systems are designed as the means by which management achieves its goals and plans in six essential steps:

- Specify and analyze

- Make decisions
- Organize men and machines
- Quality control
- Corrective action

Internal audit closes the loop on the control system. Internal audit reports to management its findings on how the system operates and in turn makes recommendations for corrective action to make the system work as planned. This broad function of internal auditing is known as operational auditing. Internal auditing also has a financial audit function, which ascertains whether the financial internal accounting controls are operative, reports the facts and finally recommends corrective action in the control areas.

In summary, the internal audit examines and evaluates the effectiveness of an MNL system of internal accounting control and the quality of performance in carrying out assigned responsibilities at authorized levels. The MNL internal audit department assesses the internal controls operative within each and every operating unit of the multinational company whether domestic or overseas. Basic tenets of internal control follow.

INTERNAL ACCOUNTING CONTROLS   Internal accounting controls are essential to the overall control of every multinational company. The control environment involves all the employees of a company. Leadership in formulating and communicating an atmosphere of control consciousness starts with the company's board of directors, audit committee, and top management. This involves creating a clearly defined organizational structure, using sound management practices, extablishing accountability for performance, and requiring adherence to appropriate standards of ethical behavior, including compliance with applicable laws and regulations.

An MNL formalizes written policies and procedures that are conducive to an environment in which internal accounting controls are understood well and operate effectively.

MANAGEMENT POLICY An MNL corporate policy manual establishes:

- Business ethics and practices.
- Objectives and requirements for an internal accounting control system.
- Objectives and requirements for accounting systems.

REPORTING PROCEDURES An MNL has reporting procedures to inform management and the board of the results of its activities:

- Reports from the internal audit function, including comments by line management on actions taken, or suggestions for alternative action to remedy the deficiencies noted in the reports.

- Reports from within the organization responsible for making changes in control procedures (e.g., data processing), including a summary of actions taken to assure that proper control procedures have been considered in the system design.

- Reports from the independent accountants describing weaknesses in control systems or recommending matters for study, including a summary of the actions taken.

- The internal monthly financial reports prepared throughout the MNL that compare planned with actual results and analyze variances. Management identifies areas where controls need to be strengthened, evaluates performance, and thereby develops an attitude of accountability at all levels of the company.

In addition, procedures include obtaining annual confirmation from executive and line management affirming compliance with policies and control procedures.

ORGANIZATIONAL STRUCTURE The organizational structure of an MNL provides the overall framework for the planning, direction, and control of the company's operations. In general, it involves reporting relationships, functions to be performed by organizational units, and the authority, responsibilities, and constraints of key positions.

245

The MNL hires competent personnel who discharge their responsibilities, its system of measure and account for performance.

• Responsibility and authority are delegated to effectively deal with goals and objectives, operating functions, organizational forms, management style, regulatory requirements, and financial reporting standards.

• Budgets and financial reports are designed to assess the discharge of assigned responsibilities and monitor activities at each level in the organization.

• Checks and balances separate incompatible activities so as to preclude absolute control by any single individual or unit, provide for supervision by higher levels of management, and provide for monitoring overall company activities.

• The company documents its organizational structure with appropriate organization charts, position descriptions, and policy statements.

Professional auditing literature states that reasonable assurance that the objectives of accounting control are met depends on the competence and integrity of personnel, the independence of their assigned functions, and their understanding of the prescribed procedures. The company has policies and procedures for hiring, evaluation, compensation, promotion, and training conductive to employing competent, honest personnel.

AUTHORITY Management delegates or limits authority in a manner that assures its responsibilities are effectively discharged. For example, the board of directors direct authority to approve long-term loan agreements but delegates authority to approve capital expenditures within established limits. Each level of management delegates authority within reasonable limits while retaining final responsibility. There is a network of personnel who are specifically authorized to approve designated transactions and who are prohibited from engaging in others.

TYPES OF CONTROLS   The terms *"internal control"* and *"internal accounting control"* are often used interchangeably. *Internal control* is the composite of all the various methods used by a company to safeguard its assets, check the accuracy and reliability of its accounting and other data, promote operational efficiency, and encourage adherence to prescribed managerial policies. *Internal accounting control* is limited to the plan of organization and the procedures and records concerned with safeguarding assets and the reliability of financial data.

There is a further distinction between administrative control and accounting controls. *Administrative control* includes the plan of organization and the procedures and records that are concerned with the decision processes leading to management's authorization of transactions. Such authorization is a management function directly associated with the responsibility for achieving the objectives of the organization and is the starting point for establishing accounting control of transactions.

Accounting control comprises the plan of organization and the procedures and records that are concerned with safeguarding assets and the reliability of financial records; consequently accounting control is designed to assure that:

• Transactions are executed in accordance with management's authorization.

• Transactions are recorded as necessary (1) to permit preparation of financial statements in conformity with generally accepted accounting principles or any other criteria applicable to such statements and (2) to maintain accountability for assets.

• Access to assets is permitted only in accordance with management's authorization.

• The recorded accountability for assets is compared with the existing assets at reasonable intervals, and appropriate action is taken with respect to any differences.

Objectives of Internal Accounting Control   The objectives of internal control can be classified into three categories—authorization, accounting, and safeguarding:

• Authorization. An internal accounting control system depends on a plan of authorization. Certain transactions are specifically authorized and others are authorized by an established policy or operating procedure.

• Accounting. This objective means that a company's accounts and records should reflect transactions as executed. Transactions should be properly described, entered in appropriate accounts, and recorded in the appropriate accounting period in the actual amounts. If these procedures are followed, it should be possible to prepare reliable financial statements from the records and accounts and to maintain accountability for assets.

• Safeguarding. The objective of safeguarding assets requires limited access to authorized persons. Depending on the type of assets involved, a variety of devices for limiting access may be used. For example, access to certain assets, such as valuable securities maintained in safe deposit boxes, might require the presence of two or more senior company officials, whereas access to cash, inventory, and other assets may require other means of cross verification. The problem of safeguarding assets requires sensitive handling because sufficient access must be allowed so that business operations are not stifled, and yet access must be restricted to authorized persons. In the process of accounting for and safeguarding assets, it is necessary to compare periodically the assets actually on hand with the amounts recorded. In a well-managed MNL, a physical inventory must be taken annually and reconciled with the books of accounts.

Elements of the System of Internal Accounting Controls

The elements of the system of internal accounting controls are divided into general controls and specific controls.

General controls pertain to the environment in which data are produced, processed, reviewed, and accumulated. They usually do not affect transactions directly, but affect the overall "control consciousness" of an organization, and therefore may have an indirect impact on the validity of data produced.

Specific controls are designed to fulfill the broad objectives of individual transactions, namely:

- The transaction has been authorized.
- The transaction has been accounted for properly.
- The asset resulting from the transaction or affected by it is safeguarded.

General Controls

General controls, the organizational structures and procedures that form the environment for controls over transactions, help establish a company's control consciousness. Three types of general controls can be identified: the general structure of the organization, the administration of accounting, and the protection of physical assets. The major considerations in evaluating each of these types of general controls are discussed below.

General Structure of the Organization

The general structure of the organization encompases those policies and procedures established to ensure that decision-making authority is vested in the proper level of management and that management decisions and policies are properly implemented throughout the organization.

The following are essential conditions to be found in the structure of an MNL:

- The corporate organization (e.g., subsidiaries, divisions, joint ventures) is appropriate for the size and scope of its various business activities.
- Senior management is subject to effective review by the organization's board of directors.
- Published organization charts show reporting lines and responsibilities.
- Authority levels and responsibilities are described in written job descriptions.
- Duties are appropriately segregated.
- Policies and procedures are effectively communicated to appropriate staff levels and organized in procedure manuals.
- Employees are hired for positions commensurate with their skills and are effectively trained before being assigned to more responsible positions.

• Job performance is periodically evaluated and reviewed with each employee.

In the company's system of internal accounting controls, appropriate segregation of duties plays an important role. In most cases, the duties related to the three broad objectives of internal accounting controls–authorization, accounting, and safeguarding—are segregated by having them performed by different individuals.

Administration of the Accounting Function Controls over processing transactions may not function properly because of human error; the following supplemental controls minimize this potential for error:

• Operating plan procedures comparing budgeted to actual results; timely investigation of variations.

• Internal financial reports, promptly issued after the close of each reporting period, covering areas of control responsibility.

• Procedures for comparing nonfinancial reports prepared by operating departments with data included in financial reports (e.g., comparison of sales forecasts to physical inventory listings to check for potentially obsolete inventory).

• Staffing appropriate in numbers of personnel needed to process the accounting data effectively, the skills required in the processing function and the integrity of the personnel.

• Accounting policies and procedures defined in current manuals, which present charts of accounts, account contents, description, record retention policies, and so forth.

Protection of Physical Assets Use of the company's assets is a necessary part of the day-to-day operations of a business but, to safeguard assets, use is limited to authorized personnel. Protection of physical assets is accomplished through various procedures, including:

• Restricting access to offices, plants, and other company premises to authorized personnel by the use of guards, fences, locked areas, and so on.

• Protecting assets subject to deterioration from the elements.

• Storing important records in facilities that are either locked or under continuous surveillance.

• Storing negotiable documents in protective containers, such as fireproof safes or vaults, to which no person has sole access.

• Maintaining written disaster plans and off-premises storage of back-up files for all critical records.

• Investigating the integrity of personnel hired to fill sensitive positions.

• Periodically reviewing the adequacy of insurance coverage.

Specific Controls   Specific controls are designed to fulfill the broad objectives of controls for any transaction, that is, authorization, accounting, and safeguarding. A common and effective approach is to view a company's controls in terms of the transaction cycles of its business.

When transactions are both frequent and similar, accounting systems and procedures are adopted to process each phase in the transaction cycle on a regular basis. The controls within the cycle are the controls over the class of transactions. Internal accounting controls within a transaction cycle may be exercised in several different departments and encompass several activities.

The transaction cycle approach to specific controls may be outlined as follows:

• Identify the enterprise's transaction cycles.

• Identify the specific objectives within the cycle to achieve the broad control objectives for any transaction—authorization, accounting, and safeguarding.

• Identify the control procedures designed to achieve the specific objectives.

The major transaction cycles typical of a manufacturing company are as follows:

251

1 *Revenue Cycle*

Transactions occur in generating revenue. Typical activities include:

Order entry

Shipping

Billing

Records of accounts receivable

Cash receipts

Sales returns

Credit and collection

2 *Expenditure Cycle*

Transactions occur in acquiring goods and services in exchange for payment. Typical activities include:

Requisitioning and purchasing

Receiving

Accounts payable

Cash disbursements

Payroll

3 *Production Cycle*

Transactions occur in producing goods for resale. Typical activities include:

Inventory recordkeeping

Material usage

Inventory costing

Manufacturing process

Cost accounting

CONCLUSION Responsibility for the system of internal accounting controls rests with management. This responsibility for supervising and monitoring the system is ongoing. In an MNL the delegation of these responsibilities falls into the following categories:

• *Board of Directors.* The system of internal accounting control is a key element in the functioning of the corporate organization. The board of directors' first concern is that the system of internal accounting controls responds to the company's needs. The board discharges its duties in a variety of ways including reviewing the system with management, reviewing the limits of authority at each level, and requiring periodic tests and reports on the functioning of the system. In practice, the board uses the audit committee for this task.

• *Audit Committee.* The audit committee of the board of directors serves as the monitoring unit for the board with respect to internal accounting controls. Its functions include discussing the system with senior corporate management and periodic meetings with internal and external auditors eliciting any recommendations to improve controls. The members of the committee receive copies or summaries of reports on controls issued by internal and external auditors.

• *Senior Corporate Management.* Senior corporate management approves the overall design of the system of internal accounting controls and establishes the limits of authority for senior officers and officers of reporting units. They evaluate results of periodic tests of the functioning of the system and the follow-up of corrective action.

• *Corporate Financial Management.* Corporate financial management is responsible for accounting control within the corporate office and for communicating control policies to reporting units. It is also responsible for determining whether reporting units have effectively implemented the control policies and whether the controls are functioning as intended.

• *Operating and Reporting Units.* The operating and reporting units establish specific accounting controls in accordance with company policy. These controls are carried out through procedures designed to safeguard assets and to maintain reliable financial records.

• *Internal Audit Department.* The internal audit department monitors the system of internal accounting controls. This includes periodic visits to reporting units and corporate office departments to test the system of controls and report on the effectiveness of procedures related to the system. Corporate management reviews its reports and important highlights are presented to the audit committee.

INTERNAL AUDITING

Internal auditing in the multinational company is an appraisal activity independent of every operational, line, and staff organization of the company. Internal auditing operates within an organization for the purpose of reviewing operations for management.

There are a number of basic guidelines for internal auditing, for example:

• To assess the adequacy of the system of internal accounting controls.

• To investigate compliance with company policy and procedures.

• To determine that the company's assets are accounted for and safeguarded from losses.

• To verify the existence of company assets by arranging and supervising inventories.

• To evaluate the reliability of the accounting and reporting system.

• To identify opportunities for improving performance.

• To coordinate its audit efforts with those of the company's public accountants.

The internal audit operations complement the scope and coverage of audits made by the independent certified public accountants; their combined efforts should provide a comprehensive cost-effective coverage for the MNL. A typical working arrangement between an MNL internal audit department and its independent CPA is as follows:

• Internal audit plans are prepared in coordination with the CPA's plans.

• Preliminary arrangements are made for the internal auditors and independent CPA to review each other's working papers.

• Every internal audit report is distributed to the independent CPA and the working papers are made available for the CPA's review.

The director of internal auditing and the engagement partner of the CPA firm are in continuous contact throughout the year; together they plan the year-end audit and the financial operational audits that follow, relying on information the internal audit department has provided for the current fiscal year. The plan for the annual year-end audit is usually finished between October and January of the succeeding period.

In a multinational company the internal audit department has a unique position. The director of internal auditing reports to the chief financial officer and is therefore independent of the group and divisional vice-presidents. The internal audit department has many unique characteristics that it accumulates over years of experience.

• It has managerial expertise and it knows how the company works. It has integrity and the support of a number of recent laws that enhance the status of the auditor.

• It understands the strengths and weaknesses of the company's procedures.

• It acts independently of the individuals and divisions that are being audited.

• More important it usually consists of a staff of very knowledgeable persons who have traveled extensively, have language skills, and at the same time can conform to the working paper techniques of the certified public accountants.

The minimum requirement of the audit department of a multinational meets the auditing standards of a typical CPA firm for reliance upon of its internal auditors. A CPA firm relies on the internal audit department of a multinational company, provided that it can meet the following standards:

• Qualification of its personnel
• Independence
• Documentation
• Performance

The Institute of Internal Auditors has described the purpose of internal auditing as an independent appraisal activity within an organization whose purpose is to review accounting, financing, and other operations as a basis of service to management. It is a managerial control that functions by measuring and evaluating the effectiveness of the company's controls.

INTERNAL AUDIT REPORTS AND RESPONSES   A principal task of the internal auditors is to evaluate internal controls, including accounting controls, and to determine whether these controls are functioning properly.

Control deficiencies noted during internal audits are brought to the attention of management in the audit report. The management of the audited unit is responsible for implementing actions, to correct these deficiencies and to respond to the audit report in writing, outlining the corrective actions taken and the target dates for their implementation.

ANNUAL INTERNAL AUDIT PLAN   The MNL internal audit prepares each year a plan to periodically audit all operating units and staff departments.

Internal auditors review and appraise the soundness and effectiveness of accounting and administrative controls and ascertain the extent of compliance with established policies, plans, and procedures. They evaluate the reliability of accounting and other data developed within the organization and determine whether company assets are accounted for and safeguarded from losses. Recommendations for improvements are formulated in the audit report issued at the end of each assignment.

To accomplish the foregoing in a cost-effective manner, a comprehensive audit plan must be prepared to ensure that all locations are audited periodically, that critical activities are audited more often than others, that selected locations with a record of sound operating controls are audited less often, and finally that the internal audit does not duplicate the audit of the independent CPA.

The internal audit plan selects the operating locations and staff departments for operational financial audits during the year and the major fields of concentration, also referred to as transaction cycles, in each audit.

The plan systematically continues the level of internal audits conducted in previous years, and complements the independent CPA's audit provided by its annual audit plan of the previous year. Particular attention must be paid to findings of previous audits and to follow-up necessary in selected critical areas. The audit activities of divisional and local internal audits are incorporated into the plan to achieve an adequate balance in their coverage of local outlets and in the operational financial audits made by corporate audit.

In recent years MNL audit plans have had features not found in the plans of previous years:

• *Transaction Cycle Auditing*

Internal audits cover all the basic business transaction cycles, rather than accounting alone. The transaction cycles are specified in an internal accounting control manual, which was distributed to location controllers throughout the company. These cycles coincide with those employed by the CPA firm, in their year-end audits and are the following:

- (a) Revenue cycle
- (b) Expenditure cycle
- (c) Production cycle
- (d) Treasury cycle
- (e) Financial reporting process
- (f) Computer controls

The audit plan requires coverage of all transaction cycles in small locations during each audit, but specifies selected cycles for larger facilities to that full coverage of all transaction cycles is achieved over a three year period.

• *System Evaluation Flow Charts*

Pursuant to the requirements of the Foreign Corrupt Practices Act of 1977, a central file of system evaluation flow charts should be established for individual operating systems and procedures. All flow charts on file are reviewed for compliance with the MNL's internal accounting control manual during each scheduled audit. Flow charts should be developed in planned audits for those cycles not yet completed.

• *Internal Accounting Control Manual*

The annual audit plan provides that auditors monitor compliance with all policies of the internal accounting control manual. Exceptions to compliance are highlighted in the audit reports, and where a location's response to the report are unsatisfactory, the matter is again referred to group and division management in a condensed, three-column, item-by-item analysis of the responses.

• *Participation in the CPA Year-end Audit*

The internal audit plan should anticipate corporate audit participation in the CPA firm's year-end audit to a considerable extent of its available man hours. The CPA firm develops its year-end audit in June and July after analyzing the company's financial position and the operational financial audits already completed; the firm then assigns specific locations to the internal audit department in the annual audit plan, which is submitted to management in August and to the audit committee in September.

Figures 28 and 29 are examples of how the current status of a plan can be summarized by location. Figures 30 to 33 are examples of the detail provided in the internal audit plan for each group, division and location; they include:

• Narrative on the facility
• Last audit—year-end significant findings
• Planned coverage by corporate audit
• Planned coverage by local internal audit

Government Products and Services

Audits planned		*Current status*
GAR Division		Planned July 1979
Dearfield division	Little River	Planned August 1979
Chain division	Baltimore	In progress
	Cold Springs	Completed 79–28
	High Miles	Completed 79–39
Education division		
EDP Systems		In progress
Core Centers		
San Jose		Planned September 1979
Morgan Town		Completed—report in process
Salt Lake		Planned September 1979
Boise		Planned August 1979

Figure 28. Internal Audit Plan.

Consumer Products

Thermal Division	
Carmel	Planned September 1979
Red River	Planned August 1979
Albany	Completed—report in process
Metric Division	
Darien	Completed—report in process
Fulton	Completed—79–33
Omaha	Completed—report in process
Headoffice	Completed—79– 9
Amsterdam	Completed—79–16
Leichester	Completed—79–20
Motor division	
Pawtucket	Planned July 1979
Cincinnati	Planned June 1979
Furniture division	
Henderson	Planned August 1979
Carson City	Completed 79–35
Linden	Planned July 1979

Consumer Products (continued)	
Harrison	Completed—Report in Process
Controls division	
Appliances	Planned July 1979
Trucks	Planned July 1979
Gary Plant	Planned July 1979
Regulation	Completed 79–38

Figure 29. Internal audit plan.

B. *Government products and services*

  2. *Dearfield Division*

The Division produces high technology navigation guidance systems and control sub-systems and related components. Sales are $144,000,000 and the number of employees totals 3750.

    2.1. Little River Operation

        Last audit: 1978 Capital Appropriation Audit.

            Corporate policy was not followed in all instances.

Planned Coverage	1979	1980	1981
Revenue cycle		X	
Expenditure cycle	X		X
Production cycle	X		X
Treasury cycle		X	X
Financial Reporting process	X		X
Computer controls		X	

    2.2. San Carlos facility

        Last audit: 1978. No major control deficiencies noted.

Planned coverage	1979	1980	1981
Revenue cycle		X	
Expenditure cycle		X	
Production cycle		X	
Treasury cycle		X	
Financial reporting process		X	
Computer controls		X	

Figure 30. Internal audit plan.

C. *Consumer products*

    4. *Furniture Division*

        4.5. Colonial Period Furniture

Colonial Period Furniture manufactures bedroom and segments of the dining room line; it receiving tables and chairs from other furniture factories. Distribution of bedroom and dining room furniture is made to all western states.

The manufacturing, administration, and marketing operations employs 217 people, located in Ojai, California, and total sales are $10 million.

Last audit: 1978 Material control weaknesses exist due to the noncompliance with established procedures.

Planned coverage	1979	1980	1981
Follow-up of 1978 audit	X		
Revenue cycle		X	
Expenditure cycle		X	
Production cycle		X	
Treasury cycle		X	
Financial reporting process		X	
Computer controls		X	

Figure 31. Internal audit plan.

B. *Joining Division*

    1. *U.S. Marketing*

The facility has a sales volume of approximately $200 million, marketing machines, equipment, furniture, and softgoods through a network of 500 owned stores and independent dealers.

Headcount: approximately 5000 employees.

Last audit: 1978 *Accounts Payable*

                Accounts Payable understated by $90,000

                Security of check vouchers is inadequate.

1978 *S and A Expenses*

        A further reduction of S&A expenses at HQ is not feasible without sacrificing controls or speed of information processing.

Planned coverage	1979	1980	1981
Revenue cycle		X	
Expenditure cycle		X	
Production cycle (inventory only)		X	
Treasury cycle		X	X
Financial reporting process	X		
Computer controls	X		

	1979	1980	1981
Planned coverage by local internal audit			
Field credit offices	X		X
Travel expenses/allowance	X	X	X
Store accounting	X		X
Advertising	X		
Tax department	X		X
General accounting	X	X	X
Personnel department	X		X
All retail stores	X	X	X

Figure 32. Internal audit plan.

C. *Joining Division—Europe*

    4. *France*

        4.3. Compeigne Factory

Situated 40 miles northeast of Paris, Compeigne produces a line of medium-priced mechanical joining machines. It also produces electric motors for the Rome and Dortmund factories, a toy joining machine and plastic carrying cases.

The factory employs 540 persons, of which 350 are direct labor. Annual sales are around $20 million.

Last audit: 1978. Intracompany accounts receivable of $340,000 are in excess of 360 days in arrears.

	1979	1980	1981
Planned coverage			
Revenue cycle		X	
Expenditure cycle		X	
Production cycle		X	X
Treasury cycle	X		X
Financial reproting process	X		X
Computer controls		X	
Planned coverage by local Internal audit function			
General accounting	X	X	
Expenditure cycle	X		X
Cafeteria operations	X	X	X
Other receivables	X		X

Figure 33. Internal audit plan.

EXTERNAL AUDITORS

An MNL pursuant to its policies and bylaws and, in the United States subject to the regulations of the Security and Exchange Commission is required to appoint CPAs to annually examine and express an opinion about the MNL's financial statements. Certain foreign operations are required to have their local financial statements audited by statutory auditors in accordance with local laws and regulations.

POLICY OF THE MNL REGARDING EXTERNAL AUDITORS

• Each year, the company's external auditors express an opinion about the fairness of the presentation of the company's financial position, the results of operations, and the changes in the company's position; the auditors also determine whether the presentation conforms to generally accepted accounting principles, consistent with those of the preceding year.

• After examining the MNL financial statements, inform management of any material weaknesses in internal control and any irregularities.

• Management letters issued by the company's independent CPAs are addressed to the vice-president and controller of the company, and copies are sent to the director of internal audit and to local, group, and division management.

• Local management is required to reply to each of the findings and recommendations included in the management letter within four weeks from the date of the letter, indicating corrective action taken and target dates for its implementation.

• Requests for changing the statutory auditors must be forwarded to the director of internal audit.

CHAPTER 13

Foreign Corrupt Practices Act Of 1977

The Foreign Corrupt Practices Act of 1977 was signed into law on December 19, 1977 (Public Law 95–213). It applies to virtually all American companies, their officers, directors, employees, agents, or stockholders acting on behalf of the companies. A fine of up to $1 million can be assessed to the company for each violation. Fines and imprisonment are stipulated for willful violations by individuals.

The first part of the act is concerned with illegal payments or bribes. In the second part, the tail really wagged the dog in that the act prescribed internal accounting controls for all companies that are required to file with the SEC. As one writer wrote at one time, an American company does not have to be either foreign or corrupt to come within the scope of the internal control section of the Act. Although the topic of internal controls is not new and auditors have been evaluating controls since the beginning of auditing, the Foreign Corrupt Practices Act of 1977 has brought the subject of internal accounting controls to the forefront of corporate and professional concern.

FOREIGN CORRUPT PRACTICES

IMPROPER PAYMENTS   A broad definition of improper payments, made or received, includes the following:

- Payments that violate laws or regulations, such as illegal political contributions.
- Payments that are falsified or not recorded in the accounting records.
- Bribes, kickbacks, or payoffs to government officials or their intermediaries, customers, suppliers, and so forth.
- Aiding and abetting another party to make or receive an improper payment.

Questionable payments include:

- Payment made in cash or a deposit in a secret bank account.
- Payment, if made in the United States, that is not necessarily illegal in a foreign country.
- Illegal payment that is not necessarily improper. Payments falsified or not recorded in the accounting records are improper. "Slush funds" and disbursements not recorded within the system of company records involve falsification of the accounting records and are deemed improper.
- Fee or commission paid to an agent to obtain business when there is reason to suspect that the agent may have used bribery to secure the contract.

Action the MNL should take to investigate a suspicious payment:

- Gather the facts: the nature, purpose, and amount of the payment.
- Determine whether it was made and to whom.

- Investigate whether the payment was illegal.
- Identify who approved the payment.
- Determine how the payment was made. Was it recorded in the books and records? Was it paid in cash or by check, or to a secret bank account?
- Ascertain whether the payment was made once or was one in a continuing series.
- Identify who knows about the payment.
- Examine potential liability due to fines, damages, taxes, penalties, and so forth.
- Calculate the risk of lost customers, increased costs, interruption or discontinuation of operations, and the expropriation of assets and resultant loss of future income.
- Management must notify the board of directors and audit committee about improper payments.
- Legal counsel and the company's independent auditors are the investigators.
- Improper payments of a continuing nature are stopped.

DISCLOSING IMPROPER PAYMENTS

When disclosing improper payments, specify:

- Amount of the payment.
- Amount of liability due to fines, damages, taxes, or penalties.
- Potential loss of customers, increased costs, interruption or discontinuation of operations, and expropriation of assets and the resultant loss of future income.

The MNL must be prepared to respond to shareholders' questions about improper payments.

SEC officials have indicated that immaterial improper payment by a registrant may constitute a material fact requiring some type of disclosure to investors that should include:

- Amount, nature, and purpose of payment.
- Method and route of payment (that is, whether the payment was made within the system of corporate accountability).

- Involvement of top management in approving or condoning the payments.
- Rectification or discontinuance of the payments.
- Potential harm to the business and employees if such payments were stopped or disclosed.

In effect, the SEC essentially seems to be using a qualitative standard of material so that even if a payment is relatively small, it may be deemed material if:

- The books are falsified.
- The internal control system is circumvented.
- Top management is involved.
- A significant part of a company's business depends on continuing the payments.

Based on the judgment of directors, legal counsel, and independent auditors, companies subject to SEC jurisdiction should consider advising the SEC about the payment and working with the SEC on acceptable disclosure and other action. Experience indicates that the SEC may be relatively lenient with those companies that voluntarily disclose improper payments. For example, such companies may not be formally charged with securities law violations and may not be required to disclose the recipients of the payments or the countries involved.

AVOIDING IMPROPER PAYMENTS The single most important way to avoid improper payments is to set a high standard of corporate conduct, exemplified by top management. Business ethics pervade an organization. Establish a sound company policy. Describe the types of payments of acts that are considered improper and emphasize the following points:

- Making or receiving improper payments is prohibited and will not be tolerated.
- Applicable laws, rules, and regulations are to be adhered to.

- Unrecorded, off-the-record funds are not to be established.

- No false entries are to be made in the books and records. All payments and receipts must be for the purposes stated in the supporting documentation.

- Any employee intentionally violating company policy is subject to dismissal and, if appropriate, prosecution by the company.

- Known violations should be reported immediately to a designated responsible official or committee.

Strengthen procedures regarding employment of agents by observing the following recommendations:

- Require signed contracts with agents who are to receive substantial fees and commissions. Describe services to be rendered and specify when management should approve contracts. Designate who should acknowledge that the agent is to perform bona fide services.

- Obtain assurance from the agent that he is not a government official or an intermediary for such an official.

- Investigate the background of the agent to determine the agent's experience, sphere of influence, and relation to potential customers.

- Make no payments to agents in cash or to a secret bank account, such as a numbered Swiss account.

- Question whether the company would be embarrassed and unable to defend itself if it became publicly known that the agent or agents in question were being used to obtain certain types of business.

To monitor the MNL policy, emphatically advise all employees of it. Require key management personnel and corporate officials to submit written statements to the effect that they have no knowledge of any improper payments made or received and that to the best of their knowledge, they and their subordinates have complied with company policy. Periodic tests of the policy should be conducted by the internal audit team, which thoroughly understands the company's policies, internal controls, and goals. In addition to having the requisite expertise for detecting violations, internal auditors build into their audit program an awareness of the possibility that improper payments may have been made. They also audit accounts and records that are likely places for concealing improper payments.

AUDITOR'S RESPONSIBILITIES

An examination of financial statements in accordance with generally accepted auditing standards is not designed to discover improper payments. Auditors recognize the possibility that such payments may have been made and have an impact on the financial statements. Improper payments reflect on management's integrity and influence the auditor's intended reliance on internal controls and representations of management.

Most CPA firms do not believe they have a professional obligation to extend audit tests to the discovery of improper payments, but they know they should advise management about such payments on all audit engagements for publicly held companies.

SPECIAL INVESTIGATIONS

Since 1975 some companies have been directed by the SEC to make "full" investigations after improper payments have been discovered, whereas others have voluntarily undertaken investigations to determine whether such payments have been made. Special investigations do not assure that all improper payments are uncovered, but they are a reasonable approach. The scope and procedures of a special investigation should be directed by the audit committee to ensure independence from management not only in appearance, but also in fact. The audit committee should have the advice of legal counsel and the independent auditors. The investigation covers suspect activities, transactions, and payments that may have occurred over a specified period of time. During the investigation, all locations need not be visited; the environment or nature of business of

269

some subsidiaries or divisions may indicate that there is little likelihood that improper payments have been made.

An efficient way to gather information is to submit a written questionnaire to each of the directors, officers, and employees whose positions would enable them to perpetrate or approve improprieties, or to obtain knowledge of improprieties committed by others. The questionnaire should request the following information:

• The chronological identification of the respondent's positions and responsibilities within the company.

• Specific knowledge of improprieties (as defined) made by the individual respondent or by another employee.

• Matters that may involve an impropriety that warrants the attention of the investigators.

• Operations that, in the respondent's judgment, are susceptible to improprieties.

Respondents must sign affidavits about their knowledge of improper payments. The written questionnaire is supplemented with personal interviews of designated directors, officers, and employees. Interviews encourage candid discussion and jog memories. Interviews should be conducted by at least one investigator, a lawyer, and an auditor. After the questionnaires and interviews, the information is evaluated for reasonableness and consistency. Inconsistencies and other questionable matters should, of course, be pursued until satisfactorily resolved.

Review in-depth the internal controls and accounting procedures as they relate to the areas under investigations, such as the controls over cash transactions including those made by wire transfer. Also, official corporate documents and records such as the bylaws, tax returns, and previous SEC filings should be reviewed to determine whether they should be modified or amended.

A "full" investigation audits certain of the books, correspondence, contracts, invoices, checks, expense accounts, logs of corporate aircraft or other facilities, especially those accounts and operating areas where improprieties are likely to occur. Investigators should also review personal financial affairs of suspect individuals, their income tax returns, bank statements, paid checks, and statements of net worth.

Following is a *representative* statement of policy on personal responsibilities of employees that might be adopted by a multinational company.

STATEMENT OF POLICY—PERSONAL RESPONSIBILITIES OF EMPLOYEES

An MNL needs the continuing support of its customers, shareholders, and employees. The MNL maintains high standards of business conduct and requires its employees as well to assume responsibility for a high standard of ethical conduct and a reputation for integrity in its business relationships.

Customers The relationship of an MNL with its customers is its key asset. Employers of the MNL are fair and honest in every dealing with its customers. Products and services are described accurately and sold only on their merits. No disparaging remarks can be made about a competitor's products or services.

Suppliers The MNL maintains strong professional relationships with its suppliers of products and services. Employees select suppliers in accordance with the best interests of the MNL, based only on needs and requirements. Reciprocity is never a condition of purchase or sale.

Competitors An MNL believes that a free and competitive economy, which American antitrust laws are designed to foster, best serves its interests. An MNL policy is to comply with the letter and the spirit of the antitrust laws of all countries where it does business.

Bribery and Political Contributions A number of corporations have made public disclosures of questionable or illegal payments. The United States is strictly enforcing all laws governing payment of bribes, kickbacks, and political contributions,

271

not only to American but also to foreign government officials and political figures. It is a crime, punishable by substantial fines for American corporations, and imprisonment for their employees or agents, for violating these laws.

• *Political Contributions.* An employee cannot directly or indirectly (through subsidiaries or agents) make any political contribution of any kind on behalf of the company except in a location where it is legal and after obtaining the approval of the general counsel of the MNL. American law, as well as most state laws, prohibit corporations from making such contributions within the United States. Corporations now are also prohibited from directly or indirectly, through foreign subsidiaries or agents, making any foreign political contributions to government officials, political parties, and candidates for the purpose of influencing any governmental act or decision to assist the corporation to keep existing business, obtain new business, direct business to others, or to obtain preferential treatment to which the company is not entitled. Employees may, of course, make political contributions from their own resources.

• *Bribes.* An employee cannot pay any governmental official, customer, or supplier (actual or potential) any bribe, kickback, or commission to obtain preferential treatment or to obtain or retain business for the company. This does not prohibit gifts of nominal value, casual entertainment as appropriate in the particular environment, facilitating payments, or commission payments to authorized agents.

• The general counsel of the MNL should be consulted if any doubt exists about the propriety of any payment, commission, gift, favor, or entertainment.

• Entertainment of some employees of American executive agencies by persons who have business with that federal agency or are regulated by such agency is prohibited by United States executive order and the implementing regulations of certain government agencies.

Facilitating Payments   In many parts of the world it is customary or even necessary for corporations to make "facilitating" payments to government officials whose duties are essentially clerical or ministerial to persuade them to perform functions or services that they are obligated to perform as part of their governmental responsibilities, but that they may refuse or delay unless compensated. A typical MNL policy strongly discourages these payments. However, it does not prohibit them if each of the following conditions is satisfied:

• The payment is not made to any government official in the following countries: the United States, Japan, Canada or countries that are members of the European Economic Community.

• The action to be facilitated by the payment must be of a clerical or ministerial nature.

• The payment must not be to obtain preferential treatment but rather to obtain action to which the Company is routinely entitled.

• Payments must be of a nominal amount. If such payments to any one official exceed $500 (or the equivalent) per year or $100 (or the equivalent) per transaction, approvals of the controller and the general counsel are necessary. Souvenirs or Christmas gifts with a value not in excess of $25 (or the equivalent) are not prohibited by this policy.

• The amount of such payments must be accurately recorded on the books and records of the local entity.

Each division of an MNL is responsible for adopting all procedures necessary to insure compliance with this policy.

Books and Records United States law requires that American corporations, including all subsidiaries, keep books, records, and accounts, which, in reasonable detail, accurately and fairly reflect all transactions. Corporations must also maintain a system of internal accounting controls sufficient to reasonably assure management control and accountability of all corporate assets and to permit the preparation of accurate financial statements. To comply with these requirements:

• Employees may not make any false, inaccurate, or incomplete entry in any book or record.

• No undisclosed or secret account, fund, or asset of the MNL may be established or maintained by or on behalf of the company in the United States or in any other country. All accounts, funds, or assets must be accurately accounted for on the MNL's books and records, and all relevant information made available to internal auditors and independent accountants.

• Any facilitating payments permitted by this policy must be accurately reported on the records of the entity making the payment. Facilitating payments may not be deducted for income tax purposes in the country where the payment is made unless unusual local circumstances require it. Because the United States Internal Revenue Code prohibits the flow through of any such deductions, a United States company must approve in advance the taking of local deductions.

273

• No employee will make any false or misleading statement or conceal any information from the internal auditing staff or any independent accounting firm.

Receiving Payments and Bribes

No employee may, directly or indirectly, accept any bribe, kickback, payment, or gift from any customer, supplier, or competitor of the MNL. This policy does not prohibit the acceptance of gifts of nominal value or casual entertainment appropriate in the particular environment.

Other Laws and Regulations

Employees are obligated to comply with the laws and regulations of those countries in which the MNL conducts business. In recent years some countries have enacted a number of new laws. Local laws and regulations are designed to:

• Preserve the environment in which people live.
• Improve the health and safety standards governing employees' working conditions.
• Prohibit discrimination in employment based on race, religion, sex, or national origin.
• Prohibit cooperation with international boycotts based on racial or religious discrimination.

Employees can never disregard these or other laws because they disagree with them or think that the best interests of the MNL would be served by violating them.

Reports to Government

Every MNL is required by American and foreign laws and regulations to prepare and file reports with local governments and agencies. Filing false or inaccurate reports may result in civil and, in some cases, criminal penalties imposed not only upon the MNL but also upon its directors, officers, and employees. Supervisory employees are responsible for assuring the accuracy of all reports prepared for filing with government units by employees under their supervision.

Trading on Inside Information

American law prohibits employees from purchasing or selling any securities of an MNL or any corporation doing business with it on the basis of so-called "inside information." "Inside information" is confidential information concerning important corporate affairs such as mergers, acquisitions, dividends, financial projections, or new products that might influence investors in trading securities. The law also prohibits giving such "inside information" to any family member, friend, or broker to profit from it by buying or selling securities.

Inside information may not be used by employees to directly or indirectly acquire any investment in real estate or other property in which the MNL has either an existing interest or the employee has reason to believe it may acquire an interest in the future.

Confidential Information

The nonpublic business information of an MNL should generally be considered confidential. Employees should never disclose nonpublic business information concerning the corporations with which the MNL conducts business to anyone, including family members and freinds. In addition, certain sensitive business information should not be disclosed to fellow employees unless their duties require that they have such information.

Assisting Other to Evade Local Laws

Employees must not engage in conduct, the likely purpose of which is to enable customers, suppliers, or their employees to evade local laws or regulations, particularly in the areas of taxation and foreign exchange.

Outside Associations and Activities

An MNL encourages its employees to actively participate in the civic, political, and similar activities that serve the public interest. Generally, however, employees so participating must not speak, or appear to speak, for the MNL but for themselves.

Conflicts of Interest and Devotion of Time and Ability to the MNL's Business

• Employees are expected to perform their duties during regular working hours and for whatever additional time may reasonably be required.

• Employment or personal business commitments outside regular hours of employment are prohibited if these would tend to impair an individual's ability to meet his or her job responsibilities.

• Employees are prohibited from taking a job with, or performing consulting services for, a competitor, supplier, or customer of the MNL. In rare cases this prohibition may conflict with local law, in which case local law will override this policy prohibition.

• Neither employees nor their spouses or minor children should hold investments in any privately held company doing business with the MNL.

• Employees may not do business with a company employing a close relative unless full disclosure is made and approval is obtained from their supervisor.

APPLICATION OF THE ACT TO SUBSIDIARIES
OUTSIDE THE UNITED STATES

The Foreign Corrupt Practices Act of 1977 requires publicly traded companies to "devise and maintain a system of internal accounting controls sufficient to provide reasonable assurances" that transactions are executed in accordance with management's authorization and are appropriately recorded and that access to assets is permitted only when authorized. Although it is clear that the provisions of Section 102 of the Act extend to a MNL's books, records, and accounting controls in the United States, it seems equally clear that Section 102 was not intended by Congress to have extraterritorial application so as to extend to a foreign subsidiary whose principal place of business is outside the United States.

Literally, Section 102 applies only to an "issuer," the MNL, and does not extend to its foreign subsidiaries. A comparison of Section 102 with Section 103's prohibition of certain payments by an "issuer" and with Section 104's prohibition of the same type of payments by "any domestic concern" (that is, any American citizen or resident and any corporation or other business having its principal place of business in the United States or organized under the laws of any state of the United States) and, further, by a subsidiary based in a foreign country, supports the conclusion that is not reached by Section 102. Finally, the Conference Report on the Act indicates that Congress decided not to extend the legislation to foreign subsidiaries whose principal place of business is outside the United States. The Conference Report explains why the House conferees rejected a House bill that applied to foreign corporations owned or controlled by American individuals or corporations in favor of a Senate bill that applied only to foreign corporations whose principal place of business was in the United States:

In receding to the Senate, the conferees recognized the inherent jurisdictional, enforcement, and diplomatic difficulties raised by the inclusion of foreign subsidiaries of U.S. companies in the direct prohibitions of the bill. However, the conferees intend to make clear that any issuer or domestic concern which engages in bribery of foreign officials indirectly through any other person or entity would itself be liable under the bill. The conferees recognized that such jurisdictional, enforcement, and diplomatic difficulties may not be present in the case of individuals who are U.S. citizens, nationals, or residents. Therefore, individuals other than those specifically covered by the bill (e.g., officers, directors, employees, agents, or stockholders acting on behalf of an issuer or domestic concern) will be liable when they act in relation to the affairs of any foreign subsidiary of an issuer or domestic concern if they are citizens, nationals, or residents of the United States. In addition, the conferees determined that foreign nationals or residents otherwise under the jurisdiction of the United States would be covered by the bill in circumstances where an issuer or domestic concern engaged in conduct proscribed by the bill.[1]

INTERNAL CONTROL—THE FOREIGN CORRUPT PRACTICES ACT OF 1977

The Foreign Corrupt Practices Act of 1977 requires publicly traded companies "to devise and maintain a system of internal accounting controls. . . ." Internal accounting controls are operative when these conditions are met:

- Transactions are properly authorized.
- All transactions are recorded in the books of accounts.
- The company's assets are safeguarded.

Following are the key provisions of the Act's accounting standards:

- Make and keep books, records, and accounts, which in reasonable detail accurately and fairly reflect the transactions and dispositions of the assets of the issuer;

[1] H.R. Conf. Report No. 95–831, 95th Cong.

• Devise and maintain a system of internal accounting controls sufficient to provide reasonable assurances that:

  (a) Transactions are executed in accordance with management's authorization;

  (b) Transactions are recorded as necessary (1) to permit preparation of financial statements in conformity with generally accepted accounting principles or any other criteria applicable to such statements, and (2) to maintain accountability for assets;

  (c) Access to assets is permitted only in accordance with management's general or specific authorization;

  (d) The recorded accountability for assets is compared with the existing assets at reasonable intervals and appropriate action is taken to reconcile any differences.

Under the Act, SEC registrants and controlling persons (i.e., any person who has the power to control the direction, management, and policies of a company) found to have willfully violated the accounting standards provisions would be subject to the general penalties contained under the Securities Exchange Act of 1934. These penalties include a fine of not more than $10,000 or imprisonment of not more than five years or both.

A typical MNL has internal accounting controls that meet the requirements of the Act. An MNL normally reports its position to the audit committee of the board of directors and outlines a plan to document evidence of the company's compliance with the Act's internal accounting control provisions. The plan is the coordinated effort of the controllers and internal audit offices, together with the MNL's independent certified public accountants.

As evidence of compliance, internal accounting controls throughout the Company have to be documented and codified:

General controls. From the board of directors to division operating levels, broad objectives and general ·controls should be outlined.

Specific Controls. Codification of bridging working papers on file in internal audit, and CPA files describing controls now in force in all major field locations and staff departments.

Internal Control Manual. A manual should be published by the MNL's internal audit department outlining minimum controls for the basic accounting transaction cycles.

Assurance. The internal audit department and its outside auditors monitor the accounting controls to assure the board of directors and senior management that the controls are operative.

INTERNAL ACCOUNTING CONTROL MANUAL

The key to conformance with the second part of the Foreign Corrupt Practices Act of 1977 is documentation of the internal accounting controls at work within the multinational company, its subsidiaries, branches, and affiliates. One means of accomplishing this is to have the multinational company publish an internal accounting control manual. The manual provides that individual locations, subsidiaries, branches, and affiliates must report to the controller of the multinational why their procedures deviate from the provisions of the internal control manual. The multinational thus states its basic principles of internal accounting control in the manual and at the same time has on file documentation that explains why individual subsidiaries, branches, or affiliates cannot comply with these provisions and what alternative measures must be taken.

The internal control manual is distributed throughout the multinational company, to all holders of its financial manual, to its internal auditors, and to selected members of its corporate staff. The purpose of the manual is to establish uniform guidelines, the minimum control measures, for internal accounting controls that apply throughout the multinational.

Responsibility for implementation obviously rests with local management, managing directors, and their controllers, who in turn are responsible for determining whether local procedures conform to the multinational's guidelines. Supplemental internal accounting controls to fill special environmental, operational, and procedural needs have to be developed and issued in writing by local management.

In some cases general control practices may not be justified because of cost or may not be applicable at certain facilities in certain countries. As provided for in the internal control manual, a local controller may obtain an exemption from the practices if he outlines the reason for his request and describes alternate controls to the division controller. The division controller forwards the request to the corporate controller who evaluates the request and approves or denies it in writing. The controller's decision is then filed in the internal accounting control manual of the local company. The preceding chapter described the company's general controls involving the environmental and leadership matters used in formulating and communicating consciousness of control, appropriate organizational structure, accountability for performance, and the basic requirement for adherence to appropriate standards of ethical behavior.

A multinational company has an organization plan with charts and a clear definition of authority for all levels of management.

A multinational has an information system with a chart of accounts with definitive explanation of the use of each account. It has procedure manuals encompassing accounting and control procedures. There are appropriate financial reporting packages, forecasting and operating strategic plans. There are also reports from internal audit including comments from line management on corrective action taken. Finally, there are reports from independent accountants, called management letters, describing weaknesses in control systems and including recommendations for action to be taken.

REPORTING DEFALCATIONS Sound internal control can only be effected when management at all levels continuously monitors compliance with established procedures. Monitoring takes place through management supervision, compliance tests, approval and control of changes in procedures, and reporting observations to the next highest level of management.

The company has a procedure for reporting all instances of proven, alleged, or strongly suspected fraudulent or dishonest acts committed by an employee acting alone or with others. This procedure requires that the director of internal audit be notified through division and group channels.

CONTENTS OF AN INTERNAL ACCOUNTING CONTROL MANUAL

The internal accounting control manual is used by the local management, subsidiary, branch, or affiliate of every multinational company. The managing director and his department heads must review existing procedures to determine whether they comply with the manual. Procedures are changed where feasible or exceptions are requested. Procedures planned for the future have to be tested for cost versus benefits against the requirements of the manual.

The internal accounting control manual provides a guide to the internal auditors of the multinational. Auditors schedule their audits so as to test compliance for each of the transaction cycles. The documentation of compliance takes the form of flow charts, also known as systems evaluation approach charts. These charts are reviewed to spot weaknesses and strengths in the controls, and particularly to determine whether controls comply with the requirements of the internal accounting control manual. Exceptions and weaknesses of control are reported in the internal audit reports and recommendations are made for corrective action. Managing directors of subsidiaries, branches, and affiliates must respond to these reports, indicating the corrective action they plan to take or alternative control measures they deem necessary because of cost-benefit considerations.

An internal accounting control manual has three basic elements:

1 *Authorization*

There must be a plan for authorizing transactions and a

description of the specific authorizations made and also a description of implied authorizations.

2 *Accounting*
The MNL's records must account for transactions as they are executed; they must be properly described, entered in appropriate books and accounts, and reflected in the appropriate accounting period; the actual amounts must be specified.

3 *Safeguarding*
There must be limited access to assets, books, records, and documents, and finally there must be a provision for periodically taking inventories of assets and material; the inventories must be compared to book balances and all adjustments should be explained.

Appendix A is an example of a comprehensive internal accounting control manual. The manual consists of a number of segments entitled *Transaction cycles* that represent basic transactions and functions performed by a typical multinational company. The following lists the transaction cycles described in Appendix A with subtitles.

- Revenue cycle—order entry, shipping and billing, sales returns, accounts receivables, credit and collection
- Expenditure cycle—purchasing, receiving, accounts payable, payroll
- Production cycle—manufacturing process, cost accounting, inventories—manufacturing, inventories—retailing
- Treasury cycle—cash and short-term investment property, plant, equipment, debt, equity
- Financial reporting process—bookkeeping records and books of accounts, generally accepted accounting principles, management control financial statements, annual report, and Form 10-K report to the SEC
- Computer controls—organization and operation, systems development and maintenance, hardware, access to EDP areas, input-output processing documentation files.

POSTSCRIPT TO THE FOREIGN CORRUPT PRACTICES ACT OF 1977

The Securities and Exchange Commission issued in April 1979 a release proposing rules that would require management and independent auditors to report on systems of internal accounting control.

Management would be required (for years ending after December 15, 1979) to show that, as of the end of the fiscal year, the systems of internal accounting control provided "reasonable assurance" that it had met the objectives specified in the Foreign Corrupt Practices Act of 1977. This representation would be required to appear in the annual report to shareholders and in Form 10-K. For years ending after December 15, 1980, the management representation and a report on the system by an independent auditor would be required, both covering the full year. To make the proposed management representation, companies would evaluate their systems using the following means:

• Evaluate the "overall control environment."
• Determine specific control objectives.
• Consider how specific control procedures, as well as individual environmental factors, contribute to achieving the specific control objectives.
• Monitor the control procedures to determine whether they are functioning as intended.
• Consider what costs and benefits might result from additional or alternative controls.

Management would be expected to document the action it took under each of these steps.

REASONABLE ASSURANCE The SEC's release maintains that "ongoing review and monitoring" of any internal accounting control system is necessary if management is to provide reasonable assurance that the objectives of controls are achieved.

With respect to years ending after December 15, 1980, the release suggests that if review procedures were so inadequate that existing weaknesses were not identified on a timely basis, one would presume that the system had not provided the requisite reasonable assurance throughout the period covered. This, it concludes, "would preclude an unqualified management opinion."

In support of its argument for ongoing review and monitoring, the release notes that errors may arise "as a result of human frailties," that systems may be "circumvented as a result of collusion or overridden by management," and that changed conditions may require changed procedures.

COST-BENEFIT FACTORS
The release indicates that the cost of a system of internal accounting control should not exceed the benefits it provides. The SEC's chief accountant has recently said, however, that management responsibilities are not limited to maintaining "controls directed to preparation of financial statements" or to "controlling only errors or irregularities that could be material to the financial statements." He indicated, therefore, that cost-benefit considerations should not be limited to amounts material to the statements.

The auditor's opinion would cover the reasonableness of management's representation regarding transactions and assets in amounts that would be material to a registrant's financial statements. The auditor would also be required to indicate whether representations made by management are considered consistent with the results of the evaluation made by management.

Although the Foreign Corrupt Practices Act requires registrants to devise and maintain a system of internal accounting controls that provides reasonable assurance that specified objectives are met, *the Act itself does not require management and independent auditors to review and report on systems.*

The concept of "reasonable assurance" means that the cost of controls must be balanced against its benefits. These judgments are necessarily subjective and must be based on management's assessments of the business risks involved, which will vary significantly from company to company. Users cannot gain an insight into the subjective nature of management's judgments from the reports contemplated, and may indeed perceive a higher degree of assurance from the management representation than is intended or warranted.

APPENDIX A

Internal Accounting Control Manual

SECTION	REVENUE CYCLE
SUBJECT	CONTENTS

The revenue cycle consists of transactions originating in the Marketing/Sales functions, and cover specifically:

- Order entry
- Shipping and billing
- Sales returns
- Accounts receivable activities
- Credit and collection

The controls in these areas cover transaction authorizations, accounting, and safeguarding of records and assets.

The Financial Manual of the MNL company contains policies and procedures pertaining to the revenue cycle as listed below.

ACCOUNTS RECEIVABLE

CREDIT AND COLLECTION

GOODS AND SERVICES ARE PROVIDED ON THE BASIS OF APPROPRIATE AUTHORIZATION.

- Customers are authorized and their orders accepted only in accordance with established local procedures.
- An approved customer master file is maintained (except for retail cash customers) and procedures for adding to, deleting from, or changing information on the master file are established.
- Procedures are required to obtain appropriate management approval for all nonroutine sales.

CUSTOMER ORDERS ARE PROPERLY ACCOUNTED FOR AND FOLLOW-UP PROCEDURES ARE ESTABLISHED.

- An order log or record is maintained covering all customer orders received and accepted.
- Procedures are established to ensure prompt delivery of orders.
- Each facility must establish a procedure to control back orders and partial shipments.
- Customer queries and complaints are followed up promptly by designated employees independent of the sales function. A log of such queries or complaints will be maintained and follow-up action indicated.

RECORDS AND OPERATING SYSTEMS ARE PROTECTED FROM MISUSE OR DESTRUCTION.

- Important records are kept in locked facilities.
- Access to records is restricted to authorized personnel.
- Important records are protected against physical hazards, (e.g. fireproof cabinets).

GOODS AND SERVICES ARE PROVIDED ON THE BASIS OF APPROPRIATE AUTHORIZATION.

- Shipping orders properly authorized by designated employees are required for all goods leaving company premises.

PRICES, TERMS, ALLOWANCES, DISCOUNTS, AND FREIGHT REQUIRE APPROPRIATE AUTHORIZATION.

- A master price list indicating approved selling prices, standard allowances, discount and shipping terms are maintained by all facilities.
- Each facility maintains a written procedure to be followed and approvals are required for deviation from established selling prices, standard allowances, discount and shipping terms.
- Periodic independent reviews by designated personnel are required to ascertain conformity with established procedures.

GOODS AND SERVICES MAY ONLY BE RECORDED AS SALES WHEN DELIVERED.

- Shipping order forms or bills of lading are prenumbered and the number sequence thereof must be controlled. (If these forms are computer generated the numbering may be made by the system. The number sequence must be controlled manually.)
- Sales invoices are prenumbered and the numerical sequence of these forms must be controlled. (If sales invoices are computer generated, the numbering may be made by the system; however, the number sequence must be controlled manually.)

- Credit memos for returned goods and allowances will be:
  - Prenumbered and accounted for
  - Supported by receiving reports for returned goods
  - Approved by a designated employee.
- The billing function must be independent of sales, shipping, and receiving.

INDIVIDUAL INVOICES ARE PREPARED ACCURATELY AND ON A TIMELY BASIS.

- Prenumbered sales invoices must be matched to related shipping documents to ensure billing of all goods shipped.
- Sales invoices will be independently checked as to terms, pricing allowances, and so on. If invoices are generated manually, the mathematical computations will be verified by a second employee.

RECORDS AND OPERATING SYSTEMS ARE PROTECTED FROM MISUSE OR DESTRUCTION.

- Important records are kept in locked storage facilities.
- Access to important records is restricted to authorized employees.
- All important records must be protected against physical hazards (e.g., fireproof cabinets, etc.).

REVENUE CYCLE RELATED ENTRIES AND ADJUSTMENTS REQUIRE PROPER AUTHORIZATION.

- The responsibility for approval of:

  Sales returns

  Credit memos

  Write-off of accounts and notes receivable

  must be assigned to specific employees. In facilities where these functions are handled by a number of employees, authorization of individuals is limited as to dollar amounts as specified by local management.
- Receiving reports for return of goods must be approved by designated employees.

SECTION	
	REVENUE CYCLE
SUBJECT	
	SALES RETURNS

ALL SALES TRANSACTIONS AND RELATED ACTIVITIES ARE PROPERLY RECORDED, CLASSIFIED, AND SUMMARIZED.

- Sales returns must be recorded in the same accounting period in which returns were received.

RECORDS AND OPERATING SYSTEMS ARE PROTECTED FROM MISUSE OR DESTRUCTION.

- Important records must be kept in locked storage facilities.
- Access to important records and forms is restricted to authorized persons.

SECTION	
	REVENUE CYCLE
SUBJECT	
	ACCOUNTS RECEIVABLE ACTIVITY

GOODS AND SERVICES MAY ONLY BE RECORDED AS SALES WHEN DELIVERED.

- A clear definition of sales must be communicated to all persons concerned. The sales cut-off procedure must be applied on a consistent basis.

ALL SALES TRANSACTIONS AND RELATED ACTIVITIES ARE PROPERLY RECORDED, CLASSIFIED, AND SUMMARIZED.

- Each facility will have a standard operating procedure to properly account for sales, discounts, allowances, freight, cost of goods sold, and related sales taxes.
- The subsidiary records for accounts receivable are reconciled on a monthly basis to General Ledger accounts.
- Customer statements will be mailed in industries or overseas facilities where this is customary. Procedures must be established to investigate and promptly clear differences reported by customers.
- Accounts receivable are aged monthly.
- Bad debt reserves are established and carried on the books in accordance with corporate policy.
- All journal vouchers and adjustment entries require approval of designated personnel.

292

- The journal voucher recording sales and related transactions is verified as to supporting documentation, account distribution, and mathematical accuracy by designated persons.
- Standard procedures are to be established by each facility to ensure that related receivables and payables are recorded within the same accounting period where shipments are made or services are rendered directly to customers by vendors.
- Cash receipts will be posted promptly to accounts receivables subsidiary records.
- Initial cash receipts recording will be compared to bank deposit slips and accounting entries by a person independent of the cashier and accounts receivable function.
- A cash receipts journal or register must be maintained.

RECORDS AND OPERATING SYSTEMS ARE PROTECTED FROM MISUSE OR DESTRUCTION.

- Subsidiary ledgers and other important records must be kept in locked storage facilities.
- Access to important records is restricted to authorized personnel.
- Subsidiary ledgers and other important records are protected against physical hazards (e.g. fireproof cabinets, etc.).

CREDIT TERMS ARE GRANTED ON THE BASIS OF APPROPRIATE AUTHORIZATION.

- A routine credit policy properly authorized by appropriate management will be maintained by each facility.
- Credit limits are to be established for all customers (except retail customers who do not maintain a revolving credit account).
- Approval of credit granted in excess of established limits must be documented.
- The responsibility for approval of credit for new customers must be assigned to specific employees.

EFFECTIVE COLLECTION PROCEDURES ARE ESTABLISHED.

- The responsibility to supervise the collection function must be assigned to a person independent of the sales function.
- Past due accounts must be followed up promptly. Collection letters will be standardized to reflect an increase in urgency as the receivable falls farther past due.
- Collection efforts will continue on accounts written off. These accounts and collections thereon will continue to be controlled, until such time when all collection efforts have been exhausted.
- Each facility will implement a procedure to investigate and follow up promptly on customer credit balances.

CASH RECEIPTS ARE ADEQUATELY PROTECTED FROM THEFT OR MISAPPROPRIATION.

- Cash receipts must be controlled by a person independent of the receivable function. Procedures are to be established to ensure that cash receipts are deposited promptly.
- Checks received are stamped immediately with restrictive endorsements and listed at the same time.
- Cash funds on hand will be counted periodically on a surprise basis by designated persons.

RECORDS, OPERATING SYSTEMS, PROCESSING AREAS, AND PHYSICAL ASSETS ARE PROTECTED FROM MISUSE OR DESTRUCTION.

- Subsidiary ledgers and other important records must be kept in locked storage facilities.
- Access to records, ledgers, and facilities is restricted to authorized persons only.
- All important records must be protected against physical hazards (e.g. fireproof cabinets, etc.).

294

THE EXPENDITURE CYCLE COVERS TRANSACTIONS ORIGINATING IN THE FOLLOWING FUNCTIONS:

- Purchasing
- Receiving
- Accounts Payable
- Payroll

The controls in these areas are delineated as to authorization, accounting and safeguarding of records.

The MNL Company has issued specific policies and operating procedures in these areas as listed below:

PURCHASING

	CORPORATE PURCHASING MANUAL SECTION
1. General Purchasing Policy	3.100
2. Corporate Purchasing Overall Responsibility	3.101
3. Purchasing Authority Assignment of Responsibility to Commit Company Funds for Acquisition of Materials and Services	3.102
4. Approval of Significant Purchases Specifying Purchasing Activities Requiring General Manager's Approval	3.103
5. Corporate Purchase Agreements Determining Conditions Under Which Common Parts, Items, Materials, and Services must be acquired under National Agreements	3.104
6. Supplier Relations Outlining Procedure for Supplier Relations	3.105

THE PURCHASING OF GOODS AND SERVICES IS INITIATED ONLY ON THE BASIS OF APPROPRIATE AUTHORIZATION.

- The purchasing activities of each facility are to be centralized in one department.
- Purchase orders are prepared and issued only on the basis of purchase requisitions or production schedules approved by appropriate management levels.
- Purchase orders are required for all purchases (except petty cash items).
- Purchase orders must clearly indicate payment terms, delivery schedules, quantities, unit prices, and total commitment.
- Competitive bids are required for purchases of materials, supplies, fixed assets, and services in excess of amounts to be specified by each facility's management.
- Written explanations are required in instances when bids were not requested, but would have been required, or where the purchase was made from other than the lowest bidder.
- A list of approved vendors is to be maintained covering all major materials purchased.
- Purchases made for employees are to be cleared in the regular manner through the purchasing, receiving, and accounting functions.
- Purchasing agents (buyers) are to be rotated in their assignments on a periodic basis.

PURCHASE COMMITMENTS MUST BE PROPERLY ACCOUNTED FOR.

- Purchase orders must be prenumbered and sequentially accounted for. Computer generated purchase orders may be sequentially numbered by an EDP system, but must be sequentially accounted for on a manual basis.
- Persons independent of the Purchasing Department will review prices paid for items on a periodic basis to determine that such prices are not in excess of current market prices.
- There must be an adequate record and prompt follow-up of open purchase orders and purchase commitments outstanding.
- Purchase orders outstanding must be clearly marked as to partial shipments received, and quantities still outstanding.
- Purchases made for employees are to be recorded as receivables due from employees.

RECORDS AND OPERATING SYSTEMS ARE PROTECTED FROM MISUSE OR DESTRUCTION.

- Important records and blank forms are kept in locked storage facilities.
- Access to important records and blank forms is restricted to authorized employees.

INCOMING GOODS WILL PASS THROUGH A CENTRAL RECEIVING POINT.

- Incoming merchandise, materials, and supplies may only be received by designated employees independent of the purchasing and accounts payable functions.

RECEIPT OF MERCHANDISE, MATERIALS, AND SUPPLIES ARE PROPERLY ACCOUNTED FOR.

- Written receiving reports are issued on all merchandise, materials, and supplies received.
  (Retail stores receiving resale merchandise directly from vendors may indicate receipt on either delivery tickets or vendor invoices, which are then forwarded for processing to the accounts payable function.)
- Receiving reports are prenumbered, are sequentially controlled, and are signed and dated by designated employees.
- A copy of the receiving report (or other permanent record of receipts, such as listings) will be kept at the receiving department in sequential order.
- Partial deliveries are clearly marked on the receiving reports.
- Merchandise, materials and supplies will be inspected for condition, and counted, weighed, or measured in the receiving department.
- Clear procedures are to be established to deal with overshipments by vendors.

DISBURSEMENTS ARE MADE BY APPROPRIATE PERSONNEL ONLY FOR AUTHORIZED EXPENDITURES.

- Check signers are designated by appropriate management levels.
- Checks, drafts, or bank transfer vouchers are prepared only on the basis of appropriate documentation.
- All items for payment require approval by persons independent of (1) the purchasing department and (2) persons requesting the specific expenditure.

AMOUNTS DUE TO VENDORS AND OTHERS FOR GOODS AND SERVICES RECEIVED ARE ACCURATELY DETERMINED AND PROMPTLY RECORDED.

- Control over prenumbered receiving reports (or other appropriate record of receipts) is exercised to ascertain that receipt of goods and services is recognized within the proper accounting period.
- A record of open purchase orders and commitments is maintained.
- All invoices are forwarded directly by the mail opener to the persons processing invoices for payment. Controls over invoices (accounts payable vouchers) are established immediately upon receipt.
- Duplicate invoices are to be clearly marked immediately upon receipt so as to prevent duplicate processing.
- The processing of items for payment include the following steps:
  (a) Verification of terms, prices, and quantities on invoices against purchase orders.
  (b) Verification of items and quantities on invoices against receiving reports obtained directly from the receiving department.
  (c) Mathematical verification of footings, extensions and discounts.
  (d) Verification of account distribution.
  (e) Check of freight bills against purchase orders, sales invoices, and so on.
  (f) Verification of invoices that do not involve materials or supplies (e.g., fees, rentals, power and light, taxes, travel, etc.) for approval by designated persons such as department heads.
  (g) A final approval for payment.
  (h) Notation on the vouchers that the above checks and approvals were made.

- Where vendor statements are received, procedures must be established to ensure prompt reconciliation, and follow-up of discrepancies.
- The Subsidiary Ledger for Accounts Payable is maintained on a current basis and reconciled with the General Ledger balances monthly.
- Unmatched purchase orders, receiving reports and vendor invoices must be investigated and cleared promptly.
- Procedures are to be installed to ascertain that return purchases are controlled and credit obtained from vendors in due time.
- Related receivables and payables are recorded within the same accounting period when shipments are made or services are rendered directly to customers by vendors.
- Adequate procedures are established covering settlement of disputes with vendors and handling partial shipments in order to avoid duplicate payment.

CASH DISBURSEMENTS ARE RECORDED BASED UPON RECOGNIZED LIABILITIES.

- All checks, drafts, or bank transfer voucher forms must be prenumbered and accounted for.
- Checks, drafts, or bank transfer vouchers can only be issued on the basis of properly approved vouchers (or check requests) by persons who do not approve the vouchers (or check requests).
- The persons who manually sign checks (at least one person where dual signatures are required) or control the use of facsimile signature plates will scrutinize supporting documentation at the time of signing.
- The persons who manually sign checks or control the use of the facsimile plates should be independent of:
  (a) The purchasing department.
  (b) Others requesting specific expenditure.
  (c) Persons approving vouchers.
  (d) Persons preparing the voucher payable register or reconciling open vouchers with the general ledger control.
  (e) Persons preparing checks.
  (f) Persons preparing the cash disbursement journals.
- If the persons who manually sign checks or control the use of the facsimile signature plates are not independent of the items listed above, the following will be implemented: (1) both signers scrutinize the supporting documentation or (2) if one signer is independent of the functions listed above he will scrutinize the supporting documentation.

- Spoiled checks, drafts, or bank transfer vouchers are to be mutilated to prevent reuse and kept on file for subsequent inspection. The practice of drawing checks or drafts to "cash" or "bearer" should be avoided wherever possible.
- Special procedures will be established (e.g. manual checks, drafts, or bank transfer vouchers) for certain types of unusual payments, such as large amounts, payroll checks, adjustment checks, etc.
- Vouchers and supporting papers will be effectively canceled upon payment by the person who will manually sign the check or control the use of the facsimile signature plate or by persons who do not prepare checks or approve vouchers for payment.
- Post office postage meter receipts will be checked to meter readings and cash disbursements by designated employees.
- Adequate procedures will be established to ensure that there is substantiation evidence for travel and entertainment expense as required by local, divisional, and corporate policies and local statutory regulations.

PURCHASES OF GOODS AND SERVICES AND CASH DISBURSEMENTS ARE PROPERLY RECORDED, CLASSIFIED, AND SUMMARIZED.

- A standard chart of accounts is in use at each facility. Adequate operating procedures are in use instructing employees clearly and in detail.
- Clear procedures will be established for accounting entries and adjustments covering transactions within the expenditure cycle, such as:
  (a) Use of standard journal entries.
  (b) Use of prenumbered forms.
  (c) Review and approval of account coding and distribution.
  (d) Utilization of clearing accounts.
  (e) Monthly reconciliation of subsidiary accounts to General Ledger balances.
- Procedures are to be established for developing, summarizing, and reporting VAT and other tax information.
- A voucher register or purchase journal is to be maintained as well as a cash disbursement journal or register.

RECORDS AND UNUSED DOCUMENTS ARE PROTECTED FROM THEFT, MISUSE, DESTRUCTION, OR MISAPPROPRIATION.

- Important records are to be stored in areas that are locked.
- Access to offices, records, and critical forms is restricted to authorized personnel only.
- The supply of unused checks, drafts, or bank transfer forms will be adequately safeguarded and will be under the custody of persons who have no access to facsimile signature plates or do not operate the facsimile signature machine.
- Checks will be mailed without allowing them to return to persons who prepare checks or approve vouchers for payment.
- The signing of blank drafts or blank transfer forms is prohibited.
- If a protectograph is available it will be useful before or simultaneously with the signature plate.
- Where a check signing machine is used care will be exercised to properly safeguard the facsimile signature plates. If the custodian of the plates is not the machine operator, the custodian will determine that only authorized checks have been signed (e.g., locked in counting device on the signing machine).

PAYMENTS ARE MADE TO AUTHORIZED EMPLOYEES FOR ACTUAL WORK PERFORMED.

- Written authorizations from responsible persons outside the payroll department are required for:
  - (a) Names added to, or deleted from, payrolls and other changes.
  - (b) Individual wage or salary rate changes, overtime, shift or department changes.
  - (c) Time cards or other documents of time worked, where such records are maintained as basis for payroll preparation.
- Payroll will be subject to a review and final approval by responsible persons outside the payroll department such as department heads, foremen, controller, and so on.
- Signed W4 forms or similar documents in foreign operations will be the basis for withholding taxes and social security deductions.
- A separate personnel department will maintain complete personnel records including wage and salary data.

EXECUTIVE PERQUISITES REQUIRE PROPER AUTHORIZATION.

- Perquisites (e.g., use of company airplanes, automobiles, etc.) require appropriate management approval.
- Significant other perquisites for individuals require appropriate management approval.

ENTRIES AND ADJUSTMENTS FOR PAYROLLS REQUIRE PROPER AUTHORIZATION.

- Approval of designated management personnel is required for garnishments, termination payments, correction to gross or net pay, special payments, and so on.

LABOR USED IS ACCURATELY DETERMINED AND PROMPTLY RECORDED IN THE PROPER ACCOUNTING PERIOD.

- Time cards, or other records indicating attendance, should be used whenever practical as the basis for preparing or checking wage payrolls and attendance must be reconciled to actual hours worked.
- When employees are paid on the basis of output, payments based on labor tickets or other output records must be reconciled with production records.
- Compensation rates must be compared periodically to rate authorizations (union contracts, personnel records, etc.)
- The persons who perform the following functions must be independent of each other:
  (a) Approve hours worked.
  (b) Prepare the payrolls
  (c) Distribute the pay
  (d) Maintain custody of unclaimed wages
  (e) Manually sign the payroll checks or control the use of the facsimile signature plate
  (f) Operate the facsimile signature machine
  (g) Reconcile payroll bank accounts.
- The details and arithmetic of the payroll preparation will be rechecked as part of the routine of preparation.
- Payroll taxes and social security withholdings will be reported and accounted for in separate liability accounts and paid to the authorities within the established time limits.
- Cutoff procedures will be established to ensure that payrolls are accrued in the proper accounting period.
- Deposits to imprest payroll bank accounts must be compared to net payroll amounts.

303

CASH DISBURSEMENTS FOR PAYROLLS ARE PROPERLY
RECORDED, CLASSIFIED, AND SUMMARIZED.

- Standard journal vouchers will be used to record payroll transactions.
- Standard journal vouchers require approval of designated management personnel and must be reviewed as to account coding
and distribution.
- Clearing accounts for payroll transactions will be established and
reconciled periodically.
- Imprest payroll bank accounts will be used for payroll purposes.
- A payroll register or journal will be maintained.

RECORDS AND UNUSED DOCUMENTS ARE PROTECTED FROM
THEFTS, MISUSE, DESTRUCTION, OR MISAPPROPRIATION.

- If payments are made in currency:
  (a) An independent pay agent (such as an armored car service)
  should be used wherever possible.
  (b) The currency will be placed in pay envelopes by employees
  who do not prepare the payrolls or approve hours worked.
  (c) Receipts will be obtained.
- Persons distributing the pay will be rotated from time to time.
- The following applies to separate payroll bank accounts:
  (a) All checks will be prenumbered and accounted for.
  (b) The supply of unused checks will be adequately safeguarded
  and under the custody of persons who do not sign checks
  manually, control use of facsimile signature plates, or operate
  the facsimile signature machine.
  (c) Spoiled checks will be mutilated to prevent reuse and kept on
  file for subsequent inspection.
  (d) Controls over the use of the facsimile signature plates will be
  adequate where a check-signing machine is used.
  (e) The signing of checks in advance of their being completely
  filled out is prohibited.
  (f) A limitation will be established on the amount for which
  checks can be drawn.
  (g) A check protector should be used wherever possible.
- Facsimile signature plates must be locked in a safe place when
not in use.
- Procedures must be established to control unclaimed wages.

THE PRODUCTION CYCLE CONSISTS OF THE MANUFACTURING PROCESS, COST ACCOUNTING, AND INVENTORIES

The MNL Company has issued a number of policies and procedures pertaining to the production cycle as listed below:

PRODUCTS ARE PRODUCED ONLY UPON PROPER AUTHORIZATION.

- Material requisitions must be used to obtain materials from store-rooms.
- Transfer forms or movement tickets will be used for movement of goods from one department to another or to finished goods.
- The production plan defining which products, how many, and when they are to be manufactured will be authorized in accordance with local and division management objectives.
- Individual production schedules or job orders require approval by designated personnel.

PRODUCTION AND OTHER ECONOMIC ACTIVITIES ARE PROPERLY CLASSIFIED, SUMMARIZED, AND ACCUMULATED.

- Journal entries or adjustments covering production accounting are approved by designated employees.
- Approval procedures must be established for adjustments to perpetual records, accounting records, operating plans, standard costs, bills of materials, and so on.
- Bills of material will be kept up-to-date.
- Manufacturing route sheets will be kept up-to-date.
- Manufacturing performance must be measured by:
  (a) Work standards or time measured standards.
  (b) Material usage
  (c) Down-time
  (d) Idle-time
  (e) Production efficiency
  (f) Lead time planning
  (g) Other criteria.
- Procedures must be established to properly account for scrap, repair, and rework.
- Each manufacturing facility will establish cutoff procedures for production and transfers to finished goods.
- Entries to record production and transfer to finished goods must be summarized for each accounting period.

RECORDS ARE PROTECTED FROM THEFT, MISUSE, AND DESTRUCTION.

- Production records, bills of material, and associated accounting records are protected from unauthorized use, theft, fire, and so on.
- Access to plants, offices, and other facilities is restricted to authorized personnel only.

THE COST SYSTEM ACCURATELY DETERMINES AND
PROPERLY SUMMARIZES AND REPORTS PRODUCTION AND
INVENTORY COSTS.

- A full absorption standard cost system or other cost systems as
  approved by Division and corporate management will be maintained as provided in the Company's financial accounting system.
- If a standard cost system is used, the following will apply:
  (a) The cost system will be periodically reviewed and evaluated
      to prevent defects in principle or application. (Symptoms of
      serious defects are significant inventory discrepancies, large
      or erratic manufacturing variances, erratic fluctuations in unit
      cost or excessive standards revaluations).
  (b) Standards will be sufficiently detailed to identify problems by
      operation, part number, machine class, and so on to permit
      appropriate corrective action.
  (c) Standards will be reviewed annually and revised where ap-
      propriate, such as significant changes in manufacturing meth-
      ods or prices.
  (d) Variances from standards are investigated and reviewed and
      properly reported monthly.
- Procedures are established to properly classify production costs
  (direct and indirect labor, material, overhead, etc.)
- The cost accounting system must provide for the accumulation of
  inventoriable costs on the following basis:
  (a) Production reports or material requisitions used to record raw
      materials put into production.
  (b) Production reports used to accumulate direct labor hours.
  (c) Direct labor hours reconciled to payroll records of actual
      hours paid.
  (d) Overhead applied at predetermined rates.

ACCOUNTING ENTRIES AND ADJUSTMENTS ARE ACCURATELY
DETERMINED AND PROPERLY SUMMARIZED, CLASSIFIED, AND
REPORTED.

- Each facility maintains a standard chart of accounts, and a procedures manual containing adequate details and clear instructions
  with regard to the journalization of transactions.
- Standard journal entries will be used. These entries are approved
  by designated employees and the accounting distribution and
  coding is reviewed.
- Entries to summarize cost accounting data are prepared at least
  monthly.

RECORDS ARE PROTECTED FROM THEFT, MISUSE, AND DESTRUCTION.
- Important records are kept in locked storage facilities and are protected against physical hazards wherever practical (use of fireproof or fire retardant cabinets, etc.).

MOVEMENT OR TRANSFER OF INVENTORIES OCCUR ONLY UPON PROPER AUTHORIZATION.
- Transfer of inventory to other locations requires approval of appropriate management personnel.
- Inventory levels are approved by appropriate management personnel.

THE INVENTORY IS ACCURATELY DETERMINED AND PROPERLY SUMMARIZED, CLASSIFIED, AND REPORTED.
- Each facility will maintain General Ledger control of inventory values.
- A perpetual inventory system (including quantities, value, maximum and minimum stock) will be in use for all major classes of inventory.
- Subsidiary records will be agreed to general ledger control balances periodically.
- Adequate records will be maintained for:
  (a) Consignment -out materials in hands of supplies and processors, materials or merchandise in warehouses, and so on.
  (b) Consignment -in merchandise on loan, and so on.
- Storekeepers will compare quantities received against receiving reports, production reports, and so on.
- Material can only be released from storerooms on the basis of approved and prenumbered requisitions or shipping orders.
- Stores personnel are required to report on obsolete, unusable, slow-moving or overstocked items on a systematic or at least annual basis.

- Disposal of obsolete, unusable, or deteriorated stock will be approved by a responsible official in accordance with company policy.
- Inventory costs are reviewed periodically.

PERIODIC VERIFICATION AND DETERMINATION OF INVENTORY QUANTITIES ARE UNDERTAKEN.

- All inventory classes on hand (including consignment inventory) will be physically counted:
  (a) At the end of the fiscal year, or
  (b) Periodically during the year, or
  (c) On a cycle count basis.
- Inventories that are on consignments-out, in hands of suppliers and processors or stored in public warehouses will be physically counted at the end of the fiscal year or confirmed with consignees or other holding agents during the fiscal year if not physically counted at that time.
- Detailed inventory records will be adjusted to reflect the results of the physical inventory counts.
- Procedures for physical counts will provide for:
  (a) Adequate written instructions.
  (b) Adequate supervision.
  (c) Clear identification or marking of such items as damaged and obsolete inventory, scrap, consigned goods, merchandise held for repairs, and so on.
  (d) Use of prenumbered tags that are accounted for.
  (e) Counting of the items and access to the tags only by employees who are not responsible for custody of the particular items.
  (f) Rechecking of counts and descriptions (dual counts) where perpetual records are not maintained or where variations from the perpetual records are significant.
  (g) Proper recognition and recording of cutoffs of production, shipments, receipts, in-transit items between Company plants, and so on.
  (h) Careful investigation of significant overages and shortages.
  (i) Prompt adjustments of records of inventory discrepancies after approval by a responsible official other than stores' personnel.
- Each facility will have a policy for valuation of inventory based on generally accepted accounting principles and covering such matters as:

309

(a) Determining and valuing obsolete, slow-moving, damaged and overstocked goods.

(b) Determination and treatment of estimated shrinkages.

(c) Determination and use of market values and

(d) Treatment of variances.

INVENTORIES ARE PROTECTED FROM UNAUTHORIZED USE OR REMOVAL AND AGAINST PHYSICAL DETERIORATION.

- Responsibilities for custody and protection of various classes of inventory are assigned to specific storekeepers.
- Goods will be adequately safeguarded against theft by keeping inventory in locked buildings, rooms, or cages, access to which is granted only to authorized personnel.
- Inventories will be adequately protected against physical deterioration.
- Separate areas will be maintained for receiving, storekeeping, and shipping functions.
- The movement of inventory will be subject to verification by the area assuming responsibility for it.

RECORDS ARE TO BE PROTECTED FROM THEFT, MISUSE, AND DESTRUCTION.

- Inventory records must be stored in locked facilities.
- Access to records is restricted to authorized personnel.

MOVEMENT OR TRANSFERS OF INVENTORIES OCCUR ONLY UNDER PROPER AUTHORIZATION.

- Transfers of inventory to marketing locations requires approval of appropriate management personnel.
- Inventory levels for each store are approved by appropriate management personnel.

THE INVENTORY IS ACCURATELY DETERMINED AND PROPERLY SUMMARIZED, CLASSIFIED, AND REPORTED.

- Each facility will maintain General Ledger control of inventory values by categories.
- A perpetual inventory system (including quantities, value, freight, and duty) will be in use for all F248 inventory categories.
- Subsidiary records (F246) will be agreed to General Ledger control balances periodically.
- Consignment inventory carried at store levels will be controlled and reporting procedures established to account for sales and cost of sales of this inventory category.
- Retail store personnel will compare quantities received against shipping documents.
- F246 will be reconciled to store records on a monthly basis.
- Retail store personnel are required to report on obsolete, unusable, slow-moving or overstocked items on a systematic basis.
- Disposal of obsolete, unusable, or deteriorated stock is the responsibility of location management and will be approved by a responsible official in accordance with company policy.
- Cost of sales percentages for general (retail value) merchandise will be reviewed at least annually and revised appropriately to reflect actual cost in inventory.
- Freight and duty percentages will be reviewed at least annually and revised as appropriate.

PERIODIC VERIFICATION AND DETERMINATION OF INVENTORY QUANTITIES ARE UNDERTAKEN.

- All inventory classes on hand (including consignments-in, etc.) will be physically counted:
  (a) At the end of the fiscal year, or
  (b) Periodically during the year, or
  (c) On a cycle count basis.
- Detailed inventory records will be adjusted to reflect the results of the physical inventory counts.
- Procedures for physical counts will provide for:
  (a) Adequate written instructions.
  (b) Adequate supervision.
  (c) Clear identification or marking of such items as damaged and obsolete inventory, consigned goods, merchandise held for repairs, and so on.
  (d) Use of prenumbered tags which are accounted for.

311

(e) Rechecking of counts and descriptions (dual counts) where perpetual records are not maintained and where variations from the perpetual records are significant.

(f) Proper recognition and recording of cutoffs of shipments, receipts, in-transit items between stores, and so on.

(g) Careful investigation of overages and shortages.

(h) Prompt adjustment of records for inventory discrepancies after approval by a responsible official other than the store's personnel.

- Each facility will have a policy for valuation of inventory based on generally accepted accounting principles and covering such matters as:

  (a) Determining and valuing obsolete, slow-moving, damaged, and overstocked goods.

  (b) Determination and treatment of estimated shrinkages.

  (c) Determination and use of market values; and determination of freight and duty contents.

- Goods will be adequately safeguarded against theft by keeping inventory in locked buildings, rooms, or cages, access to which is granted only to authorized personnel.

- Inventories will be adequately protected against physical deterioration.

RECORDS ARE TO BE PROTECTED FROM THEFT, MISUSE, AND DESTRUCTION.

- Inventory records must be stored in locked facilities.
- Access to records is restricted to authorized personnel.

SECTION	
	TREASURY CYCLE
SUBJECT	
	CONTENTS

SUBJECT TITLE	SECTION	SUBJECT
Cash and Short-Term Investments	VI	2
Property, Plant and Equipment	VI	3
Debt	VI	4
Equity	VI	5

SECTION	
	TREASURY CYCLE
SUBJECT	
	CASH AND SHORT-TERM INVESTMENTS

BANK ACCOUNTS AND CHECK SIGNERS ARE PROPERLY AUTHORIZED.

- All bank accounts are authorized by the Treasury Office or Financial Coordinator. Complete up-to-date copies of authorization are to be maintained.
- Signature authorization cards at the bank and other approval locations have to be up-to-date and purged of terminated or transferred employees.

CASH FUNDS AND FUND CUSTODIANS ARE PROPERLY AUTHORIZED.

- All cash funds will be operated on an imprest basis.
- The responsibility for each fund will be vested in only one person.
- A custodial receipt is to be obtained from the custodian upon appointment and at time of transfer to another employee.

SHORT-TERM INVESTMENT TRANSACTIONS ARE ONLY MADE ON THE BASIS OF APPROPRIATE AUTHORIZATION.

- Short-term investment transactions are authorized by the appropriate level of management and require the Corporate Treasurer's Office approval in all instances.
- A policy must be established for short-term investments covering such items as:
  (a) Type of investments
  (b) Quality (e.g. ratings)
  (c) Issues, and
  (d) Diversification.

ENTRIES AND ADJUSTMENTS TO CASH BALANCES AND SHORT-TERM INVESTMENTS ARE MADE ON THE BASIS OF APPROPRIATE AUTHORIZATON.

- All journal entries and adjustment entries to cash balances and short-term investments must be approved by designated employees.
- The transfer of funds between depositories will be approved by designated management personnel.

ALL BANK ACCOUNTS ARE RECONCILED PROMPTLY.

- Only persons who have no cash receipts or disbursements functions can be designated to reconcile the general, payroll, and any other bank or draft account on a monthly basis.
- Reconciliations have to be performed properly, that is, reconciled from bank statement balances to book balances.
  The reconciliation procedures for all bank accounts include:
  (a) The receipt of bank statements and canceled checks (or drafts) unopened by the bank reconciler.
  (b) Comparison of canceled checks (drafts) with the cash disbursements journal as to number, date, payee, and amount.
  (c) Examination of canceled checks (drafts) or authorized signatures.
  (d) Examination of canceled checks (drafts) for irregular endorsements.
  (e) Examination of canceled checks (drafts) for alterations.
  (f) Comparison of dates and amounts of daily deposits as shown on the bank statements with the cash receipts journal.
  (g) Review of completed bank reconciliations by a responsible official.
- Checks or drafts outstanding for a considerable period of time have to be investigated periodically.
- Reconciling items have to be cleared promptly.

CASH FUND DISBURSEMENTS ARE MADE UPON PROPERLY AUTHORIZED DOCUMENTATION.

- Disbursement procedure will include maximum amount for individual disbursements from each fund.
- The fund disbursements will be evidenced by supporting data properly approved.
- Replenishments will be approved by persons other than custodians upon adequate inspection of supporting data.
- Supporting data will be effectively canceled at the time of fund reimbursements to preclude their reuse.

- Check cashing for accommodation should generally be discouraged. Department or local management may, however, authorize check cashing when local circumstances require. Such checks will be presented promptly to a bank for credit.
- Funds will be checked at reasonable intervals by surprise counts made by designated persons.

SHORT-TERM INVESTMENT TRANSACTIONS ARE PROPERLY RECORDED, CLASSIFIED, AND SUMMARIZED.

- Responsibilities will be established for the preparation of entries to record investment transactions, income, and market valuations.
- Journal entries for investment transactions will be prepared on the basis of proper documentation (e.g. broker advice).
- The securities register will be:
  (a) Maintained in sufficient detail to afford a ready check on all essential data of securities at all times including the prompt receipt of income.
  (b) Kept by persons independent of those having access to the securities.
  (c) Reconciled to the General Ledger periodically.
- The income will be accrued on the basis of the investment register.
- The income received will be compared to amounts accrued. Dividends received will be verified to independent sources.
- The valuation of short-term investment will be made at the lower of cost or market, with market values based on independent sources.

CASH BALANCES AND SECURITIES ARE PROTECTED FROM MISAPPROPRIATIONS.

- Supply of blank check or draft forms have to be maintained in a secured area.
- Control must be exercised over distribution of blank check or draft forms.
- Control will be maintained over storage and use of facsimile signature plates.
- Access to cash funds is restricted to designated custodians.
- Cash must be kept in locked containers and stored securely overnight.
- Registered securities will be made out in the name of the Company or endorsed thereto.
- Securities will be kept in a safe deposit box or custodianship account at a bank or otherwise physically safeguarded.

- If a lock combination (s), key (s), and/or authorized signature (s) are required to gain access to locked up securities, the lock combination (s), lock, and/or authorized signatory (ies) will be changed whenever an authorized employee leaves his job position.

RECORDS ARE PROTECTED FROM THEFT, MISUSE, DISTRIBUTION, OR MISAPPROPRIATION.

- Important records are kept in storage facilities that are locked.
- Access to offices, file cabinets, or storage areas will be restricted to authorized personnel only.

PROPERTY, PLANT, AND EQUIPMENT TRANSACTIONS ARE MADE ON THE BASIS OF APPROPRIATE AUTHORIZATION.

- A form policy of authorization will be in effect and carried out by designated persons covering:
  (a) Additions or replacements.
  (b) Retirements
  (c) Disposals
  (d) Expenditures in excess of original authorizations.
- A clear policy differentiates types of capital expenditure from maintenance and repairs.
- A policy will be in effect specifying depreciation, amortization, capitalization, salvage, and disposition of idle assets.

ENTRIES AND ADJUSTMENTS TO PROPERTY, PLANT, AND EQUIPMENT AND RELATED BALANCES ARE MADE ON THE BASIS OF APPROPRIATE AUTHORIZATION.

- All journal entries and adjustments to General Ledger balances, subsidiary records or master files require approval of designated personnel.

PROPERTY, PLANT, AND EQUIPMENT TRANSACTIONS AND RELATED EXPENSES ARE PROPERLY RECORDED, CLASSIFIED, AND SUMMARIZED.

- General ledger balances will be supported by detailed fixed asset records, which will be agreed with the general ledger balances at least annually.
- Subsidiary records will contain sufficient information to physically identify specific assets, indicate original cost, and reflect accumulated depreciation. Fully depreciated assets that are still in use will also be identified in detailed records.
- Assets will be properly tagged.
- Expenditures will be accumulated for each authorized project.
- Post-completion audits will be made on capital appropriation projects as required by corporate policy.
- Depreciation rates will be reviewed periodically for adequacy in view of excessive use, unforeseen obsolescence, and so on, and for excessive provisions in light of experience.
- An estimated salvage value will be indicated on all retirement authorizations and followed up to subsequent realization.
- Journal entries for property, plant, and equipment transactions, including depreciation, are prepared on the basis of proper documentation.
- A period to period comparison of depreciation and amortization will be made to determine unusual variations.
- A complete physical inventory of fixed assets will be taken at least every three years.

PROPERTY, PLANT, AND EQUIPMENT IS PROTECTED FROM UNAUTHORIZED USE OR REMOVAL, AND AGAINST PHYSICAL DETERIORATION OR DESTRUCTION.

- Custodians of fixed assets are required to report to the accounting department any changes in the status of property (i.e., transfers between locations, sales, scrapping, obsolescence, excess, etc.) and the accounting records will be adjusted promptly for these changes.
- The responsibility for the determination of adequate insurance coverage will be assigned to a specific management employee.
- Access to offices, plants, and so on is restricted to authorized personnel.

DEBT TRANSACTIONS ARE MADE ON THE BAIS OF APPROPRIATE AUTHORIZATION.

- The authority and responsibility for debt financing is vested with the corporate Treasurer's Office.
- Policies are established for short-term borrowings covering such matters as:
  (a) Types of borrowings, (b) lenders, and (c) terms.
- Procedures are in effect to ensure that proposed debt agreements or borrowings are permitted within established restrictions of existing debt arrangements.

ENTRIES AND ADJUSTMENTS TO DEBT AND RELATED BALANCES ARE MADE ONLY ON THE BASIS OF APPROPRIATE AUTHORIZATION.

- Procedures are in effect covering discount amortization and interest accruals.
- All related journal entries and adjustments require approval of designated employees.

DEBT TRANSACTIONS AND RELATED EXPENSES ARE PROPERLY RECORDED, CLASSIFIED, AND SUMMARIZED.

- Detailed registers for notes payable and other debt instruments will be maintained by employees who are not authorized to sign checks or debt instruments.
- The registers will be agreed to the general ledger balances periodically.
- Redeemed notes, bonds, interest coupons, and so on will be effectively mutilated and are maintained in the Company's files.
- Responsibility will be established for preparation of entries to record debt transactions and related expenses.
- All journal entries for debt transactions are prepared on the basis of proper documentation.
- The accrual of interest expense and amortization of premiums and accretion of discounts will be made on the basis of the subsidiary records.
- Interest paid will be compared to amounts accrued.

RECORDS ARE PROTECTED FROM THEFT, MISUSE, DESTRUCTION, OR MISAPPROPRIATION.

- Important records, agreements, and so on will be kept in locked storage facilities.
- Access to these records will be restricted to authorized personnel.

EQUITY TRANSACTIONS ARE MADE ON THE BASIS OF APPROPRIATE AUTHORIZATION.

- Board of Directors, or where applicable, shareholders' approval will be obtained for equity transactions.
- Policies will be established covering equity transactions as follows:
  (a) Ensuring compliance with legal restrictions.
  (b) Use of independent registrars.
  (c) Use of independent transfer agents.
  (d) Issuance of new shares.
  (e) Stock options and other stock purchase plans.
  (f) Retirement and exchange of shares.
- Personnel to sign new stock certificates will be designated.
- A procedure is in effect ensuring review of restrictions of existing contractual agreements on proposed stock issuance or dividends.

ENTRIES AND ADJUSTMENTS TO EQUITY ACCOUNTS ARE MADE ON THE BASIS OF APPROPRIATE AUTHORIZATION.

- Approval by designated management personnel is required for all journal entries and adjustments.

EQUITY TRANSACTIONS AND RELATED COST ARE PROPERLY RECORDED, CLASSIFIED, AND SUMMARIZED.

- Responsibility is established for preparation of entries to record equity transactions and related costs.
- Journal entries for equity transactions are prepared on the basis of appropriate documentation.
- An independent registrar and transfer agent will be appointed.
- On a periodic basis registrar's and transfer agent's data are reconciled to General Ledger balances.
- Dividends declared will be accrued on the basis of registrar's and transfer agent's data.
- An imprest bank account for dividend payments will be utilized.
- A stock option ledger will be maintained and compared periodically to General Ledger balances.
- A procedure is established to control unclaimed dividend checks.

STOCK CERTIFICATES ARE SAFEGUARDED.

- Stock certificates are prenumbered and the number sequence is controlled.
- Surrendered or cancelled stock certificates are controlled.

RECORDS ARE PROTECTED FROM THEFT, MISUSE, DESTRUCTION, OR MISAPPROPRIATION.

- Keeping important records, securities, and so on in storage facilities that are either locked or under constant surveillance.
- Access to offices, records and critical forms is restricted to authorized personnel.

SUBJECT

AUTHORIZATION

ACCOUNTING PRINCIPLES USED AND THE METHOD OF THEIR APPLICATION REQUIRES APPROPRIATE AUTHORIZATION.

- The Company's Financial Manual contains accounting policies and procedures that are followed by all company units.
- The company has delineated the responsibility fo the approval of accounting principles used.
- The company has established a regular procedure for the review and approval of significant estimates and judgments used in preparing financial information.

ENTRIES AND ADJUSTMENTS (NOT AUTHORIZED WITHIN OTHER CYCLES) REQUIRE PROPER AUTHORIZATION.

- The responsibility for the preparation and approval of journal entries and adjustment is assigned to appropriate management personnel.

FINANCIAL STATEMENTS (INCLUDING DISCLOSURES) AND OTHER FINANCIAL REPORTS ISSUED REQUIRE AUTHORIZATION.

- The company has an established standard review procedure for financial statements, disclosures, and other financial reports.

JOURNAL ENTRIES ARE PREPARED ON THE BASIS OF APPROPRIATE DOCUMENTATION AND ARE RECORDED ON A TIMELY BASIS.

- A standard chart of account and accounting procedures in adequate detail are in use by the company.
- There are established procedures for the preparation of journal entries, including the required documentation.
- Standard journal entries are used whenever possible.
- Recurring journal entries are reviewed from time to time.

GENERAL LEDGER BALANCES ARE SUMMARIZED AND ACCURATELY REPORTED ON A TIMELY BASIS.

- The input of entries to General Ledger balances, including agreement with underlying records, subsidiary ledgers, account analysis, and workpapers is reviewed in a systematic manner by designated employees.
- There are standard procedures fo the reflection of necessary General Ledger corrections and adjustments on a timely basis.
- Analytical reviews of General Ledger balances are performed periodically.
- Monthly closing schedules are established and adhered to.

INDIVIDUAL GENERAL LEDGER BALANCES OF REPORTING UNITS ARE ACCURATELY CONSOLIDATED ON A TIMELY BASIS.

- The company has established a monthly financial reporting system containing all data necessary for the preparation of consolidated financial statements or other financial reports.
- Each operating unit establishes and adheres to predetermined closing schedules.
- The company has established policies for translation of financial information from non-United States reporting units into United States currency.
- Non-United States operations reconcile MNL report financial statements to local statutory reports on a periodic basis.
- The procedures for preparation of consolidation entries include:
  (a) Proper elimination of intra- and intercompany balances, profits, and so on.
  (b) Period-to-period comparison of consolidation entries.

FINANCIAL STATEMENTS AND NECESSARY DISCLOSURES ARE PREPARED IN CONFORMITY WITH GENERALLY ACCEPTED ACCOUNTING PRINCIPLES.

- The responsibility for final review and approval of financial statements is assigned to designated management personnel.
- The responsibility fo the accumulation, review, and approval of information disclosed with financial statements is assigned to designated management personnel.
- An analytical review of financial statements is performed periodically.

RECORDS ARE PROTECTED FROM THEFT, MISUSE, OR DESTRUCTION.

- Important records are kept in locked facilities.
- Access to such records is restricted to authorized personnel.
- Records are protected against physical hazards (fireproof cabinets, etc.).

<table>
<tr><td>SECTION</td></tr>
<tr><td>COMPUTER CONTROLS</td></tr>
<tr><td>SUBJECT</td></tr>
<tr><td>CONTENTS</td></tr>
</table>

SUBJECT TITLE	SECTION	SUBJECT
ORGANIZATION AND OPERATION	VIII	1
SYSTEM DEVELOPMENT AND MAINTENANCE	VIII	2
HARDWARE	VIII	3
ACCESS TO EDP AREAS	VIII	4
INPUT	VIII	5
PROCESSING	VIII	6
OUTPUT	VIII	7
DOCUMENTATION	VIII	8
FILES	VIII	9

<table>
<tr><td>SECTION</td></tr>
<tr><td>COMPUTER CONTROLS</td></tr>
<tr><td>SUBJECT</td></tr>
<tr><td>ORGANIZATION AND OPERATION</td></tr>
</table>

THE EDP DEPARTMENT IS ORGANIZED TO PROVIDE ADEQUATE SEGREGATION OF DUTIES AND FUNCTIONS.

- The EDP Department will report to an executive who has sufficient authority to ensure adequate support and effective management.
- With the EDP department the following functions are segregated:
  (a) Application programming, including design, initial development, and maintenance.
  (b) System programming, including initial generation of the operating system and its maintenance.
  (c) Operations covering all program processing.
  (d) Control and reconciliation of processing input and output, distribution of output to authorized personnel.
  (e) Control of master and data files.
- Physical as well as functional segregation is provided and personnel within a function will be rotated whenever possible.

ADEQUATE SEGREGATION OF FUNCTIONS IS ESTABLISHED
BETWEEN EDP DEPARTMENTS AND OTHER DEPARTMENTS.

- The processing will be performed by persons not involved with the following activities:
  (a) Initiation and authorization of transactions.
  (b) Initial recording of transactions.
  (c) Custody of assets, other than computer equipment.
  (d) Changes in master files.
  (e) Error correction, unless errors originated in the EDP department.
- EDP management routinely reviews processing time, master and data file usage, and scheduling reports and logs.

ADMINISTRATIVE AND OPERATIONAL PROCEDURES ARE
INSTITUTED TO ESTABLISH EFFECTIVE CONTROLS IN THE
EDP DEPARTMENT.

- Adequate procedures will be implemented for the following:
  (a) Published up-to-date organization charts.
  (b) Detailed written job descriptions.
  (c) Formal procedures for forms control and record retention.
  (d) Formal activity logging and review procedures.
  (e) Physical security.
  (f) Off-premises back-up for important master files, documentation, and programs.
  (g) Disaster planning, backup facilities, and testing procedures.

SYSTEM DESIGN, PROGRAMMING TECHNIQUES, AND
OPERATING PROCEDURES ARE STANDARDIZED TO EXTENT
POSSIBLE.

- Systems and procedures manuals, operator manuals, and user manuals will be issued.
- New system development is based on an operational plan that includes the following:
  (a) Initiation of development based on overall priority.

      (b) Involvement in the development process by EDP, user, systems, forms control, and design.

      (c) Review and approval of each significant phase of the development plan.

      (d) Documentation based on established standards.

      (e) Adequate testing.

      (f) Controlled implementation and conversion of data.

CHANGES TO PROGRAMS AFTER IMPLEMENTATION IS CONTROLLED.

- Changes to programs after implementation must be reviewed, approved, documented, and tested with the same stringent procedures and methods as used for the initial development of the system.

COMPUTER EQUIPMENT IS MAINTAINED IN GOOD WORKING ORDER.

- Control features inherent in the computer hardware, operating system, and other supporting software will be used to provide control over processing and operations and to report hardware malfunctions.
- Equipment manufacturers' suggestions will be followed for scheduled preventive maintenance and hardware testing routines to ensure that hardware is performing accurately.
- Necessary environmental controls will be provided in the computer room to protect equipment against excessive humidity and temperature. The computer room will be protected against fire hazard to extent possible.
- A formal procedure will be implemented to report hardware malfunctions.

ONLY AUTHORIZED PERSONS HAVE ACCESS TO COMPUTER HARDWARE, PROGRAMS, PROGRAM DOCUMENTATION, AND DATA FILES.

- The access to computer hardware is limited to authorized personnel by:
  - (a) Control of traffic through the computer room by using special locks, limited access ways, and when necessary by security personnel.
  - (b) Control of access to computer hardware by systems analysts and application programmers.
- Access to remote terminals is limited by:
  - (a) Physical restrictions through the use of partitions, locked doors, and so on.
  - (b) Passwords, terminal access keys, access logs, and monitored activity listings from each terminal. Passwords are assigned to individuals on a regular basis.
- Access to program documentation is limited to those persons who require it in the performance of their duties by:
  - (a) Segregation of system design and programming functions from computer operations; and
  - (b) Keeping program documentation in a secure place.
- Access to production (current application) programs and master files is limited to those individuals authorized to process or maintain particular systems.
- A librarian will be designated to control the issuance and storage of all computer files.

THERE IS ASSURANCE THAT INPUT IS COMPLETE.

- Control totals are established in the user department or control group prior to submitting data to EDP control; totals may include record counts, hash totals, dollr totals, and so on.
- Procedures will be established to verify that input data is received on a timely basis from user departments and physically controlled in the EDP department. Control may be achieved by using batch controls, document control numbers, efficient production scheduling, and so on.

• Input forms will be reviewed for completeness prior to updating master files. This can be done manually in the user department prior to submitting documents to EDP and can also be economically performed by using programmed controls (edit tests).

ERRORS OR OTHER REJECTED DATA ARE PROPERLY RE-ENTERED INTO THE SYSTEM.

• Proper control over processing rejected transactions includes:
  (a) Positive identification of rejected records.
  (b) A review of the cause for rejection.
  (c) The correction of each rejected record.
  (d) The review and approval of the correction.
  (e) A prompt re-entry of the corrections into the system at a point where it will be subject to the same input controls as the original data.

INPUT MEDIA IS DESIGNED TO REDUCE AND CONTROL ERRORS.

• Input forms will be designed in such a manner that they can be easily coded. Wherever possible preprinted and precoded forms are utilized.
• Clear instructions are issued for completing of forms.

THE MOVEMENT OF DATA BETWEEN PHYSICAL LOCATION OR DURING PROCESSING IS CONTROLLED.

• Application programs provide for verification of control totals (run to run totals, record counts, etc.).
• Data are transmitted by computer or terminals with transmission verification techniques such as message counts, answer back, character counts, and dual transmission.

SECTION	
COMPUTER CONTROLS	
SUBJECT	
PROCESSING	

DATA PROCESSED IS COMPLETE AND ACCURATE.

• Logical testing will be utilized to perform editing routines on important data fields of input records as follows:
  (a) Checks of codes or account numbers against a master file or table.

(b) Test of self-checking digits.

(c) Specific amounts or account tests.

(d) Limit tests.

(e) Tests for alphabetic characters within a numeric field.

(f) Comparison of different fields within a record to see if they represent a valid combination of data.

(g) Checks for missing or distorted data.

(h) Sequence checks.

- Data accuracy will be maintained throughout processing by using a programmed procedure such as run to run total checking, re-editing, and so on included in each job step during the job cycle.

PROPER DATA FILES ARE USED FOR INPUT.

- Application programs will check internal leader and trailer labels for data stored or magnetic (disc or tape) or control cards for data stored on cards. Leader and trailer labels generally include file identification, file volume and serial numbers, version number of generation, creation data, and expiration date.
- External labels will be checked by machine operators to ensure processing of correct files.

OUTPUT DATA IS REVIEWED AS TO COMPLETENESS AND REASONABLENESS.

- Input control totals will be reconciled to output control totals. These totals include record counts, run to run totals, and hash totals. This reconciliation may be performed with programmed reconciliation reports or manually reconciling totals on output reports with input control totals.
- The input data will be compared to output item by item to the extent considered feasible by the user or control group. Detailed review procedures are usually employed for updating important master files or for error corrections.

OUTPUT DATA IS DISTRIBUTED TO AUTHORIZED PERSONNEL ONLY.

- The persons receiving output data must be clearly identified to EDP personnel responsible for the distribution of reports.
- Report recipients will verify that all reports are received promptly.

MACHINE ACCESSIBLE OUTPUT IS PROPERLY IDENTIFIED AND CONTROLLED.

- All magnetic data files will be identified by appropriate internal leader and trailer labels, and card files are identified by control cards.

ADEQUATE DOCUMENTATION IS IN EXISTENCE FOR EACH APPLICATION.

- An acceptable level of documentation for computerized systems consists of the following:
  - (a) System flow chart — a graphic description of the flow of information through the system.
  - (b) Problem statement — a statement describing the overall objectives of the system.
  - (c) Program logic flow chart — a graphic description of the processing contained in each program.
  - (d) Program listing — a listing of the application program source code.
  - (e) Record layouts — Specifications as to the placement, length, and characteristics of data items and files on computer files.
  - (f) Transaction and activity codes — description of the codes used within the system.
  - (g) Operator's instructions — information required by the computer operator to run the program.
- Approval and change sheets — a dated record of the review and approval of new programs or revisions to existing programs.
- User manual — a description of how to prepare input to and work with output from the system.

330

SUFFICIENT BACKUP IS IN EXISTENCE TO RECREATE A FILE IF DATA IS DESTROYED DURING PROCESSING.

- Retention periods of source documents are adequate to permit repunching of transaction files.
- Tape or disc files are subjected to adequate on-premises or off-premises back-up support (son-father-grandfather for tape files).

FILES ARE PHYSICALLY PROTECTED AGAINST DAMAGE BY FIRE OR ACCIDENTAL DAMAGE AND MISUSE.

- Magnetic files are stored in temperature and humidity controlled, fireproof environments.
- All important master files are reproduced periodically and the duplicates are stored off-premises. Alternative forms of master file protection may be utilized.
- Files are under the control of librarians who control distribution of files and monitor expiration dates.

APPENDIX B

A Representative Multinational
Financial Organization

OFFICES OF THE VICE PRESIDENT-FINANCE AND
OF THE VICE PRESIDENT-CONTROLLER

Organization and Functions Charts and Position Descriptions

VICE-PRESIDENT— FINANCE

Basic Functions

Manage the financial affairs of the Company in the areas delegated by the President and Executive Committee.

Responsible to the President for developing, recommending, and administering major Company financial and investment plans, programs, policies, and objectives; for developing adequate procedures for the sound administration of Company funds; and performing special studies and projects as may be assigned by the President. Directs the Treasurer in administration of his functions.

Basic Objectives

To assure the preservation of company assets and provide maximum security for company funds. To insure the most effective utilization of resources, with a view toward obtaining maximum profit, and optimum proportion in the company's financial structure, consistent with approved objectives.

Policies and Plans

Formulate basic company policies, systems, and procedures relating to investments, cash management, credit, taxes, insurance, and property administration.

Advise on the financial aspects of company plans and programs.

Formulate policies governing the handling of Company funds and investment of assets.

Formulate policies relating to foreign exchange administration.

Plan and prepare data for use in regulation and related proceedings and represent the company as assigned.

Administration

Maintain close and effective working relationship with national and international financial institutions.

Plan and administer in cooperation with other interested company activities, the contractual obligations of the Company, including intergovernment and financial matters.

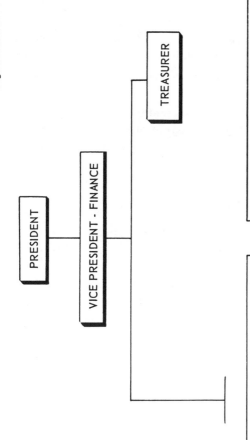

PRESIDENT

VICE PRESIDENT - FINANCE

TREASURER

• Manages financial affairs of the company.

• Develops financial investment policies and plans.

• Formulates policies relating to funds management.

• Formulates policies affecting foreign operations.

• Recommends tax and insurance policies.

• Represents the Company in negotiating financial requirements with national and international financial institutions

• Administers investment and borrowing activities of the company.

• Negotiates sale or lease of company property and surplus equipment

• Develops procedures to insure safekeeping of company funds.

• Administers tax and insurance programs.

• Regulates cash flow and transfer operations.

• Records cash transactions and report on position.

ORGANIZATION

FUNCTIONS

335

Provide for management of real properties of the Company not specifically assigned to other activities and for property management counsel to other company components.

Recommend tax and insurance policies; establish tax accounting procedures and direct tax accounting research; represent the Company on tax matters.

Forecasts and Analysis   *Direct* forecasting and analysis of economic and financial conditions; advise on investment and borrowing activities.

Direct special, finance research projects as assigned by the President.

Plan and prepare data in cooperation with Controller for use in negotiating the financial requirements of the Company and represent the Company in transactions with financial institutions as assigned by the President.

TREASURER

Basic Functions   *Responsible* to the Vice-President—Finance for the development and establishment of policies and procedures pertaining to cash management; banking; securities investment; insurance and property management; collection, custody, disbursement, and transfer of company finds.

Basic Objective   *To assist* the Vice-President—Finance in the administration of company funds and to initiate programs, policies, and procedures that will provide maximum security for assets and achieve the most effective utilization of financial resources.

Policies and Procedures   *Plan* and direct the activities of the Treasurer's office and functionally supervise such activities throughout the Company.

Negotiate the sale or lease of company real property, and surplus equipment in accordance with company approval and direction.

Develop procedures that will insure the prompt and equitable settlement of transactions for the account of the Company.

Develop company credit policies and standards, authorize exceptions to such policies and standards when necessary; and exchange credit information with appropriate Company activities.

Fund Management

As assigned by the Vice-President—Finance, develop and maintain such relationships with domestic and international banks, other financial institutions, and insurance companies as he may deem desirable and necessary for the effective discharge of the Treasurer's responsibilities and the realization of the Company's objectives.

Administer the investment and borrowing activities of the Company.

Develop policies and procedures to regulate and administer cash flow operations, including cash transfers, and short-term investments so as to profitably utilize the Company's cash resources.

In conjunction with the controller establish procedures and policies governing the accountability for cash receipts and disbursements and the maintenance of cash books and records of cash transactions.

Establish procedures for the reconciliation and transfers of bank balances.

Develop procedures and policies to insure the safe keeping of company funds and securities; maintain records of securities investments and other receivables and assure that interest and dividend payments are received.

Advise the Vice-President—Finance on investment programs involving securities; analyze company security investments and recommend changes as indicated; supervise the administration of such programs.

Establish the balances to be kept on deposit with each depository for company funds; arrange for bank letters of credit to guarantee payment to suppliers both nationally and internationally.

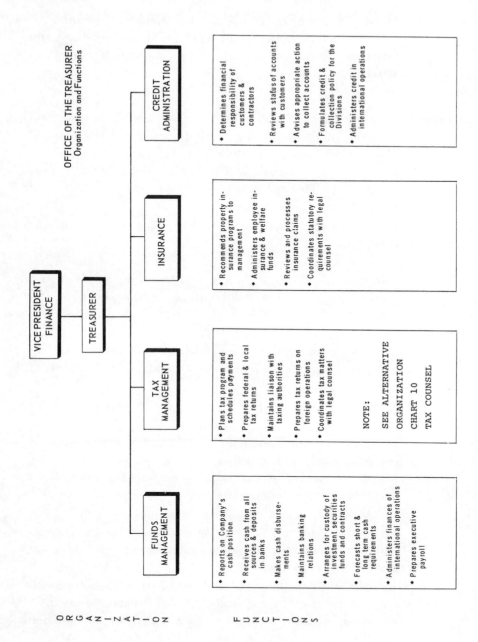

OFFICE OF THE TREASURER
Organization and Functions

ORGANIZATION

FUNCTIONS

VICE PRESIDENT FINANCE

TREASURER

FUNDS MANAGEMENT

- Reports on Company's cash position
- Receives cash from all sources & deposits in banks
- Makes cash disbursements
- Maintains banking relations
- Arranges for custody of investment securities funds and contracts
- Forecasts short & long term cash requirements
- Administers finances of international operations
- Prepares executive payroll

TAX MANAGEMENT

- Plans tax program and schedules payments
- Prepares federal & local tax returns
- Maintains liaison with taxing authorities
- Prepares tax returns on foreign operations
- Coordinates tax matters with legal counsel

NOTE:

SEE ALTERNATIVE ORGANIZATION CHART 10 TAX COUNSEL

INSURANCE

- Recommends property insurance programs to management
- Administers employee insurance & welfare funds
- Reviews and processes insurance claims
- Coordinates statutory requirements with legal counsel

CREDIT ADMINISTRATION

- Determines financial responsibility of customers & contractors
- Reviews status of accounts with customers
- Advises appropriate action to collect accounts
- Formulates credit & collection policy for the Divisions
- Administers credit in international operations

Prepare daily reports of the company cash position for submission to the office of the President.

Establish procedures to control local deposit and other banking activities.

Tax, Real Estate, and Insurance

In cooperation with the Controller, maintain a register for the payment of taxes, dividends, fees, and other expenditures and for the purchase of securities; prepare interim reports and forecasts of receipts and disbursements.

Develop, recommend, and administer an adequate company insurance program including employee, fire, casualty, indemnity, fidelity, and surety coverages.

Conduct negotiations on contracts with insurance companies, brokers, agents, and actuaries; coordinate company transactions with these companies and their representatives.

In conjunction with the Controller, develop policies and programs on insurance matters relating to reserves, rates, and necessary accounting records.

Coordinate activities with the tax accounting office in tax administration and payment and with the legal staff on custody of all legal documents including those which relate to purchase, lease, management, or sale of company property, licensing arrangements, management contracts, and so on.

VICE-PRESIDENT— CONTROLLER

Basic Functions

The Controller is responsible to the President for policies, systems, and procedures pertaining to basic accounting, financial planning, financial analysis and control; for the direction and administration of accounting functions in accordance with Company programs and objectives.

In order to serve management effectively, the Controller will:

Participate in planning and developing the necessary financial data for future operations.

Develop and maintain a reporting system to provide necessary control data.

Analyze and interpret operating results.

Report, recommend, and otherwise influence action to accomplish operating results in accordance with approved plans.

Basic Objective *To assist* the Company management to maximize profits by developing and administering policies, systems, and procedures designed to control expenses, account for revenues, and preserve the assets of the Company; to maintain records and provide reports of an accounting and, financial nature.

Plan *Develop* and establish policies, systems, and procedures pertaining to basic accounting, financial planning, financial analysis, and control.

Participate in planning and development of the necessary financial data for future operations.

Develop publish, and install systems and procedures for maintenance of adequate records of assets, liabilities, and financial transactions of the Company.

Advise management on financial aspects of company plans and programs.

Furnish assistance and advice to company executives and staffs is evaluating the financial implications of proposed or operating programs and on accounting matters.

Develop and recommend company policies and procedures for appropriations and matters relating to investments in equipment and facilities.

Develop policies and procedures relating to costing and pricing of company services.

Develop, in cooperation with Vice-President—Finance and Vice-President—Procurement, pricing, policies, and procedures relating to the disposal of surplus equipment.

Establish in cooperation with Vice-President—Procurement a system of material inventory control and procedures to insure

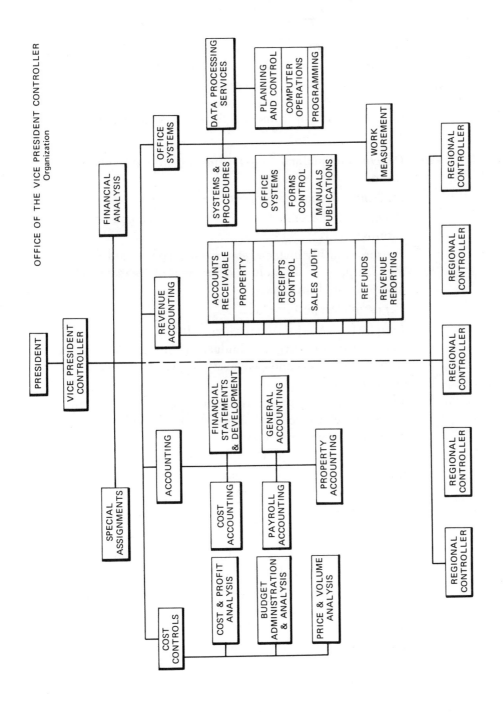

OFFICE OF THE VICE PRESIDENT CONTROLLER
Organization

adequate recording and reporting of inventories and to permit continuing inventory analysis and planning.

Plan and administer, in cooperation with other interested company activities, the contractual obligations of the Company including intergovernment and statutory financial matters.

Report   *Develop* and maintain a reporting system to provide necessary control data.

Determine the company's earnings.

Report to management on consolidated financial position and earnings.

Prepare monthly financial statements, reports, and analyzes for the Company as a whole and for each of its major operating divisions and functions.

Report on cost performance.

Prepare forecasts of capital expenditures.

Prepare the company cash budget including related studies of cash requirements and cash availability, and source and application of funds.

Prepare status reports on company facility programs and projects; review project commitments and expenditures to assure conformance with procedure.

Report on inventories. Develop in cooperation with the Auditor, Vice-President—Procurement, and division personnel procedures for taking and costing of physical inventories.

Analyze   *Analyze* and interpret operating results.

Develop short and long-term forecasts of the Company's financial position and analyze financial trends.

Prepare sepcial nonrecurring financial studies on such matters as outside financing, capitalization, and on such other matters as may be assigned by the President.

Assure investigations of abnormal inventory investments and recommend corrective action as required.

Analyze reserve requirements in relation to inventory balance and recommend adjustments.

Analyze results of operations and prepare related statistical reports for management.

Control *Report,* recommend, and otherwise influence action to accomplish operating results in accordance with approved plans.

Develop comprehensive procedures required for budgeting, reporting evaluating, and measuring company operating performance in relation to financial plans and objectives and for planning future operations.

Direct company budgeting activities and establish budget procedures.

Assist in determining allowable cost and quality standards to aid in developing budgets and measuring performance.

Provide staff assistance to headquarters and division personnel in budget preparation.

Review headquarters and division budgets to assure compliance with approved budget procedures.

Consolidate and analyze corporate budgets and recommend approval or revision.

Plan and coordinate the simplification and standardization of forms and reports and administer a forms control program.

Develop pricing policies and procedures relating to the disposal of surplus equipment.

Account and Record *Direct* and administer accounting functions in accordance with company programs and objectives.

Maintain company books of account.

Establish policies and procedures for revenue accounting, including control of receipts and accounting for earned revenue.

Develop and recommend company policies relating to properties and reserves for depreciation, depletion, and amortization.

Develop and recommend policies and procedures for cost accounting and the preparation of cost reports.

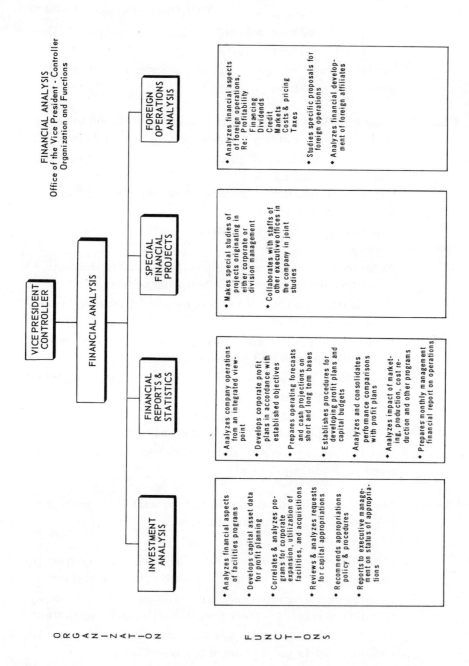

FINANCIAL ANALYSIS
Office of the Vice President - Controller
Organization and Functions

ORGANIZATION

VICE PRESIDENT
CONTROLLER

FINANCIAL ANALYSIS

INVESTMENT ANALYSIS | FINANCIAL REPORTS & STATISTICS | SPECIAL FINANCIAL PROJECTS | FOREIGN OPERATIONS ANALYSIS

FUNCTIONS

INVESTMENT ANALYSIS
- Analyzes financial aspects of facilities programs
- Develops capital asset data for profit planning
- Correlates & analyzes programs for corporate expansion, utilization of facilities, and acquisitions
- Reviews & analyzes requests for capital appropriations
- Recommends appropriations policy & procedures
- Reports to executive management on status of appropriations

FINANCIAL REPORTS & STATISTICS
- Analyzes company operations from an integrated viewpoint
- Develops corporate profit plans in accordance with established objectives
- Prepares operating forecasts and cash projections on short and long term bases
- Establishes procedures for developing profit plans and capital budgets
- Analyzes and consolidates performance comparisons with profit plans
- Analyzes impact of marketing, production, cost reduction and other programs
- Prepares monthly management financial report on operations

SPECIAL FINANCIAL PROJECTS
- Makes special studies of projects originating in either corporate or division management
- Collaborates with staffs of other executive offices in the company in joint studies

FOREIGN OPERATIONS ANALYSIS
- Analyzes financial aspects of foreign operations, Re: Profitability
    Financing
    Dividends
    Credit
    Markets
    Costs & pricing
    Taxes
- Studies specific proposals for foreign operations
- Analyzes financial development of foreign affiliates

344

Develop payroll systems and procedures for all company locations. Prepare and issue payroll disbursements and required payroll reports.

Direct data processing services.

Assist the divisions in the development of training programs for controller staff personnel.

SPECIAL ASSIGNMENTS (CONTROLLER'S STAFF)

Personnel Development and Budgets

Plan and coordinate development of headquarters and regional Controller's office personnel and concur in proposed position changes involving key personnel.

Maintain personnel records for the headquarters Controller's Office and key personnel in regional Controller's Offices and advise on position classifications and salary ranges.

Recommend organizational plans and coordinate changes.

Administer headquarters Controller's Office budgets; develop procedures for and review regional Controller's Office personnel budgets.

Develop and coordinate Controller's office training activities.

Administer supplemental compensation plans.

Audit Coordination

Review recommendations and suggestions contained in company and regional audit reports and determine action to be taken pursuant to the reports; distribute audit reports and final recommendations to field and regional personnel concerned; coordinate and follow installation of recommendations.

Prepare Controller's Office replies to audit reports; prepare monthly audit clearance status reports; participate in audit closing meetings at field locations and regional offices when appropriate.

Coordinate employee suggestion program and management proposals within the Controller's Office.

345

FINANCIAL ANALYSIS AND REPORTS

Basic Functions   *Advise* and assist the Controller in planning and directing the activities of the Controller's Office, primarily on matters relating to financial planning and control of revenues, costs, profits, assets, and the preparation of the monthly financial review and management reports.

Financial Reporting   *Recommend* action to improve the usefulness, consistency, and clarity of management reports.

Coordinate the preparation, analysis, and scheduling of management reports.

Plan, review, analyze, and edit reports issued by the Office of the Controller.

Coordinate the analysis and comments to be incorporated in the financial statements.

Analyze current operational results and prepare monthly financial review for management committees.

Prepare and coordinate statistical reports for submission to government agencies and trade associations.

Investment Analysis   *Develop* studies on financial aspects of future facilities programs.

Prepare project expenditure plans including budgets for project expense and related performance reports.

Develop fixed asset data for profit plans and price studies and prepare related performance reports.

Review proposed projects.

Conduct special studies on effective utilization of company facilities.

Develop and recommend company policies and procedures for appropriations matters relating to investments in facilities and equipment.

Assist in the development of facility programs and project appreciation and disposal requests.

Office:

Department:

Sections:

F
U
N
C
T
I
O
N
S

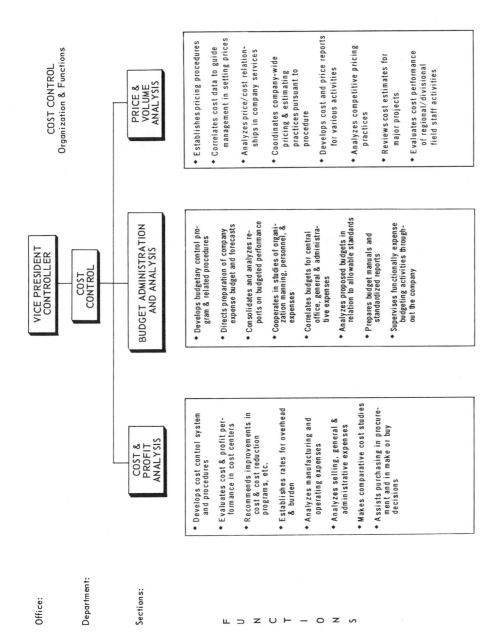

COST CONTROL
Organization & Functions

VICE PRESIDENT
CONTROLLER

COST
CONTROL

COST &
PROFIT
ANALYSIS

- Develops cost control system and procedures
- Evaluates cost & profit performance in cost centers
- Recommends improvements in cost & cost reduction programs, etc.
- Establishes rates for overhead & burden
- Analyzes manufacturing and operating expenses
- Analyzes selling, general & administrative expenses
- Makes comparative cost studies
- Assists purchasing in procurement and in make or buy decisions

BUDGET ADMINISTRATION
AND ANALYSIS

- Develops budgetary control program & related procedures
- Directs preparation of company expense budget and forecasts
- Consolidates and analyzes reports on budgeted performance
- Cooperates in studies of organization manning, personnel, & expenses
- Correlates budgets for central office, general & administrative expenses
- Analyzes proposed budgets in relation to allowable standards
- Prepares budget manuals and standardized reports
- Supervises functionally expense budgeting activities throughout the company

PRICE &
VOLUME
ANALYSIS

- Establishes pricing procedures
- Correlates cost data to guide management in setting prices
- Analyzes price/cost relationships in company services
- Coordinates company-wide pricing & estimating practices pursuant to procedure
- Develops cost and price reports for various activities
- Analyzes competitive pricing practices
- Reviews cost estimates for major projects
- Evaluates cost performance of regional/divisional field staff activities

Analyze the financial aspects of project requests.

Coordinate project requests with interested excutives prior to presentation to executive management.

Maintain company appropriation files.

Prepare monthly status reports on company programs and projects and review project commitments and expenditures to assure conformance with procedural requirements.

Furnish financial data and assistance in the development of studies of integration and expansion, and utilization of facilities and develop forecasts of company facilities and expenditures.

Functionally supervise investment analysis functions throughout the Company.

Develop an appropriations policy and procedure manual.

Special Financial Projects
Perform research into financial problems of general management interest as assigned. Such problems usually cut across the normal division of functional responsibility within both the Controller's office and other staff offices. Problems assigned to this staff customarily require coordination or joint participation with other offices and operations.

Maintain continuing statistical and financial analyses in connection with long-term studies of management reports.

Prepare nonrecurring financial studies outside the scope of other departments on such matters as pensions, corporate structure, dividend policy, outside financing, capitalization, and problems incident to labor negotiations.

Prepare the company cash budget including related studies of cash requirements and cash availability.

Prepare a monthly report and projection of sources and applications of funds.

Foreign Operations Analysis
Advise on financial aspects of programs, corporate financing, dividends, credit policies, and changes in corporate structure relating to foreign operations.

Assist in the development of the financial aspects of proposals affecting foreign affiliates.

Analyze and make recommendations on the sales and profit performance of foreign operations including such factors as pricing policies, cost performance, and assets employed.

COST CONTROLS

Basic Functions

Responsible to the Vice President-Controller for accomplishing the cost and budget control program of the company. Directs cost analysis, budget administration, and price analysis.

Cost and Profit Analysis

Evaluate costs and profits of individual cost/profit centers (producing areas).

Prepare reports and recommendations for improving cost and profit performance of specific activities.

Evaluate the cost performance of headquarters staff activities and develop appropriate procedures for measurement and control of these costs.

Evaluate the cost performance of regional/divisional field staff activities and assist these activities in the development of detailed expense control procedures.

Review and develop systems for controlling costs and profits in the regions—divisions and staffs.

Develop a system of costs and profit reports for each type of activity and consolidate and prepare comparative studies and reports.

Conduct special cost studies and provide cost information as required.

Develop burden absorption rates; furnish management expense data for price study purposes.

Coordinate preparation of cost savings analysis in all areas. Develop specific programs and submit to management for action.

Take appropriate action to assure uniform accounting relative to production expense and direct and indirect labor classifications.

Take appropriate action to assure uniform accounting relative to administrative and general expense.

Develop procedures and instructions and coordinate the preparation of the annual profit budget and four month profit forecast.

Functionally supervise all cost and profit analytical activities throughout the system.

Develop and recommend policies and procedures concerning the planning and administration of company and regional cost and profit performance.

Budget Administration and Analysis

Develop and recommend policies and procedures concerning the planning and administration of the company and regional expense budgets.

Prepare budget performance reports and special analyses as required for individual components of the company.

Furnish procedures, guidelines, and assistance to operating and staff activities for preparation of proposed general expense budgets.

Analyze proposed budgets in relation to historical experience, competitive or allowable standards, approved organizational or product plans, and other pertinent factors and make recommendations for cost savings where appropriate.

Develop a reporting system that will provide pertinent performance data. Review reasons for budget variances and recommend corrective action.

Cooperate with the company organization department in the review of existing or proposed organization and procedures affecting personnel requirements or expenses.

Cooperate with the Personnel Department in the review of salary adjustments as they relate to allowable budgeted expenses.

Develop policies and procedures for the preparation of flight operations expense budgets.

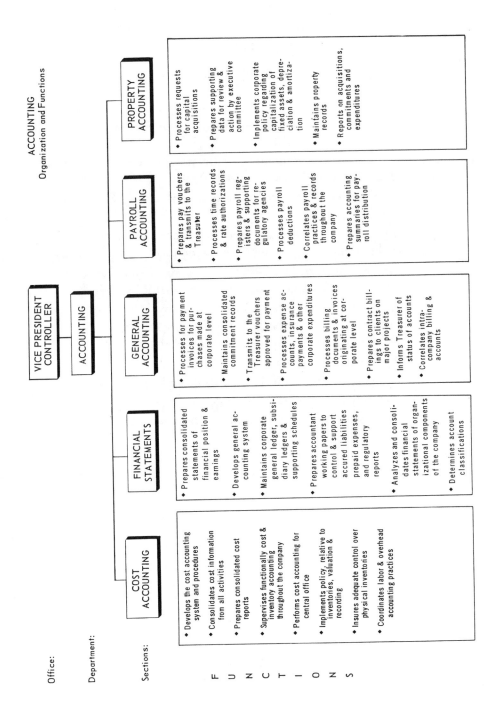

Office:

Department:

Sections:

VICE PRESIDENT CONTROLLER

ACCOUNTING

FUNCTIONS

COST ACCOUNTING

- Develops the cost accounting system and procedures
- Consolidates cost information from all activities
- Prepares consolidated cost reports
- Supervises functionally cost & inventory accounting throughout the company
- Performs cost accounting for central office
- Implements policy, relative to inventories, valuation & recording
- Insures adequate control over physical inventories
- Coordinates labor & overhead accounting practices

FINANCIAL STATEMENTS

- Prepares consolidated statements of financial position & earnings
- Develops general accounting system
- Maintains corporate general ledger, subsidiary ledgers & supporting schedules
- Prepares accountant working papers to control & support accrued liabilities prepaid expenses, and regulatory reports
- Analyzes and consolidates financial statements of organizational components of the company
- Determines account classifications

GENERAL ACCOUNTING

- Processes for payment invoices for purchases made at corporate level
- Maintains consolidated commitment records
- Transmits to the Treasurer vouchers approved for payment
- Processes expense accounts, insurance payments & other corporate expenditures
- Processes billing documents & invoices originating at corporate level
- Prepares contract billings to clients on major projects
- Informs Treasurer of status of accounts
- Correlates intra-company billing & accounts

PAYROLL ACCOUNTING

- Prepares pay vouchers & transmits to the Treasurer
- Processes time records & rate authorizations
- Prepares payroll registers & supporting documents for regulatory agencies
- Processes payroll deductions
- Correlates payroll practices & records throughout the company
- Prepares accounting summaries for payroll distribution

PROPERTY ACCOUNTING

- Processes requests for capital acquisitions
- Prepares supporting data for review & action by executive committee
- Implements corporate policy regarding capitalization of fixed assets, depreciation & amortization
- Maintains property records
- Reports on acquisitions, commitments and expenditures

Consolidate company budget proposals.

Functionally supervise budgeting activities throughout the company.

Prepare budget manuals, standardized reporting forms, and analytical reports for use throughout the company.

Price and Volume Analysis

Develop and recommend company policies and procedures for establishing product and service prices.

Coordinate the preparation of company price studies and regional proposals.

Analyze current price-cost relationships of principal company products and services and recommend changes as necessary.

Prepare company price-cost studies for discussion and proposed programs and commercial relationships.

Review and coordinate special studies involving cost estimates such as costs for pricing, costs for competitive products, and cost effects of program changes or new programs.

Supervisor acts as member of Scheduling Committee.

Review and advise on the financial implications of price-cost programs and proposals, production schedules, and so on.

Analyze the market position of the company on the major routes.

Coordinate and analyze revenue forecasts, capacity requirements, and so on for financial, facility, and equipment planning purposes.

Review and advise on the financial implications of forward programs.

ACCOUNTING

Basic Functions

Assist the Vice President - Controller in the development and establishment of Company policies, systems, and procedures pertaining to accounting activities.

Responsibilities

Maintain corporate books and publish consolidated financial statements for internal and external purposes.

Develop and establish adequate accounting records and procedures, as well as actively and functionally supervise all activities, pertaining to general accounting, cost accounting, payroll and property accounting for head office, regional offices, and establishments abroad.

Develop and establish in cooperation with the Treasurer adequate records and procedures governing the accountability for cash receipts and disbursements at head office, Regional offices, and establishments abroad

Coordinate Company policies and establish reporting procedures as regards general accounting, cost accounting, payroll, and property accounting with regional offices as well as affiliated companies.

Develop, establish, and corrdinate internal control procedures within the accounting field of activity throughout the Company.

Establish account classifications within the Company and create relevant instructions in accounting manuals and circulars throughout the Company.

Conduct special studies for the development of accounting systems and procedures upon own initiative or as may be assigned by the Controller.

Administratively supervise the office service and staff functions of Accounting Division, prepare budgets for Accounting Division, and review budgets for the establishments abroad as regards the accounting functions.

Cost Accounting

Assist (Cost Control Division) in the development of company policies and procedures for the establishment of adequate cost elements for price studies and cost control purposes.

Establish cost elements and calculate and/or estimate costs to be used for price quotations, cost comparisons, and studies of cost effects of various programs and plans.

Develop company policies and procedures for the accounting (registration) and reporting of actual costs throughout the Company.

Develop company policies and procedures for the allocation of general and administratives expenses throughout the Company.

Conduct reviews of the application of Company policies and procedures for the cost accounting as well as cost practices at regional offices and affiliated companies.

Coordinate cost accounting matters between regional offices and provide technical assistance as required.

Actively and functionally supervise all cost accounting and material accounting activities throughout the Company.

Review profit and loss statements from regional offices and affiliated companies and prepare consolidated profit and loss statements.

Currently follow the development and research of cost accounting systems and practices.

Review material accounting systems in effect in all locations to ensure the establishment of adequate physical controls and proper recording and reporting of all kinds of material.

Review and analyze periodic material inventory reports and supporting data from all locations to ascertain trends. Conduct investigations in respect to abnormal inventory conditions and recommend corrective action as required.

Consolidate material inventory reports for inclusion in Balance Sheet and for submission to Materials Management.

Participate in the development of material inventory reserve policies; analyze reserve requirements in relation to inventory balances and recommended adjustments.

Develop procedures and techniques for the taking and costing of annual inventories at all locations; administer the application of such procedures and consolidate annual material inventory reports.

Supervise the maintenance of inventory records and maintain controls over the material under the direct jurisdiction of headquarters.

Price and summarize requisitions for productive inventories and expense materials.

Financial Statements and Development

Maintain General Ledgers; prepare and publish financial statements (Balance Sheet, Profit and Loss Statement and supporting schedules) for all activities under the direct jurisdiction of head office, Regional offices and organizations abroad.

Determine the acceptability of Financial Statements submitted by regional offices as well as affiliated companies.

Prepare and publish consolidated Financial Statements for internal company purposes as well as external needs, for example, for lenders, authorities, and industrial organizations, and so on as may be required.

Prepare four month financial forecasts and develop special financial reports and analyses of a pure accounting nature, as requested.

Develop company policies and procedures for the preparation of Financial Statements, forecasts, and recommendations, as well as assist in the development of company practices and procedures within the accounting field of activity.

Develop and determine all accounts classifications within the company and administer the Accounts Catalogs issued by head office.

Review internal controls for specific fields within head office Accounting Division and recommend as well as assist in the development and coordination of internal control procedures throughout the Company.

Upon request, conduct special studies within the accounting field of activity, involving proposals for new or revised accounting procedures, issuance of relevant instructions, assistance in establishing the procedures, as well as a proper follow-up of the profitability of the project.

Develop and administer accounting manuals, handbooks, and circulars, as well as forms issued by Accounting Division.

Reveiw and coordinate the creation of required procedures and instructions having accounting implications in manuals, handbooks, and circulars issued by other divisions and departments.

Assist in the planning and arrangements of internal meetings, conferences, and training courses held by Accounting Division.

Conduct special studies in the field of machine accounting and developments in the accounting concepts in cooperation with Office Systems Division.

General Accounting

Process suppliers' invoices for payment and accounting; maintain necessary records and prepare reports of accounts payable.

Process all outgoing/incoming interoffice invoices and accounting respectively.

Invoice customers and clients, maintain adequate records and claims procedures, and prepare reports of accounts receivable.

Process and control sales and expense reports.

Process and control accounting reports from establishments abroad.

Process incoming intracompany billings and issue and process outgoing intracompany billings, maintain necessary records and prepare reports intracompany accounts.

Payroll Accounting

Prepare monthly payroll reports for payments and accounting of salaries and payroll accruals.

Prepare weekly payroll reports for payment and accounting of weekly/hourly wages and payroll accruals.

Maintain adequate payroll records.

Check and price clock cards and reconcile with time sheets.

Prepare labor distribution for cost accounting purposes.

Control travel expense reports and perform accounting of travel expenses.

Prepare payroll deductions/additions in settlement of sales incentives and miscellaneous receivables and payables relating to personnel.

Property Accounting

Maintain property records for fixed assets of all kinds in possession throughout the company.

Assist regional and district offices in establishment of property records.

Develop and administer procedures and techniques for taking of inventory as regards fixed assets.

Develop and administer procedures and techniques for correction of deficiencies in property records.

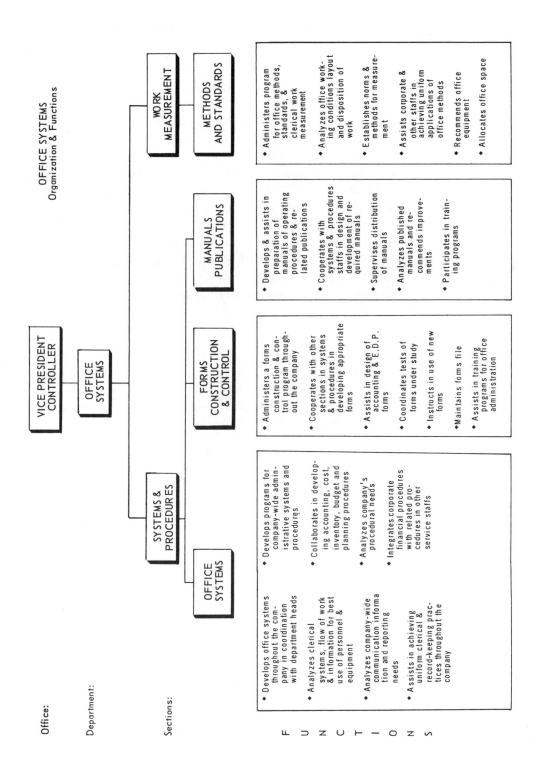

Prepare consolidated analysis of fixed assets to be included in periodic financial reports.

Calculate depreciation for fixed assets.

Develop and recommend Company policies and procedures relating to fixed assets and reserves for depreciation, depletion, and amortization.

Conduct special studies of depreciation rates and reserves.

Coordinate property accounting matters with tax, treasury, and legal offices.

Actively and functionally supervise all property accounting activities throughout the Company.

Issue work orders in construction and maintenance.

Review appreciations and disposal requests and prepare reports.

Review the accounting aspects of appropriations and disposal requests.

OFFICE SYSTEMS

Basic Functions *Responsible* to the Vice President - Controller for development and revision of office systems, procedures, and manuals for the guidance and economic and efficient performance of office tasks throughout the Company.

Responsibilities *Construction* and control of forms to assure optimal usefulness and uniformity in design; proper integration and continuity in the flow of information; desired accuracy and elimination of unnecessary duplication.

Determination of office machine requirements in terms of the tasks to be performed, the type of equipment to be procured, and the standards of performance to be maintained. This responsibility will be discharged in full cooperation with the Data Processing Planning activities and other interested groups as indicated.

Establishment and or revision of objective work measurement systems, development of performance standards, systems, and reports for the evaluation of performance against standards.

Administration of the data processing services.

Participation in and assistance to management in effecting cost reduction program.

Relationships The Manager of Office Systems and Controls is directly responsible to the Comptroller.

The Manager is responsible for the administration of the data processing activities at headquarters office and a staff of analysts who work on systems related to above-mentioned major functions.

The Manager works in clsoe relationship with the data processing planning activities in order to assure the desirable degree of understanding and cooperation.

The Manager functionally supervises all office systems and activities of the Company by regional and departmental staffs of analysts.

The Manager performs assigned tasks as a service agency, informs, advises, and technically assists supervision and management in question dealing with above-mentioned major functions.

The Manager contacts administrative management personnel in other companies, as desirable, in the exchange of information on problems under study.

The Manager also maintains contacts with outside associations and technical groups in his fields of activity as an aid in the performance of his functions.

Systems and Procedures

Major Functions and Objectives *Administer* programs of clerical work analysis for the improvement and/or development of office systems, procedures, manuals, forms, construction, and control throughout the Company to assure efficient utilization of office personnel and assets.

Analyze and recommend policies as may be requested to achieve more effective utilization of office personnel and assets and assist in the implementation of approved policies and program.

Coordinate and assist in the installation of clerical cost reduc-

359

tion programs resulting from the adoption of work simplification methods.

Relationships

The Superintendent of systems and procedures is directly responsible to the Manager of Office Systems and Controls.

The Superintendent maintains close working relationships with the Managers of work measurement, data processing services and data processing planning activities in the performance of his assigned functions.

The Superintendent performs assigned tasks as a service agency, informs, advises, and technically assists supervision and management in questions dealing with above-mentioned major functions.

The Superintendent contacts administrative management personnel in other companies as may be deemed desirable by the manager of Office Systems and controls or at the request of the data processing planning activities in the exchange of information on specific problems under study.

Office Systems—Major Functions

Within the definitions and relationships indicated above for the Superintendent of office systems the office systems activities shall comprise the following functions.

System Design

Analyze clerical systems and the flow of work and information to assure best possible utilization of personnel and assets.

In cooperation with headquarters, regional and department heads analyze policies pertaining to office systems for financial implications and prepare appropriate recommendations or concurrencies.

Assist in the development of required accounting systems within the Comptroller's Office and coordinate the activity of the various departments as needed.

Inform, assist, and instruct locations in the use of new record-keeping reporting systems and assist in the Company-wide application of new systems.

Establish and maintain files pertaining to offices systems in use in the Company.

Plan, manage, and follow up training programs for supervisors in office administration and procedures and especially within the Comptroller's Office.

Procedures *Analyze* the Company's the Company's procedural needs, develop detailed office procedures as required and establish means of measuring the efficiency of established procedures.

In cooperation with headquarters, regional and department heads analyze policies pertaining to clerical procedures for financial implications and prepare appropriate recommendations or concurrences.

Cooperate with work measurement activities and methods analysis in the development and follow-up of procedure.

Assist in the development of required accounting procedures within the Comptroller's Office and coordinate the activity of the various departments as needed.

Coordinate the installation tests of systems and procedures under study at selected locations.

Analyze results of installation tests of new procedures and recommend adoption of improved systems and procedures.

Inform, assist, and instruct locations in the use of new record keeping, reporting procedures, and so on and assist in the Company-wide application of new procedures.

Establish and maintain complete files of the Company's office procedures.

Participate in the training programs for the supervisors in office administration and procedures and especially within the Comptroller's Office.

Office Machines *Review* improvements in the business machine field for application within the Company. Establish contacts with vendors after consultation with office equipments planning activities.

Coordinate installation tests of new machines under study at selected locations.

Analyze results of installation tests and recommend adoption of improve equipment and related methods.

Advise, assist, and instruct locations in the use of new equipment and related methods and assist in the Company-wide applications.

Establish and maintain files on pertinent data of office equipment.

Recommend types of equipment to be procured and develop a

361

suggested master plan for the procurement and standardization of office equipment throughout the Company.

Participate in the training programs for supervisors in office administration or procedures and in particular within the Comptroller's office.

Forms Construction and Control–Major Functions

Within the definitions and relationships indicated above for the superintendent of office systems the activities of forms construction and control shall comprise the following functions.

Administer a forms construction and control program for head office as well as for all forms received by head office for further processing or consolidation.

Cooperate with work measurement activities and methods analysis as well as of office systems and procedures activities in the development of forms.

Assist in the development of required accounting forms within the Comptroller's Office and coordinate the activity of the various departments as needed.

Coordinate the installation tests of forms under study at selected locations.

Analyze results of installation tests of new forms and related methods and recommend adoption of improved forms.

Inform, assist, and instruct locations in the use of new forms and assist in the Company-wide application of new forms and related methods.

Plan, assist in, and coordinate the control and simplification of reports.

Establish and maintain files of forms of the Company.

Participate in the training programs for supervisors in office administration and procedures and in particular within the Comptroller's Office.

Manuals and Publications –Major Functions

Analyze, develop, and assist in the construction and layout of clerical manuals and related publications to assure economic processing and distribution, efficient performance, and easy readability.

Administer the Comptroller's Office publication system, including manuals and related publications, to assure above-mentioned objectives.

Cooperate with the work measurement activities, methods analysis, and data processing services, as well as the other activities of office systems and procedures, in the development of manuals and procedures.

Analyze the effect of issued manuals and publications and recommend improvements.

Establish, supervise, and assist in the development of an effective system of distribution and proper briefing of personnel in the use of published manuals and related publications.

Instruct locations in the use of new manuals and related publications and assure their Company-wide utilization.

Establish, maintain, and review files of office manuals and related publications of the Company.

Participate in the training programs for supervisors in office administration and procedures and and in particular within the Comptroller's Office.

Work Measurement

Major Functions and Objectives

Administer programs of work measurement for clerical functions and procedures throughout the Company and develop programs to assure effective utilization of clerical personnel and office assets.

Analyze and recommend the best working conditions, layout, and disposition of work to achieve optimal performance.

Develop, recommend, and establish standards for repetive, semimechanical or other types of clerical operations that permit a quantitative and/or qualitative evaluation and measurement.

Develop, recommend, and establish norms for the relationships of quantitative standards to service levels, quality of production, and so on.

Develop and establish systems to measure performance of clerical operations under established standards and revise standards as required.

Establish and maintain a master file of standards for clerical operations and evaluate these standards and applications with regard to circumstances under which they prevail and should prevail.

363

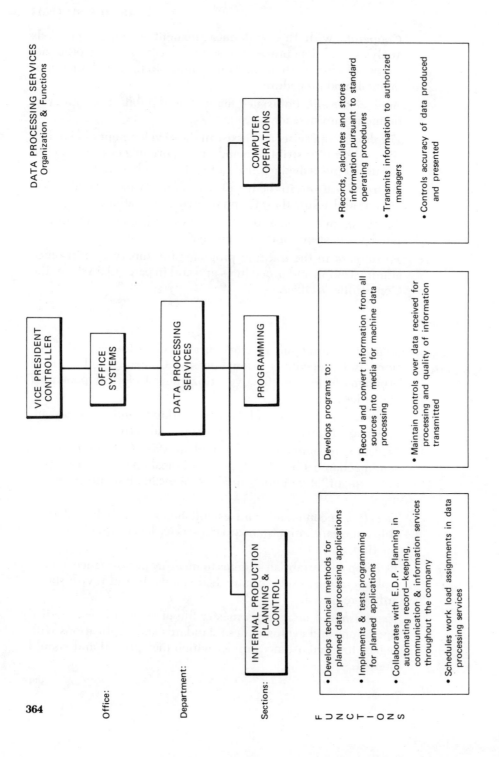

DATA PROCESSING SERVICES
Organization & Functions

Office:

Department:

Sections:

VICE PRESIDENT
CONTROLLER

OFFICE
SYSTEMS

DATA PROCESSING
SERVICES

PROGRAMMING

COMPUTER
OPERATIONS

INTERNAL PRODUCTION
PLANNING &
CONTROL

FUNCTIONS

• Develops technical methods for planned data processing applications

• Implements & tests programming for planned applications

• Collaborates with E.D.P. Planning in automating record—keeping, communication & information services throughout the company

• Schedules work load assignments in data processing services

Develops programs to:

• Record and convert information from all sources into media for machine data processing

• Maintain controls over data received for processing and quality of information transmitted

• Records, calculates and stores information pursuant to standard operating procedures

• Transmits information to authorized managers

• Controls accuracy of data produced and presented

Assist management as requested in achieving uniform application of standards or performance.

Relationships The Superintendent of work-measurement is directly responsible to the Manager of Office Systems and Controls.

The Superintendent maintains close working relationships with the Managers of data processing services office systems, and data processing planning activities in the performance of his assigned functions.

The Superintendent performs assigned tasks as a service agency; informs, advises, and assists supervision and management in questions dealing with above-mentioned major functions.

The Superintendent contacts work-measurement management personnel in other companies as may be deemed desirable by the Manager of office systems and control in the exchange of information on work-measurement specific problems under study.

The Superintendent keeps current and close contact with Personnel Department in studies that may effect the relationship between the employees and the Company.

DATA PROCESSING SERVICES

Major Functions *Responsible* to the Controller for managing data processing services to assure effective administration and utilization of machines and manpower. Provide adequate, timely, and equitable service to all activities using the service.

Responsibilities *Operate* established systems and equipment located at Headquarters office according to assigned programs and schedules.

Plan and supervise the distribution of work-load and responsibility within the department in order to assure most efficient services.

Cooperate with the data processing planning activities and other interested groups, as indicated, in the development or revision of data processing applications.

Relationships The Superintendent of Data Processing Services is directly responsible to the Manager of Office Systems and Controls.

OFFICE OF THE INTERNAL AUDITOR
Organization and Functions

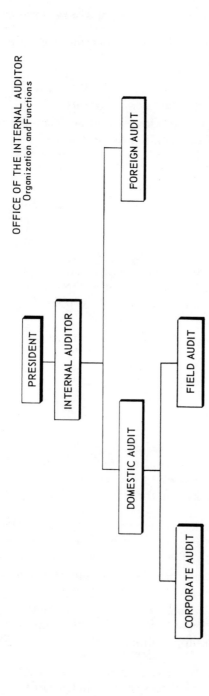

ORGANIZATION

PRESIDENT

INTERNAL AUDITOR

DOMESTIC AUDIT — FOREIGN AUDIT

CORPORATE AUDIT — FIELD AUDIT

FUNCTIONS

Corporate Audit:
- Examines statements of financial position and earnings
- Audits supporting accounts & records, including data processing information
- Audits bank transfers, investment & fund transactions
- Reconciles bank accounts for payroll & other payments
- Reviews operations of Controller's & Treasurer's offices
- Recommends internal control procedures

Field Audit:
- Audits accounting and cost records of organizational components of the company
- Reviews intra-company pricing structure
- Audits payrolls
- Reports on audit reviews for conformance with accounting and operating procedures
- Audits purchasing and inventory practices
- Evaluates internal controls

Foreign Audit:
- Audits periodically accounts & records in foreign offices
- Reviews operations for conformance with accounting & operating procedures
- Evaluates internal controls
- Examines cash & exchange transfers for conformance with legal and procedural requirements

The Superintendent maintains close working relationships with the Managers of Work-Measurement Office Systems and the Data Processing Planning activities in the performance of his assigned functions.

The Superintendent performs as a service agency assigned tasks; informs advises, and assists supervision and management in questions dealing with above-mentioned major functions.

The Superintendent contacts data processing management personnel in other companies as may be deemed desirable by the Manager of Office Systems and Control or the Data Processing Planning activities in the exchange of information of specific data processing services under study.

Internal Production Planning and Control– Major Functions

Within the definitions and relationships indicated above for the Superintendent of the Data Processing Services the internal production planning and control activities shall comprise the following functions.

Plan and develop procedures, supervise the machine programs and schedule within the department, and give technical assistance to customers as requested.

Develop and supervise schedules in cooperation with customers in order to assure proper coordination in areas of common interest and between the customers and the Data Processing Services.

Control the input and output of data before processing and delivery to customers to assure good quality of production and adherence to established procedures and standards.

Suggest to the Superintendent of Office Systems changes in forms construction and control, methods of control, flow of work or operations to achieve more effective work, higher quality, and shorter processing time.

Computer Operations— Basic Functions

Within the definitions and relationships indicated above for the Superintendent of the Data Processing Services the activities shall comprise the following functions.

Process received documents according to established procedures, schedules, and quality standards.

Recommend to the internal production planning and control group changes in schedules, operating methods, and so on in order to achieve more effective work, higher quality, and shorter processing time.

Computer Operations— Major Functions

Operate the computer equipment according to established procedures, schedules, and quality standard.

Assist in test runs of new or revised systems as requested.

Recommend to the internal production planning and control group changes in schedules, operating methods, and so on, in order to achieve more effective work, higher quality, and shorter processing time.

INTERNAL AUDITOR

Basic Functions

The Internal Auditor provides assurance to the President and the stockholders that the financial responsibilities of the management are carried out according to company policy and procedure. The Internal Auditor accomplishes this by examining financial statements, records, practices, and related internal controls. He examines generally all company activities for conformance with standard operating procedure.

Duties

Examine corporate, subsidiary, and intracompany statements of financial position and earnings.

Cooperate with company's professional auditor in conduct of the annual examination.

Audit supporting accounting records in corporate, division, and foreign plants and offices.

Audit cash and funds in custody of treasurer.

Review company activities for conformance with established accounting and operating procedures.

Audit cost records and inventories.

Review company and intracompany pricing practices.

Examine purchasing practices.

Audit payrolls.

Evaluate and recommend internal control procedures.

Audit bank transfers investments and fund transactions.

Examine foreign cash and exchange transactions for conformance with legal requirements.

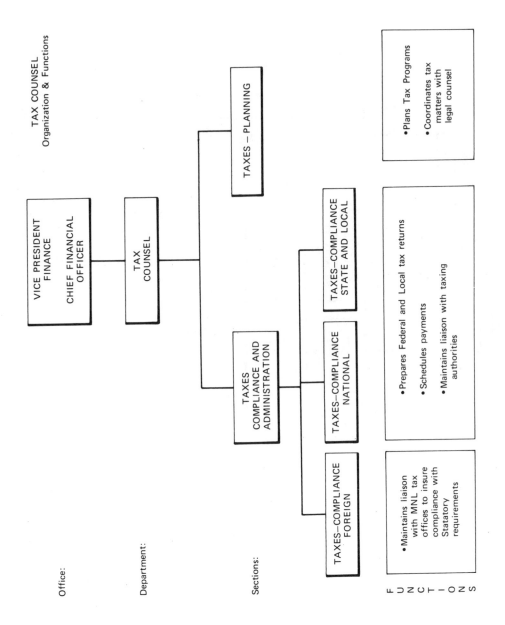

TAX COUNSEL
Organization & Functions

Office:

Department:

Sections:

VICE PRESIDENT
FINANCE

CHIEF FINANCIAL
OFFICER

TAX
COUNSEL

TAXES — PLANNING

TAXES
COMPLIANCE AND
ADMINISTRATION

TAXES—COMPLIANCE
FOREIGN

TAXES—COMPLIANCE
NATIONAL

TAXES—COMPLIANCE
STATE AND LOCAL

FUNCTIONS

- Plans Tax Programs
- Coordinates tax matters with legal counsel

- Prepares Federal and Local tax returns
- Schedules payments
- Maintains liaison with taxing authorities

- Maintains liaison with MNL tax offices to insure compliance with Statatory requirements

369

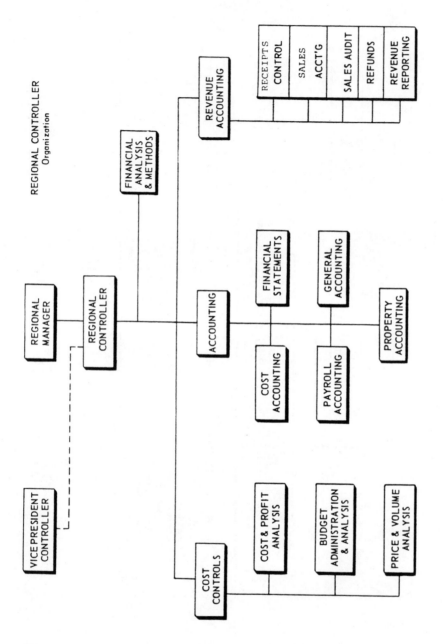

REGIONAL CONTROLLER
Organization

VICE PRESIDENT CONTROLLER

REGIONAL MANAGER

REGIONAL CONTROLLER

FINANCIAL ANALYSIS & METHODS

COST CONTROLS

ACCOUNTING

REVENUE ACCOUNTING

COST & PROFIT ANALYSIS

BUDGET ADMINISTRATION & ANALYSIS

PRICE & VOLUME ANALYSIS

COST ACCOUNTING

FINANCIAL STATEMENTS

PAYROLL ACCOUNTING

GENERAL ACCOUNTING

PROPERTY ACCOUNTING

RECEIPTS CONTROL

SALES ACCT'G

SALES AUDIT

REFUNDS

REVENUE REPORTING

INDEX